KT-116-787

The Really Helpful Cookbook

The Really Helpful Cookbook

Ruth Watson

EBURY PRESS
LONDON

First published in Great Britain in 2000

3 5 7 9 10 8 6 4

Text © Ruth Watson 2000

Photography © William Lingwood 2000

Ruth Watson has asserted her right to be identified as the author of this work under the Copyright, Designs and Patents Act 1988.

All rights reserved. No part of this publication may be reproduced, stored in a retrieval system, or transmitted in any form or by any means, electronic, mechanical, photocopying, recording or otherwise without the prior permission of the copyright owners.

First published by Ebury Press, an imprint of Random House, 20 Vauxhall Bridge Road, London SW1V 2SA

Random House Australia (Pty) Limited
20 Alfred Street, Milsons Point, Sydney,
New South Wales 2061, Australia

Random House New Zealand Limited
18 Poland Road, Glenfield, Auckland 10,
New Zealand

Random House South Africa (Pty) Limited
Endulini, 5A Jubilee Road, Parktown 2193,
South Africa

The Random House Group Limited Reg. No. 954009

www.randomhouse.co.uk

A CIP catalogue record for this book is available from the British Library.

Editor: Kathryn Holliday
Design: Vivid Design
Photographer: William Lingwood
Food Stylist: Sunil Vijayakar
Stylist: Helen Trent

ISBN 0 09 187798 9

Papers used by Ebury Press are natural, recyclable products made from wood grown in sustainable forests.

Colour separation in Milan by Colorlito

Printed and bound by Imprimerie Pollina S.A. in France

For Darling (and Jessie & Jack)

Acknowledgements

A big thank you to: Delia and Michael for giving me a golden opportunity eight years ago; the smashing team at Sainsbury's *The Magazine*, especially (past and present) cookery editors, Aggie MacKenzie, Sarah Randall and Jane Curran, and Chief Sub, Eirwen Oxley Green; Andrew Wallace, who nagged me remorselessly into writing this book; Rosemary Scoular, a heaven-sent agent; Denise Bates, who had the superlative sense to want this book, and is patience personified; William Lingwood for fabulous, in-focus photography; Sunil Vijayakar for his exuberant food styling; Kathryn Holliday for tireless subbing (and hardly any of the threatened fireworks); Paul Blow, who did the brilliant covers; Kim Hart and Joyce Hutchinson, who are exemplary recipe testers; Lindsey Savage, my terrific (and far too part-time) assistant; Leah Klein, with great regrets and loving thanks; Chloë Hutchinson, my lovely niece for giving me her home, time, computer and talent when I needed them most; Nigel Slater, who could not have been more supportive and kind if he were a cookery writer himself (!); and lastly my mother who, if she didn't teach me how to cook, certainly taught me how to eat.

Contents

Introduction 10

Important Things 12

Favourite Foods 16

Know How 22

Favourite Kitchen Kit 28

Chapter 1
Wintry Starters 38

Butternut and chickpea soup with basil rouille
Spinach, two-pea and leek soup
Celeriac, greens and potato soup
Soy-glazed grilled aubergines
Deep-fried onion bhajis with mint, coriander
and ginger yoghurt
Harry's Dolce fagioli in saor
Pear and pine nut salad with roquefort and
honey
Nearly sashimi
Tiger prawn tempura with lime, chilli and
tamarind dipping sauce
Smoked salmon with pancetta, horseradish
crème fraîche and blini
Thai-style gravadlax
Cockle, chicory and bacon salad with mustard
dressing
Griddled squid with coriander hummus
Gratin of mussels Basque-style
Mussels with red curry sauce

Chapter 2
Wintry Main Courses 60

Twice-baked spinach and parmesan soufflé
Seized cod with white bean and parsley purée
Griddled scallops with Seville orange chutney
Scallops with whipped garlic butter
Cod with saffron mash and gremolata
Mussel and fennel broth
Crevettes with flat mushrooms and garlic
Dover sole meunière with saffron pancakes
Fritto misto
Steak and kidney pie
Fried chicken with hazelnut sauce
Confit of duck with pearl barley stew
Not Betty's hotpot

Chapter 3
Wintry Puddings 86

Seville Pond pudding
Butter-fried bananas with orange and coconut
syrup
French apple tart
Lemon meringue pie
Baked plums on panettone
Damson and almond cobbler
Pumpkin cheesecake with pumpkin seed and
maple praline
Hazelnut and apricot meringue cake
Coconut pancakes with maple, pecan and rum
butter
Deep-fried mincemeat and ice-cream parcels
Coffee, rum and cardamom trifle
Hot fruit salad brûlée
Chocolate and stem ginger pavé
Chocolate zuppa inglese
Bread and butter pudding with honey
Afghan rice pudding with cardamom,
rosewater and pistachios
Marzipan baklava

Chapter 4
Wintry Lunches 116

Burritos with spicy beans and avocado salsa
Macaroni con brio
Roast butternut squash, garlic and oregano
risotto
Savoy omelette with peas, pepperoni and
potatoes
Omelette Molière with parmesan and gruyère
Livarot, rocket and potato tart
Flat mushroom, red onion and mascarpone
pizza
Ham and fontina pancakes
Stuffed mushroom crostini with smoked
mozzarella
Smoked haddock Bénédict
Linguine with clams, parsley and garlic

Chapter 5
Wintry Suppers 138

Mum's minestrone soup
Buckwheat noodles with squash, soy and
sesame seeds
Pappardelle with squash and sage pesto
Linguine with caramelised onions and fried
breadcrumbs
Casarecce with porcini and pinto beans
Borlotti bean and goat's cheese pasteles
Italian beans on toast
Haggis, potato, bacon and apple fry-up
Penne with kale, mascarpone and pancetta
Deep-fried mussel and vegetable tangles
Smoked haddock chowder
Ham and haddie
Spiced lamb patties with roast vegetables

Chapter 6
Summery Starters 158

Chilled sweet potato vichyssoise
Chilled cucumber and coconut milk soup
Leek salad with tarragon, caper and parsley
dressing
Feta and watermelon salad
Griddled asparagus with sesame sauce
Asparagus and girolles crostini
Spinach salad with avocado and pancetta

Old-fashioned egg mayonnaise
Fried mozzarella with pesto and chilli
Little Gem salad with egg and bacon dressing
Warm smoked salmon escalopes with potato
and sorrel salad
Seafood and chickpea salad crostini

Chapter 7
Summery Main Courses 176

Gado-gado salad with peanut sauce
Le petit aïoli
Escalope of salmon with champagne sauce and
tomato, ginger and basil salsa
Cold lobster with tarragon mayonnaise and
chips
Crab cakes with coconut and tamarind
Warm salmon salade Niçoise
Grilled lobster with Café de Paris butter
Griddled prawns wrapped in basil and parma
ham, with lemon risotto
Cioppino
Scallops with sauce vierge and crisp pancetta
Pinenut-crusted chicken stuffed with basil
butter
Chicken escalopes with salsa verde
Hot gammon with parsley sauce and broad
beans

Chapter 8
Summery Puddings 204

Sweet French toast with peach, lime and mint salsa
Apricot frangipane tart
Blackcurrant bavarois tart with chocolate pastry
Zabaglione and raspberry cake
Piña colada roulade
Raspberry mess
Poached strawberries with five-pepper ice cream
Pavlova with cherry compôte and sloe gin syllabub
Cherry custard fritters
Fresh pineapple with passion fruit sorbet
Apricot and amaretto trifle
Floating islands with nectarine custard
Banana split
Baked egg custard

Chapter 9
Summery Lunches 232

Linguine with raw tomato sauce
Roast red pepper, garlic and saffron risotto
Egg and bacon pie with cos salad and mustard dressing
Lentil salad with soft-boiled eggs and tapenade toasts
Courgette, potato and herb frittata
Feta and Med veg tart
Chargrilled squid, potato and onion salad with lime dressing
French bean, tuna and shallot salad
Baked chicken stuffed with Boursin
Smoked haddock and watercress tart
Grilled coconut chicken with noodles and satay sauce
Chicken and courgette risotto
Tomato, mozzarella and pesto galette

Chapter 10
Summery Suppers 258

Risi e asparagi
Tomato, avocado and basil omelette with garlic breadcrumbs
Scrambled eggs alla parmigiana
Grilled goat's cheese salad with balsamic and sultana dressing
Potato, goat's cheese, pea and mint tart
Buffalo mozzarella with pears
Prawn, mushroom and parsley crostini
Tiger prawn, leek and red pepper stir-fry
Warm taleggio, mushroom and fennel salad
Gorgonzola, broad bean and dill risotto

Directory 278

Index 284

Introduction

Does the world really need another cookbook? After all, there are literally millions of recipe books gathering dust on bookshelves from Sydney to Sydenham, and at least 90 per cent of them are never opened, never used. So why should I add another one to the pile? Well, the answer has to be that food is vitally important – literally – and, whatever has been said about it already, the subject can never be exhausted.

Food is the operative word. *The Really Helpful Cookbook* might be essentially a collection of recipes and cooking instructions, but what it's really about is the stuff you put in your mouth. Why else bother to cook? There's only one reason, and that's to take some good ingredients and turn them into something wonderful to eat. I know a cake can look prettier than Monet's garden but if you only want to sit and admire it, save on electricity and paint waterlilies instead.

Actually, some of my favourite food doesn't need cooking at all; if you live near a good deli (particularly an Italian one), you'd be mad not to have at least one or two bought-in meals each week. I can't think of a better summer lunch than a few paper-thin slices of sweet, nutty parma ham, each mouthful accompanied by a shard of ice-cold unsalted butter or some really ripe, jammy figs. (An even more sensational treat would be the Spanish, acorn-fed, pata negra ham, which is so expensive you could wear it to the theatre.)

Much cheaper, but equally saliva-stirring, are salamis and other cured meats – coppa, mortadella and bresaola, to name a few – with salty black olives and a hunk of really chewy sour dough bread. Buffalo milk mozzarella makes another fabulously simple meal, the soft, fresh, milky cheese accentuated by peppery-sweet tomatoes and aromatic basil or better still, by a perfectly ripe Comice pear quickened with freshly ground black pepper and a slurp of fruity olive oil.

Buying in delicatessen food is not the same as buying in ready-meals. The variety and number of the latter might be endless but, with certain honourable exceptions (especially the Indian ranges), most of them are pretty horrible. Look at the ingredients list and you'll see why. When did home-cooked food ever include xanthum gum, modified starch, stabilisers and sundry E numbers?

No, if your stomach is groaning for a real meal, but your brain is screaming at the thought of having to make it, then the answer lies in a bowl of pasta or a one-pot meal. It only takes ten minutes to cook a hank of linguine, which gives you plenty of time to fry a few cloves of crushed garlic in a little olive oil, add a jar of drained clams and toss in a handful of chopped parsley; or to sauté a chicken breast with a few sliced mushrooms, add a dash of Madeira and a pot of cream, and whisk the juices into a rich, toffee-coloured sauce.

If you're not convinced you can cook something even this simple, well, there's no need for self-immolation. God doesn't wave a magic wand over every new-born (female) baby and guarantee she's going to be the next Delia, any more than he blesses every (male) child with David Beckham's right foot. We each have our own skills, talents and interests and there's no reason on earth why cooking should be one of them. The snag is that – unlike playing Sunday morning football – we eat every day, and while breakfast and lunch can be covered by a bowl of cereal and a sandwich, most of us want something a bit more substantial for our main meal.

That's where this book comes in. I have written it for people who love eating but need recipes for inspiration and instruction. Not just recipes, either, but information about where to buy particular foods; why one ingredient might be better than another; which bit of equipment is most useful or will best stand the test of time; and, how to deal with tricky things like squid and scallops. And as well as tasting good, these recipes really do work. Many of them have come through the gruelling obstacle course known as Sainsbury's *The Magazine*. Believe me, if they pass muster there, it's unlikely you'll end up with the trifle fully decorated – and wondering where you were meant to put the custard.

The Really Helpful Cookbook is also for the millions of working people who don't cook much during the week, but are quite happy to spend a few hours in the kitchen at the weekend. After all, I am that woman. (I don't want to exclude men from the joy, and burden, of cooking but let's not kid ourselves too much.) I know about wanting to crash out in front of *Coronation Street*, and have a delicious, tasty dish appear magically in front of me – and I don't mean Mike Baldwin. I know how difficult it can be to summon up the energy even to think about what to cook when you've been toiling away all day. But I also know that spending a few calm hours on a Sunday cooking, then eating a meal you thought only the likes of Jamie, Gary or Rick could make is truly satisfying.

There's something else I should point out, and that's the paucity of meat recipes in this book. My original working title was Bugger-all Meat, but I was persuaded (wisely) to change it. The fact is that while I'm certainly not a vegetarian – I'd only have to think about a hot, fat, crispy bacon sandwich to throw in the green gauntlet – neither am I wild about the conventional meat-and-two-veg. On the whole I like timid meat – crunchy shards of pancetta tossed in a minerally spinach, avocado and mushroom salad – but not hunks of venison or legs of lamb. (The fact that I love steak and kidney pie is either an example of gross hypocrisy, or wanton contrariness.) There's no moral issue at stake here – though of course I think all animals should be reared (and killed) with kindness – it's simply that a slab of roast beef is not for me. I don't think I'm alone: I've made countless meals for family and friends where the lack of meat has gone completely unnoticed, and in my restaurant (The Trinity bistro at the Crown and Castle, Orford) the number of customers ordering fish far exceeds those ordering meat – except on Saturday evening, of course, which has been 'steak night' since time immemorial. I suppose it's partly because my hotel is on the Suffolk coast, and the water stirs up atavistic reminders of our sea-circled heritage: more mundanely I think it's because hardly anybody knows what to do with a whole fish any more.

I hope I've taken some of the mystery out of preparing shellfish and fish in this book. But whatever the ingredients, there is no need for cooking to be either a terrifying or cheerless chore. The recipes in *The Really Helpful Cookbook* are not always short, but they are always easy to follow and, on the whole, they can be prepared in advance. The bottom line is quite simple – if a recipe is easy to follow, and the food tastes good, then the preparation and cooking can be almost as pleasurable as the eating. Almost – let's not get too carried away.

Ruth Watson

Important things about this book

Measurements

Trust me on this one – there are very few recipes where it really, really matters if the measurements are heroin-dealing accurate. Cakes, meringues, pastry, yes, but not much else. Having said that, even as an experienced cook I realise how disconcerting it is to be left worrying whether the recipe will be ruined if you use a level tablespoon of chilli powder instead of a heaped one. My recipes are based on standard 5ml teaspoons and 15ml tablespoons, but I only make the distinction between level, rounded or heaped spoons if it matters. Otherwise, just fill the spoon as it comes, and go with the flow. Be warned, though, that old-fashioned tablespoons have almost twice the capacity of modern ones.

When it comes to measuring freshly chopped herbs accurately, again, life's too short. Most of the time, all you need to know is whether to chop a large handful or a small handful of parsley, or pop in a few sprigs or lots of sprigs of thyme – and if there's a bit more parsley or a bit less thyme, the world won't stop revolving. Okay, the recipe will give a fair indication, but it won't really matter if you've chopped a bit more or a bit less.

As for metric vs imperial, although I instinctively think in pounds and ounces myself, it is an inescapable fact that only people who can remember Fanny Craddock are more comfortable with imperial measurements. And, as it's now illegal for shops to sell food in anything other than metric quantities, it hardly seems helpful to keep pursuing the past. Anyway, if you think about it, there are very few of us who can judge 8oz sugar by eye, and it's no more more difficult to put a metric weight on the scales, than an imperial one. In other words, none of us has to understand metrication to use it.

How many will it feed?

There are some very tidy cookbooks out there, in which every recipe serves four people. The problem is that some recipes are so obviously suitable for one or two people, and others scream out to be made in quantity. Making a small amount of soup, for example, strikes me as batty; it takes no longer to make a big pot, and there's nothing nicer to have in the fridge or freezer. I also like it when there's some pudding left over to have the next day.

As for the exact numbers a recipe will serve, it varies, depending on individual appetite, how big the rest of the meal is going to be, and the occasion. So if you come across a tart which says 4-plus, you'll know that it will feed four at a minimum, but might well go further.

Hot or cold

All food has its optimum serving temperature. Salad leaves and vichyssoise, for example, are fine served very cold, but anyone who has bought a supermarket sandwich will know just how horrible it is to eat bread straight from the chiller cabinet. Of course, food hygiene is important. I'm not suggesting you make a bowl of tuna fish salad and leave it to fester in a hot kitchen for eight hours, it's simply that many dishes taste better at room temperature. So do remember to get something like cheese out of the fridge a little while before it's needed. Similarly, food that should be served piping hot should be served piping hot. Far better that the people eating it have to wait a few moments, if necessary.

Equipment

It's helpful to know which bits of equipment are essential for a particular recipe, either because it makes the preparation so much easier, or because it's almost impossible to make the dish without them. So, at the start of every recipe I've highlighted the equipment that's really necessary – but not every single size of pan, or whether you need a palette knife. I have also assumed that you own a food processor/electric mixer and liquidiser, on the basis that anyone who can afford this book is not short of a few bob.

Warming plates

It makes a huge difference to the enjoyment of hot food if you remember to warm the plates and serving dishes first. Don't think it's something only professionals do, and a pointless over-complication – it's not. As modern cookers nearly always have two ovens, it's not such a difficult exercise, but if you do have limited facilities (or if you forget), then all is not lost; simply leave the plates to soak in a sink of very hot water for a few minutes.

Advance preparation

I take a revoltingly smug pride in never ever having kept a meal warm in the oven: it just isn't necessary. But I've no more desire to stand over a hot stove while friends glug down a bottle of champagne than you, nor do I want to miss my favourite soap in order to dish up dinner to a tardy partner. With a bit of forethought there's no need to do either. Immediately before the list of ingredients in each recipe, it will clearly state whether, or how far ahead, you can make the dish. All you have to do is choose a recipe that suits the circumstances, and take full advantage of any pre-preparation that can be carried out. Or use an '*à la* minute' recipe which only takes minutes to cook from start to finish. That way, neither you, nor the food, should be left languishing.

Clingfilming food

I probably don't need to say that any food kept in the fridge for longer than half an hour should be clingfilmed. It might be worth explaining, however, that this is partly to prevent something smelly (such as fish) tainting other foods, and partly because the air in a fridge is very dehydrating. That's why you should never store bread or cakes in a fridge as they will go stale twice as quickly as if kept in a bread bin or airtight cake tin.

Organic food

Given the choice, I always buy organic produce. Unfortunately, the choice is still not that big, and some organic foods – particularly vegetables – don't always look as tempting as they might. Having said that, if biting into physical perfection means downing a dose of organosulphates at the same time, give me

Steptoe-looking fruit and veg any day.

It's also true that organic food does not always taste noticeably better than normal food (hang on, what's normal about the 40-odd herbicides and pesticides that can be legally sprayed on carrots). But eating is not exclusively about sensory satisfaction. There's the nutritional aspect, too, and while we involuntarily ingest a thousand times more rubbish than our ancestors did, it makes sense to eat good, wholesome food when we have the opportunity. I try to buy organic cream, eggs, milk, butter and yoghurt whenever I can, as well as cereals, flour, sugar, pulses, ketchup and, of course, baked beans.

Genetically modified or engineered foods

The subject of genetically engineered or modified foods is vastly complex. Personally, I think there should be a generation's moratorium on proceeding with the planting of genetically engineered seeds so the impact on the environment, and our health, can be fully assessed. This is not the place, nor am I qualified to discuss the issue, but anyone interested in learning the facts should contact Friends of the Earth, the Soil Association or Greenpeace.

All I will say is that genetically engineered foods are created by a crude and imprecise technology; no commercial organisation (or government body) should be able to hold a patent on nature and the time-honoured way in which we feed ourselves; supplying sterile seeds to farmers in the emerging nations is cynical in the extreme; seeds that only respond to a herbicide made by the company which sells the seeds is monopolism of the worst kind; and ladybirds – man's best friend in the war against 'bad' aphids – that have been fed aphids, which in turn have been reared on genetically engineered foods, live half as long as ladybirds fed on normally nourished aphids. Now let's talk about something nice.

Why bother?

Cooking a meal can be exciting, stimulating and satisfying – with the added bonus that you don't have to wear a condom, and can share the pleasure with family and friends. But, like sex, it's no good if your mind is on other things, or you don't feel confident, or you take it too seriously. It's just cooking, after all. Eating might be pretty important in the sense that if you stop you're likely to keel over after a while, but cooking – well, people survive who've never wielded a wooden spoon in their lives, so don't get too worked up about it. As long as you use decent ingredients, even disasters can be quite edible, and your friends don't love you because you can cook well. Many years ago Wendy Craig, in a very funny sitcom called *Butterfly*, showed us how endearing, funny and attractive a lousy cook can be.

Making food fit to eat can be great fun, and eating it certainly is, but if cooking is going to make you sick with worry, far better that you buy in some good cheese, bread and fruit, instead.

Favourite foods

'Tinned anchovies in olive oil are fine, but the 'if you've got it, flaunt it' rule applies as much to food as it does to big boobs, and bottled anchovies tend to be the best'

Oils

In the past few years, every last Luigi with an olive tree in his back garden has produced a swanky, boutique oil. My favourite extra-virgin olive oils are Collona, Tenuta di Saragano and Lungarotti, all of which are well-flavoured but without the very grassy flavour that I find faintly repellent. However, for everyday cooking where you need a good, but not excessively characterful olive oil, Waitrose and Sainsbury's own-label extra-virgin olive oils are more than acceptable. I am also very fond of Sainsbury's Santa Sabina, Dauno and Tuscany extra-virgin olive oils.

The trick is to match the particular character of the oil – grassy, peppery, fruity or whatever – to the food. And to do that you'll have to taste it. Dab a piece of plain white bread into a saucer of oil, and trust your own palate as to what tastes right. After all, it's you who will be eating the food.

When it comes to the really exceptional, oddball varieties, there's nothing quite like Collona lemon oil for swishing over griddled fish or shellfish (especially squid – which is actually a cephalopod, but who cares). I'm also very struck with Merchant Gourmet's Austrian roasted pumpkin seed oil, which looks like cough linctus but makes a devastatingly rich, nutty dressing. For recipes where I don't want the flavour of the oil to dominate the food, I use groundnut oil (aka peanut or arachide oil). This is partly because it's virtually tasteless, and partly because groundnut oil burns at a higher temperature and is less likely to go rancid than many other oils – it's also habit, if I'm being honest. Of course, you must not use groundnut oil if you're allergic to peanuts; replace it with a good-quality vegetable oil or sunflower oil.

Sea salt

Salt is not just salt. Sea salt, whether it's the fragile, snow-white, crystalline flakes from Maldon (not everything from Essex is tasteless), or the dingy-looking crystals from Guérande, isn't just salty, it's positively awash with flavour. The reason is quite simple; sea salt is not refined and so tastes of its habitat. It not only contains sodium chloride (that's salt-salt), but magnesium

chloride, magnesium sulphate (that's Epsom salts), potassium sulphate, calcium carbonate, potassium bromide and sodium bromide. It's this complexity which gives sea salt a subtlety and flavour completely lacking in refined salt. And, although it costs more you don't need to use so much. Use coarse sea salt in soups, casseroles and for cooking veg, or where the crystals add to the taste sensation – hard boiled eggs dipped in crunchy sea salt are wonderful. For 'dry' cooking, or to adjust the seasoning at the end of a recipe, fine sea salt is better.

Black pepper

Any cookery writer worth her or his salt (ha!), will specify freshly ground black pepper in a recipe. The reason is quite simple: the moment you crush a peppercorn all the subtle aroma and flavour starts to dissipate, and you're left with monotonic heat. Black peppercorns are the whole berries, whereas white peppercorns have been stripped of their skins: the former are more

aromatic, and should be used in all but a handful of recipes where black specks would spoil the appearance.

Eggs

Free-range eggs are so infinitely nicer to eat than battery eggs, they're worth every extra penny. And as there's precious little (expensive) meat in these recipes, you might even consider buying organic free-range eggs. Unfortunately, the packing date is not a particularly accurate indication of how fresh the eggs are, as they could have been laid days (weeks?) before. Best to buy your eggs from somewhere you can trust.

Tomatoes (tinned and fresh)

The best tinned tomatoes are undoubtedly Italian. But even more superb are the little ring-pull cans of 'chopped Provençal tomatoes with tomato purée' that Sainsbury's sells under the unlikely name chair de tomate – 'chair' being

French for flesh, not a seating requisite. The tins appear pretty expensive, but there's so much flavour you don't need a large quantity.

As for fresh tomatoes, enough has been said about tomatoes 'grown for flavour' to fill a greenhouse. But, really, is there any point in buying anything else? Tomatoes on the vine cost even more, but stay fresher. Give me one sweet, peppery, aromatic tomato a week, rather than three tasteless toms a day.

Blini

A lot of supermarkets as well as specialist delicatessens and food shops sell packets of 4 large or 16 cocktail-size (their words) ready-made blini. They're not bad, although I think the price of the little ones is a bit cheeky. If you can't find any, Marks & Spencer's fresh pikelets would make a good replacement, as would the big, floppy North Staffordshire oatcakes.

Smoked salmon

Supermarket smoked salmon is all right (just – and M&S is the best), but none of it compares with the Scottish oak-smoked salmon the Craig family prepare in their smokehouse in Knipoch. Equally good is the Suffolk-smoked, but Irish-born wild salmon produced by the Pinney family at Butley-Orford. They also sell the best smoked cod's roe I've ever eaten.

Tempura batter

Having a box of tempura batter in the store cupboard is more useful than you might think. It's particularly handy if you're faced with having to knock up a vegetarian meal without notice; deep-fried potatoes, mushrooms, courgettes, carrots, French beans and the like, taste a damn sight more interesting than plainly boiled veg. Of course, it doesn't take more than a few minutes to make your own tempura batter, but Japanese flour is different from English flour, which is one of the reasons why the authentic Hime-brand batter mix tastes good.

Thai fish sauce

Fish sauce is as fundamental to Thai food as soy sauce is to Chinese, adding an indefinable boost to the other core Thai flavours of lemon grass, galangal, lime leaves and coriander. There are quite a few brands of fish sauce (nam pla) available, of which Blue Dragon is the most common; it's all right, but I prefer the Squid brand stocked in most specialist Asian shops – weird though the name is.

Stock powder

Put Marigold Swiss vegetable bouillon powder at the top of your store cupboard list (and spelling bee). Unlike many other brands, it doesn't produce a virulent orange scum, nor does it taste like some sort of chemical brew. It's even good enough to use in a risotto, a real test given that this is a dish where any lack of flavour (or off-flavours) will show up dramatically. Marigold used to be available only in health food shops, but I am pleased to say most supermarkets stock it now. Great stuff.

Horseradish

Despite stricter legislation, food labelling can still be outrageously misleading. Sunny Delight (which contains the magnificent sum of 5 per cent real fruit juice), is my particular bête noire, but next time you buy a bottle of horseradish sauce, check the ingredients label. If the first ingredient – and, therefore, the greatest quantity – is turnip, you might prefer to return it to the shelf.

Freshly grated horseradish can sometimes be found in the chiller cabinet of a health food shop. Good bottled horseradish sauces are Tracklement's Strong Horseradish and Cream Sauce, and Sainsbury's Special Selection Horseradish and Cream. I'm a bit of a wimp about raw heat, so I normally add a touch more cream, sugar and lemon juice to mitigate the pungency.

Mozzarella

If you are going to swamp it with strong flavours, then cow's milk mozzarella will do, otherwise I insist you use buffalo milk mozzarella. (I'm not called Miss Rod for nothing.) Albeit a very mild-flavoured cheese, genuine 'mozzarella di bufala' has a slightly sour, yoghurty flavour, and a fabulous stringy-milk texture. While nothing beats eating dripping-fresh mozzarella in Naples, many specialist cheese shops and grocers have weekly deliveries of buffalo mozzarella which they store in bowls of whey (to keep the cheese moist.)

The best branded buffalo mozzarella I've found is Bontà di Bufala Campana (which is packed in plastic pouches, similarly filled with whey), followed by Polenghi or Rusticone Pomella Ciociara. And Invernizzi cow's milk mozzarella has infinitely more flavour than most of its rivals.

Anchovies

Cheap anchovies (packed in dubious oil) are horrible, and probably the reason that so many people would rather clean a ferret's teeth than eat them. They are certainly a lot saltier than anchovies packed in olive oil. In addition to the cost, another indication of quality is whether the anchovies are in bottles or cans. Tinned anchovies in olive oil are fine, but the 'if you've got it, flaunt it' rule applies as much to food as it does to big boobs, and bottled anchovies tend to be the best.

Tinned red peppers

The El Navarrico, wood-roasted, whole piquillo peppers from Lodosa are packed in their own juices and are seriously good, even if they are less thick and fleshy than home-roasted peppers. I nearly always have a tin on the go – decanted into a non-reactive, sealed container, they keep for about two weeks – and I find them an excellent standby for crostini, bruschetta, risotto and pilafs.

Duck (or goose) fat

Not only does duck and/or goose fat make the best roast potatoes you'll ever eat, it's also essential if you're going to cook confit of duck. You can buy the fat from specialist butchers, and in cans from grocers specialising in French products, and some of the more adventurous supermarkets.

Tiger (or king) prawns

The raw tiger prawns that most supermarkets stock nowadays are farmed, fresh-water, Asian prawns. They are sold with shells both on and off, and are the ones to use for Thai hot and sour soups, Japanese tempura, Chinese stir-frys or Indian curries, where ready-cooked prawns will not do. If you have a choice, the tiger prawns with a rusty-coloured shell taste better than those with a blue-black shell, although they all end up pink when they're cooked.

Greenland (or North Atlantic) prawns

Cooked Greenland prawns are the ones that used to be sold by the pint in the days before we became a European shire. Latterly eclipsed by warm-water tiger prawns, these cold-water prawns are actually far superior in flavour – if you buy them whole. The flaccid, pink commas sold already peeled in plastic trays are not even worth speaking about in the same breath as the sea-sparkling flesh of a firm, juicy prawn newly extracted from its shell. Not only that, all the debris – shells, heads, tails, the lot – can be used to make a (nearly) free shellfish stock of marvellous sweetness and intensity. As a guide, 225g of whole prawns releases about 100g of usable flesh, so take this into account when calculating the weight required.

Pulses

Dried pulses, including beans, lentils and chickpeas, are the backbone of my store cupboard (along with rice and pasta). Not only are pulses cheap, they add substance to casseroles and soups. Although you might think one bean is much the same as the next, they do vary in quality. Among the very best dried beans are the Spanish ones harvested by hand to make sure each pod is picked at the peak of perfection. They're packed under the Tormesina brand-name, and my absolute favourites are the huge, creamy, tender Judion beans which are almost big enough to double up as a spectacle case.

Of course, the drawback with most dried pulses is that you have to soak them for about eight hours before you can cook them: this is when tinned pulses come into their own. As with the dried pulses, the quality is variable, but Suma and Waitrose own-label organic tinned beans are particularly good.

Lenticchie Umbre
I used to think that Puy lentils – the charcoal-flecked, dark-green ones that look like miniature Westmorland roof slates – were the best, but not since coming across these Umbrian lentils. They don't look so beautiful, but the flavour and texture are fabulous. They're available in specialist Italian shops, and Sainsbury's.

Natural (golden) caster sugar and organic cane sugar
If you haven't tried golden (or natural) caster sugar before, it will be a revelation. Natural golden sugar looks like milky-coffee-coloured caster sugar, but instead of the monotonic sweetness of white sugar, it has a wonderful, complex, slightly toffeeish flavour. I love Billington's natural, organic cane sugar, too, but because the crystal-size is not as rigorously exact as with natural caster sugar, I wouldn't recommend using it in any recipe where precision is paramount – such as meringues. Always buy light and dark muscovado sugar, too; if the packet merely says light or dark brown sugar, it's refined sugar that's been coloured, rather than the real raw McCoy.

Jam and fruit compôtes
French jams, such as Bonne Maman, tend to have less sugar than British ones. This makes for a runny consistency that's great for spooning over yoghurt, fromage blanc and rice pudding (but also means that the jam has to be refrigerated after opening). I also like to keep a few jars of compôte – fruit that's been gently

stewed in its own slightly sweetened juices – in the store cupboard, particularly apricot and cherry.

Dried apricots

Whatever you do, don't buy those sweet, nothingy, ready-to-eat apricots for cooking – or eating, for that matter. The gloomy-looking, unsulphured apricots stocked in health food shops or specialist grocers taste light years better, although Hunza apricots are the real acme of dried apricots. These are small, leathery, wizened-looking things, with stones that are nigh-on impossible to remove, but they have a fantastic flavour and are well worth the hassle.

Vanilla pods

The price shops charge for single or twin-packed vanilla pods is nothing short of scandalous. Not only are they rarely very fresh (the pods should be moist, bendy and highly aromatic), but the price is astronomical. As a caterer I can buy a

thick bundle of vanilla pods for about one-eighth of the retail cost. I'd say this is one instance where it is worth establishing a co-operative with fellow cooks, and buying them wholesale.

White (béchamel) sauce

At the moment it's known as 'cuisine cream' (pretty ghastly, huh), but this ambient, ready-made Italian white sauce, more properly known as besciamella, is excellent. Imported by Parma Britishlat there's no hint of those chemical undertones you can taste in so many bottled, canned or boxed sauces. Why should there be, with only whole milk, cream, flour, corn starch and salt in the ingredients? A useful store cupboard standby, it should soon be in more general distribution than at present

Risotto rice

You can't use any old rice for risotto; it must be a proper Italian one that absorbs loads of liquid

but still retains its texture. Arborio is the bog standard risotto rice, and perfectly good it is, too. Vialone nano is small-grained and a traditional northern Italian favourite, but my own preference is for carnaroli, a larger-grained rice which is very good-tempered and reliable. The Gallo brand is freely available in most supermarkets.

Dried pasta

I'm a great fan of De Cecco dried pasta in its distinctive turquoise packaging – although sod's law says that by the time you read this it will probably have changed to brown kraft (that's German for 'force' by the way) paper. Not only does this pasta come in a fantastic range of shapes and sizes, it performs superbly well. Having said that, the quality of supermarket own-label pasta is immeasurably better than it used to be. The best is produced in Italy (and will say so on the label).

Butter

I always use unsalted butter, not just in cakes and desserts, but even in recipes which need salt. It has a sweet, creamy, fresh flavour quite unlike slightly-salted butter and, in my view, is well worth the extra dosh. I only make one exception to this rule, and that's for buttered crumpets which, for some reason, are hopeless unless you plaster them with salted butter.

Bottled clams

It's odd how some foods slump into despondency when they're packed away in a bottle or tin, while others lounge around like Sleeping Beauty waiting to be woken with a can-opener. Clams are particularly container-happy, especially if they've been packed in their own juices: just one little bottle coupled with some oil, garlic and parsley, and a hank of linguine, makes a super-speedy, very good supper for two. The Medusa brand is particularly good, and Carluccio's vongole con guscio (with shells).

Lobster

Please don't ever waste your money on Canadian lobster – the flavour is as elusive as a check-out packer on a Saturday morning (but not at Tesco's – respect). Unfortunately Canadian lobsters don't look very different from British lobsters, although the colour is perhaps a little darker red (when cooked), and the shell is slightly more plastic-looking. The real clue is that our own superb native lobsters are only available from April to September. Buy a lobster at any other time, and it's almost certain to be a Mountie.

The other important thing is that freshly boiled lobster – which, I am afraid, means lobster you've killed yourself – is stupendously better in both flavour and texture than ready-cooked lobster. If you really can't bring yourself to commit homaricide, at least try to ensure the sun hasn't set on the day the bought-in lobsters were dispatched.

Plum sauce

My favourite instant dip for spring rolls, crab cakes, prawn won tons, or any other dryish Asian-style food, is a splodge of Sharwood's plum sauce mixed up with a little hot chilli sauce. Apart from the sweet, zippy flavour, I like the fact that the ingredients are remarkably innocent – if you can forgive the sugar content. (And I can.)

Palm sugar

Palm sugar is very sweet, richly-flavoured, toffeeish – and worth every calorie. I first had it (the sugar, that is) in Bali, where it was playing a starring role in one of the most sublime desserts I've ever eaten – black rice pudding. God, it was gorgeous. Unfortunately, I made the mistake of asking for some rice and sugar to bring back. One year later, I was still regularly throwing out the entire contents of the store cupboard in an effort to rid it of the little black bugs that kept tipping up in packets of rice and pasta, sealed or not. Nowadays palm sugar is readily available in Asian stores, and major supermarkets (and black rice is making an appearance).

Olives

I've rarely seen such an extravagant and great-tasting array of olives as the ones marketed by the Fresh Olive Company (although I am very partial to the oven-dried black olives with orange peel, sold by Waitrose). I nearly always prefer ripe, black olives to the sharper, youthful, green ones, but the marinades and stuffings employed by the Fresh Olive Company are so good, it hardly matters.

German mustard

I've become very fond of German mustard recently, finding it milder and less vinegary than Dijon mustard. I prefer it in sandwiches and with ham and sausages.

Pancetta

Heaven knows what we did before pancetta appeared in our lives. Of course, I know exactly what we did – we used streaky bacon. But there's no denying that Italian, salted belly of pork (pancetta) is finer-flavoured and less bumptious than streaky bacon. Pancetta can sometimes be found on the deli counter in a big piece, but supermarkets tend to sell it in packets, either in small dice or thinly sliced. Use pancetta as a base ingredient in soups and stews, fried to a crisp and tossed into salads; or braised with vegetables and pulses.

Peaches, apricots and nectarines

It's a complete waste of time buying any stone-fruit that isn't flagged up as 'tree-ripened'. Otherwise, all that happens is that you take home some rock-hard peaches, lovingly nurse them for a few days, and then find they've achieved the botanical feat of being both simultaneously rotten and still under-ripe. Alternatively, they ripen (a little bit), but still taste of old blankets. Pay the extra, and buy peaches, nectarines and apricots that are ready to eat – and that you're likely to enjoy.

Limes

Think about it: most fruits that are green are under-ripe. Limes are no exception. So next time you're in the supermarket, instead of spurning the yellow-splashed limes, buy them; they'll be riper (and juicier) than the dark green ones.

Full-fat dairy products

My philosophy is quite simple: I'd rather have a dollop of rich, luscious, full-fat mascarpone, crème fraîche or cream once a month, than a tub of timid, low-fat cream every week.

Avocados

Don't be seduced by ultra-large, smooth-skinned avocados; they look good but tend to be watery and tasteless. The Hass variety is by far the creamiest and richest-flavoured avocado readily available, and can be easily recognised by its pimply, dark purple-green skin. As for ripeness, those labels suggesting the avocados are ripe and ready to eat are, in my experience, optimistic to the point of lying: avocados nearly always need a day or two at room temperature before they're worth eating.

Yoghurt

If you want a really thick, rich, tangy, plain yoghurt there's only one to buy, and that's Greek yoghurt. But make sure it's genuine Greek yoghurt, not Greek-style yoghurt. The most common brand is Total, and it's very good, particularly if you can find their sheep's milk yoghurt, which is truly sublime. Otherwise, Loseley and Rachel's Dairy both make an excellent range of plain and flavoured yoghurts, and Marks & Spencer's Channel Island yoghurts are quite superb.

Know-how

'If the custard does curdle, there's an easy remedy: pour it into a food processor, lumps and all, add an ice cube and whizz until smooth. To all intents and purposes this does the trick, but try not to bugger it up in the first place'

To let down

This isn't what your partner does to you when he turns up at the firm's Christmas 'do' wearing Brut and grey shoes, but a culinary term which describes the process of making a thick liquid thinner. So, for example, if a custard is too thick, you let it down by adding more milk.

Zest

There are two parts to the skin of a citrus fruit. The outer, coloured layer is called the zest, and the soft, fibrous layer underneath is called the pith. It's the zest that contains the aromatic oils, and it's these oils which can add so much flavour to a recipe. You can use a sharp knife to remove the zest, but it's easier and more efficient to use a little tool called a zester.

Keeping it warm

Recipes very often include an instruction to keep something warm. If you've got a four-oven Aga this is a doddle because you can use the lower left-hand oven. But for those who don't own a Volvo and a black Labrador, I suggest you wrap a piece of foil loosely around the dish, and leave it near, or above, the stove. To prevent food drying out, always cover it with foil or clingfilm – surprisingly, the latter doesn't melt, as long as the heat is no higher than 100°C.

Toasting nuts

I prefer to spread the nuts on a baking tray and brown them in a hot oven, but they can be toasted just as effectively under the grill or in a heavy frying pan. Whichever method you use, it's imperative that you don't kid yourself you won't forget them. Nuts with little substance – flaked almonds or pine nuts, for example – only take 2-3 minutes to brown in a 200°C oven, and less under the grill. Once you've chucked the third tray of burnt nuts in the bin, you'll realise this is one occasion when you *must* put the pinger on.

Folding in

I don't suppose there are too many reflexology clients who have spent the last five minutes of their treatment standing semi-clad by the couch, holding an imaginery spoon, and demonstrating the art of folding to their therapist. Never mind, once darling Dee (*the* best reflexologist in London) realised that stirring was not the same as folding, it sent her sponge cakes soaring.

Firstly, you need a large metal spoon, at least three times the size of a tablespoon. Now for the action: cut down sharply with the side of the spoon to the bottom of the bowl, then bring it back to the surface in a light, looping action – as if you were drawing the outline of a wheel. By scooping the contents from the bottom of the bowl and bringing them to the surface, you incorporate air, as well as mix the ingredients together. Stirring, conversely, bashes out the air and will leave your sponge cake, meringue or mousse as flat as the proverbial pancake.

Melting chocolate

I'm spoilt by having an Aga, because all I have to do is put the broken chocolate into a saucepan and leave it on the warming plate where it melts to perfection. You can also melt chocolate very successfully in a microwave, but the normal, gadget-free method is to break the chocolate into a bowl and perch it over a pan of hot water that's not quite simmering (or use a double saucepan, if you have one). The chocolate will take five to ten minutes to melt. What you must never ever do is let the chocolate come into contact with high heat, or it will turn into an ugly, grainy (irredeemable) mess.

Clarifying butter

There's a very good reason for bothering to clarify butter – it burns far less quickly than butter straight from the packet. And, although it sounds like something only a real cuisine-swot would do, clarifying butter is dead easy. Put the butter into a small saucepan, melt it over a low heat, then pull the saucepan to one side and let the contents settle. After a few minutes you will see a milky, curdled-looking mass (just some harmless solids and impurities) skulking underneath the clear, liquid, golden butter. Gently pour this liquid off – discarding the milky sediment in the bottom of the pan – and there's your clarified butter. As it keeps for several weeks in the fridge it's worth making in quantity. Then, next time you want to fry some fillets of plaice, you won't end up with sooty-black-speckled fish.

Making croûtons

First, slice a fairly thick piece of crustless bread into small or medium dice (the recipe will make the distinction). You can either deep-fry the cubes of bread at 180°C, or shallow-fry them for about 2 minutes in a frying pan over a medium-to-high heat, tossing and turning them almost constantly. Alternatively, you could spread the cubes on a baking sheet, drizzle them with oil (olive oil for Mediterranean-inspired recipes, groundnut for everything else), and cook them in a preheated oven, 160°C (fan), 180°C (conventional), gas mark 4, for about ten minutes.

Drain the croûtons on a pad of kitchen paper before using them. Any that are surplus can be kept for a few days in an airtight container lined with fresh kitchen paper, and used at a later date to scatter over salads, egg or pasta dishes and soups.

Peeling garlic

I tried one of those newfangled plastic tubes that are meant to peel garlic, and thought it was hopeless. I can't be bothered with a garlic press, either – by the time you've cleaned it out and washed it up, you could have read *A Brief History of Time*. No, all you need is a heavy knife. Slice off the little root end, cover the clove with the blade turned horizontally, and give it a good thwack with your fist. In one fell swoop the clove is crushed and the skin thoroughly loosened. Now, all you have to do is chop the clove, as required.

If the garlic is going to remain raw, or you want a particularly mild flavour, don't crush the clove first, just chop it. Crushing accentuates the flavour by breaking down the cell walls and allowing the essential oils to mingle to maximum effect.

Cooking pasta

On the packet it always tells you to cook pasta in plenty of boiling, salted water. That means p-l-e-n-t-y of water, lots and lots. In other words, more than a pint or two in a tiny saucepan. Imagine a half-filled bucket – two-thirds filled, maybe. That much. Second tip: when the water comes back to the boil, stir the pasta thoroughly so it doesn't stick together in ugly clumps. Now an even better tip: good-quality dried pasta can be cooked in advance, thoroughly rinsed under cold running water, and then 'held' for several hours in a pot of cold water. To reheat it, all you have to do is to plunge the pasta into a pan of very hot water, leave it to soak for a couple of minutes, then drain again.

Finally, the best tip of the lot: instead of adding more cream or oil to let down a pasta sauce, use some of the cooking water instead. Just a small ladle or two will transform an ugly, too-dry-and-stiff tangle into a silky rhapsody.

Sweating

Not exactly an elegant turn of phrase, but sweating is nothing to do with dart players, and everything to do with cooking vegetables very gently, and slowly, in butter or oil so they soften – indeed, almost melt. This culinary term is used mostly in connection with the onion family, and other pot vegetables, but not exclusively so.

Storing flavoured butters

A rather esoteric little technique, this one, but useful none the less. Whether it's a savoury garlic butter or a sweet brandy butter the method is the same: scrape the mixture on to the centre of a piece of clingfilm in a rough, sausage-shape, wrap the clingfilm around the length of the butter, then gather up the two ends and twist them in opposite directions. This not only moulds the butter into an almost perfect sausage shape, which can be neatly sliced later on, but ensures the packet is airtight.

Coating food for frying

There are two simple but effective ways to make this chore less messy. Firstly, use only one hand throughout to coat the food; this leaves the other hand free to flick away that irritating strand of hair, and prevents you ending up with egg in your ear. Second, line up the dishes containing the coating ingredients (milk, egg, flour and breadcrumbs, for example) in the same order you are going to use them. Organisation is a wonderful thing.

Dusting with icing sugar or cocoa

While it's quite permissible to dust a cake or tart with icing sugar or cocoa powder, only time-warped chefs dust the actual plate: it's pointless and unsightly, and woe betide anyone who tries it on in my restaurant. But if you do want to dust said cake or tart, the easiest way is to put the powder in a flour-shaker or a small sieve. To make a pattern, lie a paper template over the surface of the food and shake the sugar or cocoa over the top; when you remove the template, hey presto, a neat design.

Peeling a pineapple

You can't do this without a very sharp, medium-length knife. Cut a thick slice from the top and bottom of the pineapple, reserving the saucy top-knot for decoration, if you like. Stand the pineapple on a work surface, and slice down fairly thickly to remove both the peel and most of the little tufts that are embedded in the pineapple flesh. Any that remain can be nicked out with the edge of the blade. (If you take the skin off too finely, it will mean having to go over the whole surface with a potato peeler to remove the tufts. Not only is this very tedious, but you'll end up with a pineapple that looks as if it's the son of Ventress. Heartbeat fans will get my drift.

Although you often see pineapple cut into rings, this isn't a very clever idea because pineapples vary in sweetness from one end to the other – lucky the person who gets the stem end. It is far better to cut the pineapple lengthways into fine slices. Slice it in quarters lengthways. Remove the core from each section, turn each piece flat-side down on the work surface, and cut thin slices from top to bottom. Of course, you could cheat and buy one of those clever gadgets that, apparently, remove the skin and core in one fell swoop. I wouldn't know.

Cleaning mussels

Commercial, rope-grown mussels are nothing like as dirty as wild mussels. Nevertheless, they still need a vigorous sloosh in a sinkful of clean cold water. After you've washed them – or scrubbed them, if they're very dirty – pick up the mussels one by one and rip off the tough, hairy 'beard' (byssus) which the mussel uses to anchor itself to the ropes. Scrape off any barnacles with a small robust knife (or the shell of another mussel), and give any open mussels a sharp tap. If they remain open they are dead, so discard them. Once the mussels have been cooked, however, do the reverse, and chuck out any that remain closed.

Spanking fresh mussels will keep for a day in the fridge with a thick piece of wet newspaper over the top of them. Ignore all that rot about feeding them with oatmeal – they'll just keel over and die, even bold Scottish mussels.

Sorting out squid

A whole squid might look rather horrific, but once you steel yourself for preparing the ghoul-white, slippery creatures there's a perverse enjoyment to be had. The first thing is to pull off

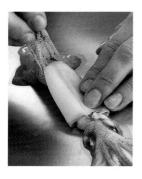

the fine, transparent membrane which embraces the entire squid, and remove the two triangular wings – the latter can be quite tough and, generally, I prefer to use them for stock. Pull out the tentacles from the body, if they are still attached. Chop off the bit that was inside the white sac and discard it, leaving a small circular band to which the purplish tentacles are attached. Cut any freakishly long tentacles into two-inch lengths. Scrape out and discard anything left inside the sac – normally just a bit of creamy stuff or, with larger squid, an amazing cellophane blade. Finally, neaten up the crinkly-edged opening to the sac.

Cut the sacs into strips, rings or squares, according to the recipe, but only use small or medium-sized squid for rings as larger squid will be too tough. For squares or strips, first slice the sac down its natural, thickened join to open it out. If the squid is large, use the point of a knife to cross-hatch the inner surface – it helps to tenderise the flesh, and prevents the squid curling up too much when it's cooked.

Preparing scallops

It's unusual to see scallops still in their shells nowadays, but if you do come across any the fishmonger will be quite happen to open them for you. Normally scallops are sold already

shucked, but still in a fairly messy state. Using a small knife, or your fingers, pull off the pinkish corals (the roe), remove the rubbery band which attaches them to the scallop, and the small, thickish white pad that adheres to the side of the scallop meat. You should now have a small pile of corals and some pristine, small drums of ivory scallop flesh. (Discard or reserve the other trimmings for a fish stock). If the scallops are extremely large you can cut them in half horizontally, but I prefer to leave them whole.

Although the coral is incredibly pretty, some people don't like its soft, pappy texture. Whether you serve the corals or not is up to you, but it seems a shame to waste them.

Peeling (and blanching) tomatoes

For rustic dishes, I think it's crazy bothering to remove the skins from tomatoes, but there are some recipes where a certain elegance is required. In those rare instances, boil a kettle of water, pour it into a heat-resistant bowl, then plop in the tomatoes and leave them for 1 minute. Drain off the water, leave the tomatoes to cool, and you'll find the skins slip off as easily as an ice-cream wrapper.

The same technique can be used for removing the skin from peaches, nectarines and apricots.

Surviving chillies

The fierce oil that renders chillies hot will remain on your fingers even after washing them thoroughly. To avoid any agony from inadvertently rubbing your eyes, nose or – heaven forbid, while you are cooking – any other sensitive parts, wear thin, disposable plastic gloves while you prepare the chillies, or cover your hand with a small plastic bag (or a piece of clingfilm). Use the protected hand to discard all the trimmings, and the blade of the knife to transfer the chopped chillies to the recipe. The seeds are particularly hot so always discard these unless you want a scorching heat. And, remember, drinking water or beer only exacerbates the pain; assuage the heat with something fatty instead, such as milk, lassi or yoghurt, all of which will calm things down far more effectively.

Cracking crab

It might look completely impenetrable, but it's actually easier to get into a crab than a bottle of aspirin. Firstly, wrench off the legs and claws and break them apart at the joints; discard the pointed, furry feet. Put the claws and legs in a strong plastic bag, and crack them with a meat mallet or hammer. The glorious white meat can now be picked out very easily.

Turn the legless crab upside down, and pull off and discard the flap (apron) that curls underneath the shell. (By the way, a wide,

stubby apron signifies a female – more flavour – and a thin, longer apron, a male crab – more white meat.) Insert a short, sturdy knife between the shell and the body of the crab, and twist the two sections apart. Pull off and discard the sharp-edged mouth area, and the grey feathered gills which surround the dome of fine-shelled white body meat. (These are known as dead man's fingers, which sums up their appearance pretty well.) Chop the body into quarters and, if you're preparing the crab for a fruits de mer in which everybody does their own work, leave it at that. If it's for a recipe, then pick out all the white meat from the body, cracking each little hollowed segment open as you go.

The terracotta-brown meat inside the shell can be used for dressed crab, bound with mayonnaise, breadcrumbs and seasoning. Or freeze it, and add it to a sauce or stock at a later date. Being strong-flavoured and close-textured, it's not to everyone's taste.

Poaching eggs

Absolute freshness is the only secret to successful poached eggs. Unfortunately, commercial egg producers are only compelled to mark the date the eggs were *packed* on the cartons, not the date the eggs were laid. I reckon you could sometimes take a world cruise in between the two dates. So unless you know for certain that the eggs are really fresh (which means no more than 3 days old), you'll have to rely on the old trick of adding a tablespoon of vinegar to the poaching water: better still, cook something else.

Happily, eggs can be poached in advance and then reheated: slip the cooked eggs into a bowl of ice-cold water to stop the cooking process then, when they're completely cold, transfer them into another bowl of ice-cold water. The eggs can now be kept for up to 24 hours in the fridge. To reheat them, put the poached eggs into a heatproof bowl, and very gently drown them in boiling-hot water. Leave them for one minute, then drain, and serve as normal.

Mixing and tossing

I can't tell you how much easier it is to mix things with your hands, rather than with an implement. Well, I can, and have. Of course, your hands must be as clean as a whistle (how on earth did that particular expression come about, given that the average whistle is bubbling with spittle?), but then you're grown up and know that. And, if you're grown up and don't know that, you probably work on a shellfish stall at the races. (Or is it just me who's always served by a bloke who doesn't skip a beat between fingering the lobster and having a fag round the back?) Anyway your infinitely dextrous, pristine hands, as fashioned by the Great Designer, are the best things ever invented to mix anything from a fruit cake batter to a salad.

Preparing Herbs

There is as much, or more, flavour in the stalks of herbs as in their leaves, but when to use the stalks depends very much on the recipe. Take parsley: if it's for a stock, where flavour is all and texture nothing, then by all means put the stalks in, as well as the leaves. If I'm making a parsley sauce for an old-fashioned fish pie, I always use a fair proportion of the stalks (finely chopped). But if the recipe calls for a final, decorative scattering of chopped parsley, the flavour and texture of the thick stalks can be too brutal, so only use the very fine upper stalks and the leaves. The same rule applies to all the 'soft' herbs – coriander and dill, for example.

If, on the other hand, you are using a 'woody'

herb, such as thyme, marjoram, oregano or rosemary, the stalks should always be discarded; you can either strip the leaves off and chuck out the stalk from the outset, or put the entire sprig in the dish, then fish out the denuded stalk at the end.

Use a knife to chop most leafy herbs, except basil: the cut edges turn brown very quickly so it's better to tear the leaves, unless the chopped leaves are going to be used in a sauce where any discolouration won't be noticed.

Peeling broad beans

Eating a broad bean that's been peeled of its inner skin is like the difference between wearing Giorgio Armani and George. Unlike Italian couture, however, it won't cost you a zillion lira to put on the style, just a bit of elbow grease. Peel the beans after they've been cooked, when the skins will slip off very easily: simply pinch the bottom of the greyish shells, and the bright green kernels will pop out. If you're serving the beans hot, toss them in a little melted butter to reheat them.

Rescuing curdled custard

You don't need to use a double-boiler to cook real custard, but you do need to stir it constantly, and you do need to remove the saucepan from the heat just before the custard boils, or the eggs in it will curdle. (This only applies to cornflour-less custard.) But custard isn't quite as alarmingly sensitive as it might seem, and you can certainly allow a few small bubbles to rise to the top, before you need panic. If the custard does curdle, there's an easy remedy: pour it into a food processor, lumps and all, add an ice cube and whizz until smooth. To all intents and purposes this does the trick, but try not to bugger it up in the first place.

Oiling baking tins

If the recipe asks you to oil a tin or baking sheet, always use an appropriate oil – olive oil for something like a pizza where the flavour of the oil will enhance the food, and a tasteless oil (preferably groundnut) for sweet or mild-tasting food, where you don't want any taint of oil to be left at all.

Re-using oil

As long as you neither over-heat or burn it, deep-fat frying oil can be re-used several times. Always scoop out (and discard) any fragments of cooked food or batter from the oil before re-heating it – another instance where a Chinese spider comes in very handy – or pass the cold oil through a sieve, if you prefer.

Pastry

The secret of good pastry is to use as little liquid as possible, and as much fat as it will take: this is what makes pastry meltingly crumbly, rather than tough. My recipes include egg yolk, because this is a way of introducing fat, but in liquid form. I've always used a spot of icing sugar, too, but have to confess that it's only habit – there's not enough to flavour the pastry, but I cling to the idea that it helps the texture. You will also find a constant admonition not to stretch the pastry when you are lining a tin. This is simply because when the pastry cooks it contracts, and you'll be left with a pastry case that's as useless for filling as a shrunk duvet cover.

Favourite kitchen kit

'You could write a book about kitchen equipment, and people have. Apart from the frequently stated (and sound) advice to invest in top quality saucepans, here are a few of my favourite tools'

Tongs

A pair of professional chef's tongs – and I don't mean those silly tweezer-like things made out of a single piece of bent metal – make life a lot easier. The ones I'm talking about are hinged and open as wide as a crocodile's mouth, with a scalloped-edged 'grabber'. I use them all the time, not just for turning bacon or sausages, but for extracting hot pans from the oven, taking lids off saucepans, nicking a piece of pasta out of the pot to taste, or putting in an egg to boil. They are like a heat-proof extension of my own fingers, and quite brilliantly useful.

Chinese spider

The long-handled, open-wire-meshed ladle called a 'spider' has a value quite out of proportion to its monetary cost: when your hand is a long way from the business end, it's quite safe to fish things out of boiling liquid, or skim bits of batter from the deep-fat fryer. And because the scooping part is so capacious, you can shovel up large quantities in one fell swoop. Spiders aren't often stocked in conventional kitchen equipment shops, but if you're ever in a supermarket or a hardware shop in Chinatown, you'll find them in sizes ranging from a saucer to a dinner plate.

Zester

Far from being one of those useless gadgets that ends up lying forgotten in the kitchen drawer, a zester is a precious little tool. Edged with a line of tiny, sharp-edged holes that remove the zest from citrus fruit in thin, perfect, pith-free strips, it's a cheap 'must' for any cook, especially one who wants to make lemon meringue pie – what more inducement do you need.

Oroshigane

A dedicated root ginger grater probably sounds too esoteric for words, but if you value your knuckles, it's really worth spending a fiver, or so, on a Japanese oroshigane. This small hand-held plaque bristles with raised ceramic pimples that

are harmless to the operator. Where the ginger is concerned, though, it has the same grating capability as Barbara Windsor singing 'You've Got a Friend'.

Whisks

It would be a mistake to think that whisks are only good for whipping cream or egg whites. They're also brilliant for making sauces: a whisk can delve into the corners of a saucepan far more effectively than a wooden spoon, and is often better at the basic task of combining ingredients, too. Balloon whisks come in all shapes and sizes; I'd recommend buying two – one about 32cm long, the other about 22cm. Whatever the size, the most important thing to look out for is the quantity and springiness of the metal loops. A stiff whisk with only a few loops is okay for stirring, but useless for incorporating air into something such as meringue. As a straightforward mixing implement, though, one of those wire-looped, horseshoe-shaped 'magic' whisks is admirable.

Pestle and mortar

The mortar is the bowl, the pestle is the bashing bit, and they come in many different sizes and materials – wood, marble, ceramic or stone. I own one large ceramic pestle and mortar which I find works as well for pounding small amounts as large ones. (And the rough internal surface assists the grinding process far more effectively than a smooth surface.) If you don't have a pestle and mortar, a liquidiser or blender will do, but use the pulse button: if a recipe recommends a pestle and mortar it's because the food should retain a rough, grainy texture, rather than be reduced to a smooth, characterless purée.

Saucepans

I'm fully aware that the most boring part of any cook book is the one that exhorts you to buy good quality knives and saucepans. Yawn, yawn, bring me my copy of *Hello!*, I'm going to paint my nails – do you prefer Rouge Noir or

Dragon Red? Well, sorry to be tedious, but there's nothing that will enhance your ability to cook well more than a decent range of saucepans – decent in terms of both quality, and size. Which means you must have at least one big sauté pan, and you must have a saucepan capacious enough to poach a whole kitchen – whoa, where did that come from – I meant chicken. (I wrote out a cheque for 70 foods yesterday; writing this book is definitely getting to me.) I've had my aluminium-based, stainless-steel, Cuisinox saucepans for nigh on 20 years, and they still look brilliant – literally – and function impeccably. Naturally, they cost an arm and a leg, but if you consider how long they last, they're cheap at the price. (A good-quality non-stick pan is vital for scrambling eggs, though.)

Bakeware

The best quality metal bakeware I've found is sold under the brand name La Forme, has a 5-year guarantee and, despite its French-sounding name, is Luftwaffe-grey, and made in Germany. After nearly 10 years, my springform cake tins are still going strong, as are a variety of other La Forme baking tins, none of which sticks or buckles, and all of which bake evenly. Vorsprung durch Küchentechnik, as they say.

Blini/egg pans

A very personal foible, this one, but I love my tiny cast-iron blini pans, not just for making fat little buckwheat pancakes to go with caviar, but for the everyday task of frying eggs. Admittedly it helps that I've got a solid top stove, but I can cook six eggs separately in six pans, knowing that they're all going to turn out perfectly – and round. I can't bear those hacked-up, squarish eggs you get when several have been cooked together in a big frying pan.

Spoons

A slotted spoon has little holes drilled in the bowl. It's incredibly useful for allowing fat or liquid to drain off food, and every cook should own at least one. They're not expensive, and will last a life-time, especially if the handle and bowl are crafted from the same piece of metal. Another essential is a big metal spoon (at least three times the size of a standard 15ml tablespoon) for all-round general use, and for 'folding' in egg whites and sponge mixtures.

Cake lifter

If you only make one elaborate cake or tart a year, it will still be worth buying a dedicated cake lifter. Simply a large, flat, sheet of metal, it takes all the stress out of transferring a precious, vulnerable cake from its baking tin to the serving plate – and I speak as someone who once dropped a huge pavlova on the floor three hours before Delia was coming to lunch. (Yes, I did make another one.)

Non-reactive containers

More of an explanation than an exhortation to buy, non-reactive containers are made of material which does not interact with food. Generally speaking, non-reactive means plastic, glass or ceramic; it is vital that food (especially anything acidic), is not stored in aluminium, copper or iron.

Meat mallet

Mainly intended for bashing out veal or chicken escalopes, a wooden mallet is also great for cracking open crab or lobster claws. You can also use it for bashing amaretti (or other biscuits) into sweet oblivion when you need a crumb lining for a cheesecake or suchlike. (Remember to put the biscuits in a stout plastic bag first.)

From left to right: Draining spoon, oroshigane, meat mallet, Chinese spider, zester, chef's tongs, blini pan and balloon whisk.

Wintry starters

When I eat out in a restaurant, I often choose two (or even three – I'm very greedy) starters, rather than a conventional meal. Starters always seem more frivolous, more daring, and less weighty – both in quantity and intention. It's as if the chef thinks, Oh I'll have a bit of fun before I get down to the boring business of stuffing stomachs. The starters here look almost frighteningly eclectic, but they're definitely not gimmicky; all of these dishes burst with flavour and pizzazz, which is exactly what you need in the depths of winter.

The beauty of this soup – apart from its sassy flavour and bright colour – is that, like a day at the races, it can be as smart or downhome as you like. The basic blend of squash, chickpeas, tomato and aromatic spices is perfect for a family soup, but knock up an unctuous basil rouille (a spin on the rust-coloured mayonnaise traditionally served with Mediterranean fish soup), and it becomes a seriously splendid affair. I feel slightly embarrassed including basil in a wintry recipe, but it's silly to pretend fresh herbs are not available year round – albeit your own home-grown summer basil will be far more intensely flavoured.

The soup can be made well in advance, and will linger in the fridge for a fair few days, but the basil rouille would be better kept cool and served within 24 hours.

Butternut and chickpea soup with basil rouille

TO SERVE 6-plus

FOR THE SOUP
50g unsalted butter
1 large shallot, peeled and finely chopped
1 clove of garlic, peeled, crushed and finely chopped
1 mild chilli, deseeded and finely chopped
1 medium butternut squash, peeled and cut into roughly 3cm cubes
1 level tsp ground cinnamon
1/2 level tsp ground cumin
1/2 level tsp ground coriander
1 (420g) tin chickpeas, drained and rinsed
4 rounded tsp Marigold Swiss vegetable bouillon powder
2 (200g) tins chair de tomate
about 1.2 litres cold water

FOR THE BASIL ROUILLE
about 20 fresh basil leaves
1 large free-range egg yolk
1 large free-range egg
a pinch dry mustard powder
150ml extra-virgin olive oil
150ml groundnut oil
a squeeze of fresh lemon juice
1 (420g) tin chickpeas, drained and rinsed

YOU WILL NEED
a very large saucepan, with lid

Heat the butter in a large saucepan over a medium heat, and gently fry the shallot, garlic and chilli for 2-3 minutes. Tip in the squash, toss the cubes around, and continue to cook for about 5 minutes, stirring frequently. Add the spices, and cook for a further minute to release the flavour. Take the pan off the heat, stir in the chickpeas, Marigold powder, chair de tomate and water, and season well with salt and pepper. (If you cannot find the chair de tomate, you can use a 400g tin of Italian tomatoes, drained and chopped, with 1 teaspoon of tomato purée.) Put the pan back on to a high heat and bring the contents to a boil, with the lid on. Now reduce the heat and simmer the soup for 30-40 minutes, half-covered, until the squash is tender.

Remove the saucepan from the heat, take off the lid, and allow the soup to cool for 10-15 minutes. Pour it into a liquidiser (in several batches) and whizz until smooth. If you are not making the rouille, the soup can now be reheated and served, family-style.

To make the rouille, first boil a saucepan of water, put the basil in for 20 seconds, then drain and 'refresh' the leaves under cold running water, to fix the colour. Put the whole egg, the egg yolk and the mustard in a liquidiser and whizz for 30 seconds. Season, add the basil, and whizz for another 30 seconds, then scrape down the sides. Mix the oils together in a jug. With the motor going, pour the oil through the lid, a few drops at a time, then after 1 minute in a thin, thread-like stream. Only when at least half the oil has been incorporated and the mayonnaise has thickened can the thread be increased to a string-like stream. Stop the machine halfway through to add a squeeze of lemon, and scrape down the sides. Once the oil is incorporated, taste, and adjust the seasoning, perhaps adding more lemon juice, or salt and pepper. Finally, scrape the rouille out into a bowl and fold in the chickpeas. Float a dollop of rouille in the middle of each bowl and serve at once.

A lot of my recipes come about through desperation at the apparent lack of food in the fridge. Sometimes they turn out to be rather good, well up to offering friends and family as bona fide food.

This soup is best freshly made because the spinach gets quite dowdy-looking as time wears on.

Spinach, two-pea and leek soup

TO SERVE 6-plus
4 tbsp olive oil
3 large cloves of garlic, peeled, crushed and finely chopped
2 large leeks trimmed, rinsed and chopped into medium dice
4 sticks celery, rinsed and chopped into medium dice
1 large onion, peeled and chopped into medium dice
1 tbsp Marigold Swiss vegetable bouillon powder
1.5 litres boiling water
1 (420g) tin chickpeas, drained and rinsed
200g leaf spinach, trimmed, cleaned and roughly torn
about 150g peas, fresh or frozen

YOU WILL NEED
a very large saucepan, with lid

Put the saucepan over a medium heat and pour in the oil. When it's warm, stir in the garlic, leeks, celery and onion. Cook for about 10 minutes, stirring occasionally, until the vegetables have softened, but don't let them brown.

Spoon in the Marigold powder, and pour on the boiling water. Bring the contents of the saucepan to the boil, covered. Add a large pinch of salt, reduce the heat and simmer the soup, half-covered, for about 25 minutes.

Finally, add the chickpeas, spinach and peas, season with pepper, and simmer for a further 10 minutes, uncovered. Taste the soup to check the seasoning, then serve.

This is a no-nonsense, homely type of soup which is easy to make and very satisfying to eat. Feel free to use any other type of leafy green cabbage (kale or Savoy cabbage, for example) in place of the greens, but the muted-celery flavour of celeriac – that large, knobbly, swede-like root – is mandatory.

The soup can be made in advance, and will keep refrigerated for several days. But it needs to be reheated very gently, or the potatoes will turn to mush; the greens, too, become a bit dingy after 48 hours or so. If you prefer you can use a tin of (drained and rinsed) cannellini beans instead of the potatoes – the soup will taste equally good.

Celeriac, greens and potato soup

TO SERVE 8-plus
about 500g greens
about 500g not-too-floury
potatoes (eg Desirée)
1 celeriac root
15g unsalted butter
2 tbsp olive oil
1 medium onion, peeled
and roughly chopped
3 cloves of garlic, peeled,
crushed and finely chopped
1 mild green chilli, deseeded
and finely chopped
2 shallots, peeled and
finely chopped
3 tbsp Marigold Swiss
vegetable bouillon powder
2 litres boiling water

YOU WILL NEED
a very large saucepan, with lid

Strip the greens from their stalks, and discard any very tough or damaged leaves. Wash thoroughly, then bundle the leaves together and slice into ribbons roughly 1cm wide. Peel the potatoes and cut into bite-sized chunks. Peel the celeriac and cut it into small cubes. Leave to one side.

Combine the butter and oil in the saucepan and heat it over a low-to-medium flame. Tip in the onion, garlic, chilli and shallots and fry gently for 6-8 minutes, stirring occasionally, until they have softened.

Add the celeriac and fry it gently for 5 minutes, stirring occasionally, then toss in the potato and fry for a further 2 minutes. Add the Marigold powder and the water. Give the soup a good stir and season well with salt and pepper. Raise the heat, and bring the soup to the boil, with the lid on.

Immediately reduce the heat to a strong simmer, and cook for 15 minutes, half-covered. Now throw in the greens and bring the soup back to the boil. Reduce the heat again, and carry on simmering for 15-20 minutes, still with the pan half-covered, until all the vegetables are tender. Finally, taste the soup, and adjust the seasoning.

'Sparky ginger, coriander and garlic permeate the aubergine flesh like a cuckoo commandeering a wren's nest: the intense soy glaze completes the assault'

There is no better gastronomic blotting paper than aubergines, even if they don't have much taste themselves – or perhaps *because* they don't. But when it comes to sopping up and enhancing other flavours aubergines are the business. In this recipe, sparky ginger, coriander and garlic permeate the aubergine flesh like a cuckoo commandeering a wren's nest: the soy glaze completes the assault. (Etymologists might like to know my US Spellcheck preferred aborigine flesh.)

The aubergines will positively relish a long soak in the marinade, but must be served immediately after they've been cooked.

Soy-glazed grilled aubergines

TO SERVE 4
a large-thumb-sized knob of root ginger
2 large cloves of garlic, peeled and crushed
a small handful of fresh coriander (including stalks), coarsely chopped
1 tsp black peppercorns
1 tsp coarse sea salt
2 medium aubergines, trimmed, and halved lengthways
2 tbsp dark soy sauce
2 tbsp miso paste (medium or dark)
2 tbsp groundnut oil
1 level tbsp natural cane sugar

YOU WILL NEED
a pestle and mortar; a heavy baking tray

Preheat the grill just before cooking the aubergines.

Prepare the marinade. Peel and coarsely chop the ginger. Grind it with the garlic, coriander, peppercorns and salt in a mortar, or pulse in a blender until the ingredients have been smashed to a paste.

Cut off a small slice from the rounded side of each half-aubergine to form a flat base. Cross-hatch the flesh into roughly 2cm diamonds, scoring deeply but without cutting through the skin. Using clean hands, work the gingery paste into the flesh. Put the aubergines on a baking tray, clingfilm tightly, and leave to marinate for 2-8 hours.

Whisk the soy sauce, miso paste, oil and sugar together, and paint the aubergine flesh with just over half the glaze. Put the baking tray under the grill, at least 25cm from the elements, and cook the aubergines for 15 minutes. Remove the tray, and brush the aubergines with the remaining glaze. Grill for a further 10 minutes, or until the flesh is as soft, brown and wrinkly as an old leather coat.

If you've only had onion bhajis from a supermarket or in a so-called Indian restaurant – they're normally Bangladeshi – you're in for a fantastic treat. With their crisp batter, fresh herbs and sensitive spicing these home-made bhajis are quite sublime, and as different from restaurant bhajis as the Taj Mahal from the Dome. For occasions when you can't be bothered to make the mint yoghurt exactly as described, dip the crunchy-soft, aromatic bhajis into some chilled plain yoghurt – it will still be a near-divine experience.

The yoghurt dip can be prepared up to 24 hours ahead, and kept refrigerated. The dry ingredients for the bhajis can be mixed up to 24 hours ahead, and kept in a sealed polythene bag; add the herbs and water at the last moment.

Deep-fried onion bhajis with mint, coriander and ginger yoghurt

TO SERVE 6

FOR THE BHAJIS
225g chickpea (gram) flour
1 rounded tbsp rice flour
1 rounded tbsp toasted sesame seeds
2 level tsp hot chilli powder (or cayenne pepper)
1/2 level tsp turmeric
1 rounded tsp fine sea salt
about 200ml cold water
2 large Spanish onions, halved and finely sliced
a small handful fresh coriander leaves, chopped

FOR THE YOGHURT
275ml plain Greek yoghurt
a medium handful fresh mint leaves, finely chopped
a small handful fresh coriander leaves, finely chopped
a thumb-sized knob of root ginger, peeled and grated
1 mild green chilli, deseeded and finely chopped
2 tbsp pomegranate molasses (optional)

YOU WILL NEED
a deep-fat fryer, or a large saucepan or wok half-filled with groundnut oil

Preheat the oil in the deep-fat fryer to 180°C; place the saucepan or wok over a moderate heat.

Mix all the yoghurt ingredients in a bowl, and season to taste. Divide among six small serving bowls and leave to one side.

Sieve the chickpea flour into a large bowl, then add the remaining dry ingredients. Mix thoroughly, and pour in most of the water. Stir the mixture and, if necessary, slowly add more water to make a thick, just-pourable batter. Add the onions and coriander, and stir really thoroughly until the onion is completely covered with batter.

To fry the bhajis, take a large spoon and drop golf ball-sized clumps of the mixture into the hot oil. You will probably only be able to fry a few bhajis at a time. When the bhajis are crisp and completely golden-brown (you might need to turn them halfway through), take them out with a pair of tongs and drain them well on a pad of kitchen paper. Repeat with the rest of the mixture, keeping each batch warm. Serve as soon as possible, with the cool yoghurt dip.

Any visitor to Venice is a tourist, no matter how highfalutin they may be, and a Bellini made from white peach juice and prosecco is as compulsory as a tramp round the Doges' Palace. But once the obvious sightseeing has been done, take the vaporetto to Giudecca and enjoy the tranquillity of a slightly dull residential quarter. Crouched next to the S Eufemia stop, you'll find Harry's Dolce, the sedate restaurant that some aficionados think serves better food than its more famous parent, Harry's Bar. Certainly, the bread, fritto misto, carpaccio, and this simple starter with its sweet, tart, earthy flavours, are all splendid.

The 'saor' refers to the slowly simmered, sweet-and-sour onions (fagioli are the beans). You could use ordinary Spanish or Dutch onions in place of the red and white ones, but don't even think of using tinned beans, or anything other than a fine, well-flavoured extra-virgin olive oil.

The onions can be cooked 24 hours in advance. The beans must be soaked for at least 8 hours before being cooked, and must be warm when they are combined with the onions. The whole salad will keep happily in the fridge for a day or two, but remember to bring it to room temperature before serving.

Harry's Dolce fagioli in saor

TO SERVE 6

FOR THE BEANS
250g dried borlotti (or pinto) beans
1 (200g) tin chair de tomate
2 large shallots, peeled
1 medium carrot, peeled
2 sticks celery
3 sprigs flat-leaf parsley
1 sprig fresh rosemary
2 tbsp well-flavoured extra-virgin olive oil

FOR THE ONIONS
3-4 tbsp well-flavoured extra-virgin olive oil
1 large red onion, peeled and sliced into fine rings
1 large white onion, peeled and sliced into fine rings
3 bay leaves
3 tbsp red wine vinegar

YOU WILL NEED
a rustic earthenware or pottery serving dish

Rinse the soaked beans, then fill a large saucepan with cold water and bring them to the boil, covered. Reduce the heat and simmer for 2 minutes, then drain off the water and start again. Put the beans, the chair de tomate, vegetables and herbs into a large saucepan and cover with about 1 litre of cold water. Do not add salt or the skins will toughen. Bring the beans to the boil, then reduce the heat and simmer, with the pan half covered, for 30-35 minutes. The length of time it takes for the beans to become tender depends to a large extent on their age; a long 'best before' date means the beans are fresher, and they will cook more quickly.

Meanwhile, prepare the onions. Heat 3 tablespoons of the olive oil in a fairly large frying pan over a low flame and fry the onions, stirring to coat the onions and break up the rings. Stir in the bay leaves, season with salt and pepper, and add a little more oil, if necessary. Fry the onions for about 25 minutes, stirring occasionally, until they are soft and slightly golden. Turn the heat up to medium, pour in the vinegar, and sizzle for 1 minute, stirring constantly. Remove the pan from the heat and leave it to one side.

When the beans are tender, drain them in a colander. Using a pair of tongs, discard all the vegetables and herbs – including the rosemary needles, if you have the time and the patience – but not the tomato bits. Tip the warm beans into the dish and scrape in the onion mixture, including all the oily juices, together with the extra 2 tablespoons of olive oil. Season well, then stir gently but thoroughly. Leave the beans for 2-3 hours at room temperature to soak up all the juices, stirring occasionally. Serve with lots of crusty bread.

Ripe, fragrant, juicy pears and cheese – whether it's Stilton, Lancashire or mozzarella – make a fantastic partnership, but the pears must be full of flavour. That means iron-hard, subfusc Conference pears don't get an invitation to the party. Not that you're likely to find a ripe pear in a shop anyway, as they bruise as easily as little boys' knees and Shopkeepers United don't like that. So you'll need to bring the unripe pears home and let them burgeon into luscious, aromatic perfection in the warmth of the kitchen. It won't take more than a couple of days – and that's about the most exerting part of this absurdly simple salad.

Pear and pine nut salad with roquefort and honey

TO SERVE 4

2 medium-sized romaine or Cos lettuces, outside leaves discarded

3 heads white Belgian chicory, outside leaves discarded

a handful of watercress, trimmed

2 ripe-but-firm Comice pears (or 3 Williams or Rocha)

30g pinenuts, toasted

about 2 tbsp runny honey (preferably heather)

FOR THE DRESSING

1-2 tbsp red wine vinegar

3 tbsp extra-virgin olive oil

100g roquefort (or other blue cheese), roughly diced

about 150ml sour cream (or whipping cream)

Break up the lettuce leaves, the larger roughly into three, and the smaller into two, and put them in a large bowl. Remove the chicory leaves one by one (discarding the core), and add to the lettuce, together with the watercress. Season with salt and pepper, then toss the leaves together.

For the dressing, whisk 1 tablespoon of vinegar with some black pepper, add the oil and whisk until emulsified. Mash in the roquefort, add the sour cream and whisk to a thick, fairly smooth dressing. Taste, and add a little salt, or more vinegar, if necessary: if you're using ordinary cream, it will probably need a touch more. Set aside.

Peel, core and cut the pears into sixths (or quarter them, if using the smaller Rocha or Williams pears). Do this at the last moment to prevent the pears browning.

Divide the salad leaves among the plates, artfully tuck the pears in and around, and season with black pepper. Trickle the roquefort dressing over the top, then scatter on the pinenuts. Finally, drizzle a little honey over each wedge of pear. Serve immediately.

Strange though it may seem, this esoteric, almost-raw-salmon starter was one of the most popular dishes at my erstwhile restaurant, the Fox and Goose Inn in Fressingfield. I'm pretty sure it was inspired by that friendly dynamo of a chef Antony Worrall Thompson; certainly the vivacity and freshness of the quickly seared salmon and scallops, not to mention the Japanese flavours, are typical of Antony's cooking. However it came about, it's a very clean-tasting, snappy starter.

As with most Far Eastern-style dishes, presentation is really important. If you haven't got any authentic Japanese plates, at least use flat, unfussy, modern-looking ones – gilt-edged dishes with intertwined rosebuds and ivy just won't do. As for the weirder-sounding ingredients, you should be able to find them in the better supermarkets, as well as specialist Asian and Japanese shops.

The salmon can be prepared and marinated up to 36 hours in advance, and refrigerated. However, I do think this dish is at its best served about 12 hours after the salmon goes in the final marinade.

Nearly sashimi

TO SERVE 4
about 350g salmon fillet, preferably the back not belly
4 large scallops, trimmed
a little groundnut oil
175ml sake (or very dry sherry)
1 tbsp sesame seed oil
1 tbsp mirin
1 tbsp Japanese soy sauce
a large-thumb-sized knob of root ginger, peeled and cut into very fine strips
1 rounded tsp miso paste (medium or dark)
about 4 heaped tbsp Japanese pickled ginger (gari)

YOU WILL NEED
a large heavy griddle pan, or iron frying pan; a dish of ice cubes; a plastic container just large enough to take the fish

The salmon fillet should be free of all skin and bones – just a long 'barrel' of perfect flesh.

Put the griddle pan over a very high heat and leave it until shimmeringly hot. Lightly oil the salmon and the scallops, then place the salmon in the pan. Sear the fish for a few seconds, then turn it and sear the other side; the surface should be sealed and blackened, but the inside raw. Remove the salmon immediately, and place it on the ice cubes to cool. Do the same with the scallops, then put them both in the plastic container.

Whisk the sake, sesame seed oil, mirin, soy and root ginger together, then pour this marinade over the salmon and scallops. Seal the container and put it in the fridge for 2-6 hours.

Pour off the marinade (except the ginger) into a small sauce saucepan (keeping the fish in the plastic container) and bring it to the boil over a high flame, uncovered. Leave it to bubble until the marinade has reduced by about a quarter. Take the saucepan off the heat, and stir in the miso paste and the reserved ginger. When the marinade is cool, pour it back over the salmon and scallops, seal the container and replace it in the fridge.

To serve, arrange a clump of pickled ginger in the middle of each plate, and perch a scallop on top. With a very sharp knife, cut the salmon into slices 1cm thick and arrange them neatly on the plates. Spoon a teaspoon of marinade over each piece of fish and a few shreds of the pickled ginger. Serve immediately.

'You'd be mad trying to cook tempura for more than four people. Even then, they should be real friends – the sort who won't care how deeply unattractive you look when sticky-fingered with batter and red-faced with heat'

I gorge myself on ebi (prawn) tempura whenever I go to a Japanese restaurant, normally the horrendously expensive but superb Suntory in London's St James's Street. I'd rather have a meal there than go to New York for the weekend which, with one picture-perfect plate of sashimi costing nearly £40, is just as well. Suntory serves a traditional dashi stock-based dipping sauce as an accompaniment to their text-book execution of huge juicy prawns deep-fried in an almost ethereally light, crisp, lacy batter. At home I'm just as fond of this hybrid Asian/Eastern concoction. It is based on Simon Hopkinson's dipping sauce in his excellent *Roast Chicken and Other Stories* but, like most interfering old bags, I've tinkered with it a bit, reducing the fairly fierce quantity of chillies and lime juice, and adding a splash of sour tamarind.

You can omit the prawns and use a mixture of vegetables and tofu for a more than acceptable (and much cheaper) vegetarian meal. But, as deep-fried food is always best eaten straight away, you'd be mad trying to cook tempura for more than four people. Even then, they should be real friends – the sort who won't care how deeply unattractive you look when sticky-fingered with batter and red-faced with heat.

I've suggested using Hime tempura batter mix because it uses authentic Japanese flour – and it's quick. Otherwise, whisk up a batter made from 1 large egg, 3 tablespoons of plain flour, 1 tablespoon of cornflour and 125-175ml ice-cold water, starting with the lower amount – the batter should be just thick enough to coat the food. The essential Japanese secret is to use it within 10 minutes, and leave some little lumps in the batter; it's these that create the authentic, exploded look.

A word about the sauce: to achieve the right balance of flavours to suit your palate it needs to be tasted quite a few times. 'But how do I know if it's right, if I've never tried it before,' I hear you bleat. The answer is quite simple – do you like it? Ask yourself – would I like it better if it were more acidic, less sugary, less fishy, more herby, more chilli-hot? – then adjust the quantities accordingly.

The sauce will keep in the fridge for up to 5 days, but add the herbs only a couple of hours before serving.

Tiger prawn tempura with lime, chilli and tamarind dipping sauce

TO SERVE 4

1 packet Hime tempura batter mix

8 huge or 12 large raw tiger prawns, shelled, but with tails still on

4 shiitake and 4 pieces of red pepper (or aubergine, courgette, etc)

FOR THE DIPPING SAUCE

2 large cloves of garlic, peeled, crushed and finely chopped

1-2 mild green chillies, deseeded and finely chopped

1 heaped tbsp caster sugar

2-3 tbsp fresh lime juice

150-175ml Thai fish sauce

1-2 tbsp tamarind juice

175ml cold water

a handful of fresh coriander leaves, finely chopped

the leaves from 6-8 sprigs of fresh mint, finely chopped

YOU WILL NEED

a deep-fat fryer, or a large wok or saucepan half-filled with groundnut oil

Preheat the oil in the deep-fat fryer to about 180°C; place the wok or saucepan over a moderate heat.

For the dipping sauce, start with the minimum amounts given here and add more if desired. First, combine the garlic, chilli and sugar in a bowl, then add the lime juice. Whisk vigorously, then add the fish sauce, tamarind juice and water and whisk again. Taste, and adjust the quantities before stirring in the chopped herbs.

Make up the batter according to the instructions on the packet, or my blurb in the intro. Holding on to the prawn tails, dip them in the batter, shake off the excess, then release them one by one into the hot fat. Give a little stir with a long chopstick or a similar implement to ensure the prawns don't clump together. When the batter is a light, golden brown, fish the prawns out and drain them on a pad of kitchen paper. Continue with the vegetables, battering and frying the the shiitake first, then the red pepper. Drain the vegetables on kitchen paper as they emerge from the oil.

Serve on plain Japanese-style flat plates lined with paper napkins; put the sauce in individual small bowls, and eat as soon as possible.

There are good combinations of food, and there are perfect combinations, and this is one of the latter. The soft, rich, silky texture of the smoked salmon contrasts brilliantly with the salty crispness of the Italian-style bacon, and the stab of peppery horseradish and sourish crème fraîche puts the icing on the cake – which, for entirely inappropriate metaphors, takes the biscuit. Ouch.

Home-made blini are infinitely more delicious than commercial ones, but there's no getting away from the fact that they do take some time to make. If you can't find blini, try pikelets, or a packet of those dreary, pancake-looking, dampish Staffordshire oatcakes, available in most supermarkets; they taste infinitely more appealing than they look.

You will notice 'about' figures rather a lot in this recipe. That's because it's up to you how strong you want the horseradish cream to taste, and how generous you want to be with the salmon and pancetta. The horseradish sauce can made at least 12 hours ahead, and the final assembly only takes minutes.

Smoked salmon with pancetta, horseradish crème fraîche and blini

TO SERVE 4
4 large blini (or pikelets, Staffordshire oatcakes)
about 150ml crème fraîche
about 2 level tsp strong horseradish cream, or 1 tsp grated fresh horseradish
about 1 tsp white caster sugar
about 1 tsp Dijon mustard
4 large slices smoked salmon
about 150g thinly sliced pancetta, cooked until crisp
4 good-looking sprigs of watercress

Preheat the oven to 130°C (fan), 150°C (conventional), gas mark 2.

Firmly seal the blini (or pikelets, etc), in a loose but tightly sealed foil pouch and place in the oven for 20 minutes.

Whisk the crème fraîche until softly peaked. Gently stir in the horseradish, sugar and mustard, starting off with the level measures, and tasting as you go. When the cream seems right to you, season with a little salt.

To serve, swirl the smoked salmon over the blini with a degree of panache. (Which is not an ingredient by the way.) Season with pepper, then dollop a spoonful or two of horseradish cream on the smoked salmon, followed by some crisp pancetta. Finally, perch a sprig of watercress on top. Serve immediately.

Asian gravadlax might sound like a complete contradiction in terms but the principle of dry-pickling a whole salmon remains true to the original Scandinavian recipe. Although we British are in danger of becoming food fashion fetishists, the classic Thai flavours of lime, ginger (or galangal), coriander and lemon grass should not be dismissed as old hat just because they've been around for a few years – after all, Thai people still like them.

Gravadlax is ideal for a dinner-party starter, not least because the pickling process must start at least 2 days, and up to 4 days ahead. The sauce, too, can be made 48 hours in advance.

Thai-style gravadlax

TO SERVE 8
1 whole salmon, about 1.5kg

FOR THE PICKLE
3 rounded tbsp caster sugar
3 rounded tbsp fine sea salt
a large-thumb-sized knob of root ginger, peeled and grated
3 stalks lemon grass, sliced very finely
1 rounded tsp Thai 7-spice seasoning
2 rounded tsp black peppercorns, coarsely crushed
1 red chilli, deseeded and finely chopped
the grated zest of 3 fresh limes
a handful of fresh coriander leaves, finely chopped

FOR THE SAUCE
2 large free-range egg yolks
2 tsp Dijon mustard
2 tsp natural cane sugar
225ml groundnut oil
a thumb-sized piece of root ginger, peeled and grated
the juice of 1 large (juicy) lime
a small handful of fresh coriander leaves, chopped

YOU WILL NEED
a non-reactive dish just large enough to take the salmon; a board and some weights; tweezers

Ask the fishmonger to scale the fish, remove the head and fins, split it lengthways into two sides, and remove the backbone. If you don't want to make quite so much, buy a thick tail-piece instead, and halve both the pickling and sauce ingredients.

Make sure that there are no fine pinbones left in the salmon. These lurk in a long line down the middle of the back fillets (not the belly). Simply smooth your fingers down the flesh to find them, then pull them out with a pair of tweezers. You should now have two sides of salmon, completely free of head, bones, fins, but with the skin still on.

Combine all the pickling ingredients in a bowl. Mentally quarter the mixture. Spread one quarter in the bottom of the non-reactive dish. Lie one of the sides of salmon over the pickle, skin-side down. Now smear two quarters of pickle evenly on to the flesh. Place the second side of salmon on top of the first, to make a 'whole' fish. Rub the remaining quarter of pickle into the skin.

Cover the salmon with foil, place a board on top, and then pile some weights on to it. Put the salmon in the fridge and leave it to marinate for at least 2 days, turning the 'whole' salmon each day.

To make the sauce, vigorously whisk the egg yolks, mustard and sugar together. Slowly whisk in the oil to make a smooth, viscous sauce. Stir in the ginger, lime juice and coriander, and season to taste, adding more lime if necessary.

Don't worry about how you are going to slice the salmon: for each person, cut 2 or 3 short, diagonal escalopes across the fish as thinly as you can, and leave the long diaphanous slices to the experts. Serve with a good dollop of sauce.

'The pearly-white chicory leaves napped in a mustard dressing tasted as if the New Zealand rugby team were hoisting a series of perfect reverse passes from my mouth to my belly'

I think it was in one of the Conran restaurants that I first had a side salad of pearly-white, slightly bitter chicory leaves napped in a smooth, sweetish mustard dressing. But though the salad worked brilliantly as a side dish, I thought it needed something extra as a starter. Eventually I came up with the idea of adding bacon and cockles. Now, it doesn't always work when you start fiddling with recipes – in fact, it's often a disaster – but in this case I think the result is a bloody triumph. Faint hearts, who think they don't like cockles (which taste sweetly of the sea, and are much nicer than they look – unless they're in brine, which are horrible), can substitute prawns. The recipe tastes best as it is, though.

The dressing will keep for 2-3 days in the fridge, but it might need a little warm water whisked in to bring it back to pouring consistency. The chicory can be prepared and kept in a plastic bag in the fridge.

Cockle, chicory and bacon salad with mustard dressing

TO SERVE 4
4 heads Belgian chicory
8 thin rashers dry-cured streaky bacon, crisply cooked
125-175g cockles, either frozen and defrosted, or fresh
2 tbsp chopped fresh chives

FOR THE DRESSING
1 tbsp smooth Dijon mustard
1 tsp natural cane sugar
1 tbsp cider vinegar
2 tbsp groundnut oil
150ml whipping cream

To make the dressing, whisk the mustard, sugar and vinegar together, then whisk in the oil, and finally the cream. The dressing should be smooth, thickly pourable and piquant. Adjust any element to please, and leave to one side.

Peel the leaves off the chicory, discarding any damaged outer leaves and the inner core, and arrange them on four flat dinner plates. (Try to resist that awful spokes-of-a-wheel design.) Break up the bacon (the ready-cooked, bought-in stuff will do), and sprinkle the shards over the chicory. Scatter on the cockles, and season with sea salt and black pepper. Trace the dressing generously over the salad, then finish with a final flourish of chopped chives. Serve immediately.

This recipe came about after I'd struggled with a squid and chickpea salad some years ago at the then trendy Orso restaurant in Covent Garden. I loved the flavours but found it utterly maddening trying to balance the bouncy chickpeas on the same fork as the squid. To solve the problem I came up with the following recipe which is extremely satisfactory on all counts, especially if you can get hold of some Collona lemon oil for the final flourish.

If you don't like squid, nothing I say will persuade you that it's fabulous. But next time you see squid on the menu in a good restaurant (and I do mean good, not some dubious suburban trattoria), please try it. You'll discover that properly cooked squid is not tough and chewy, but delightfully firm and smooth-textured, with a sweet clean flavour. It's also cheap. If you're still not convinced, substitute strips of grilled chicken for the squid, or use the hummus alone as a vegetarian dip and serve it with pitta bread.

The hummus can be made up to 48 hours in advance and kept clingfilmed in the fridge: bring it to room temperature before serving, and stir in a splash of water if the texture has become too solid. The squid must be cooked to order.

Griddled squid with coriander hummus

TO SERVE 4

about 500g squid including tentacles, prepared

1 (425g) can of chickpeas, drained and rinsed

2 cloves of garlic, peeled and crushed

a large thumb-sized knob of root ginger, peeled and roughly chopped

2 level tsp of Indonesian sambal manis (or 1 tsp chilli sauce and 1 tsp dark soy sauce)

1 medium handful of fresh coriander, leaves and stalks

about 150ml groundnut oil

a handful of salad leaves or watercress, dressed

a little Collona lemon oil (or extra-virgin olive oil)

a small handful of flat-leaf parsley, chopped

YOU WILL NEED

a large griddle pan or large, heavy frying pan (definitely not non-stick)

Cut the squid sacs into roughly 7cm square pieces. If the squid is quite thick, lightly crisscross the inside surface with the point of a small sharp knife – this not only helps to tenderise bigger, thicker squid but also stops it curling up when you cook it. Cut any ultra-long tentacles into less freaky pieces. Leave the squid in the fridge.

Tip the chickpeas into a food processor together with the garlic, ginger, sambal manis (or soy and chilli sauce), coriander, and half the groundnut oil. Whizz for 30 seconds or so, then scrape down the sides. Now, using the pulse button, add more oil bit by bit, until you have a slightly rough-textured, but soft, creamy mass. Finally, season to taste with a generous amount of salt and pepper. Dollop some hummus on each plate and garnish with a handful of dressed salad leaves or watercress just before you cook the squid.

Heat the griddle pan over a very high heat until it is searingly hot. Toss the squid in a little groundnut oil, and season it with salt and pepper. Drop half the squid into the pan and cook for no more than 90 seconds in total, turning the pieces with a pair of tongs – any longer and it will toughen. As soon as the squid is opaque, remove it and cook the second batch.

Pile the squid on top of the hummus and drizzle over a little lemon oil or olive oil, then scatter on some parsley. Serve immediately.

That dreaded ingredient, anchovies, figures in this recipe. Enough to put most people off, I know. But anchovies are fantastically useful as a flavour enhancer – just think of a classic Caesar salad dressing. Of course, that won't make a blind bit of difference to anyone whose experience of anchovies is confined to those massively salty little brown worms that are strewn on third-rate pizzas. But if I tell you that many traditional British sauces, such as Worcester or Daddy's, include anchovies - what then? They are just as undetectable in this recipe, but similarly vital to the final flavour. Slightly Spanish in style, the combination of tomatoes, basil, garlic (and anchovies) is as classic as they come.

The whole dish can be prepared up to 12 hours in advance, and kept refrigerated. Bring the mussels to room temperature before the final grilling.

Gratin of mussels Basque-style

TO SERVE 4
125ml dry white wine
about 48 big mussels, or 80 small mussels, cleaned
about 125g well-flavoured, ripe tomatoes, peeled, deseeded and chopped into fine dice
2 large cloves of garlic, peeled, crushed and finely chopped
about 25g anchovies, finely chopped, the oil reserved
a small handful of fresh basil leaves, finely shredded
a small handful of flat-leaf parsley, finely chopped
1 tbsp, plus some more, robust extra-virgin olive oil
about 2 tbsp fresh, fine white breadcrumbs

YOU WILL NEED
a very large saucepan, with lid; 4 medium gratin dishes; a heavy baking tray

Preheat the grill before browning the mussels.

Pour half the white wine into the saucepan, place it over a very high heat and throw in the mussels. Put on the lid, and cook for 4-5 minutes, shaking the pan occasionally, and using a thick oven cloth to keep the lid clamped on. When the mussels have opened, remove the pan from the heat and leave it to one side for 2-3 minutes, uncovered.

As soon as the mussels are cool enough to handle, discard any that remain closed, and remove and discard the empty half-shells from the others. Put the mussels on their half-shells in the gratin dishes, in a single layer. Leave them to one side, loosely clingfilmed.

To prepare the stuffing, combine the tomatoes, garlic, anchovies, basil, parsley and reserved anchovy oil in a mixing bowl. Season with freshly ground black pepper, but don't add any extra salt.

Heat a tablespoon of olive oil in a small, non-stick frying pan over a medium heat. Add the stuffing mixture and cook for 2-3 minutes, stirring frequently. Raise the heat, pour in the remaining wine, and leave to bubble for 2 minutes, stirring occasionally. Pull the pan off the heat, and leave the mixture to cool for about 10 minutes.

Using a teaspoon, dab tiny amounts of the stuffing on top of each mussel. If you want to make this recipe ahead of time, this is the point to stop: clingfilm the gratin dishes and put them in the fridge.

To finish the dish, sprinkle the breadcrumbs in a thin, even layer over the mussels and drizzle them generously with olive oil. Place the dishes on a very sturdy baking tray, slide it under the grill, and blitz the mussels for about 3 minutes, or until the stuffing is golden and bubbling. Transfer the dishes on to cold under-plates, and serve at once with good, crusty bread – and a warning about the hot dishes.

Mussels slopping around in a Thai broth of coconut milk, lemon grass and ginger are excellent, but I thought it would be nice to try to reduce some of those flavours into a more intense, clinging sauce. Frankly, I think the result is stunningly good, and I found myself cleaning my plate rather too assiduously for elegant behaviour. On the other hand, no one who cared about smart table manners would serve mussels anyway. Like most shellfish, mussels are made for abandoned, gutsy slurping.

I am bound to say that mussels are always better if they are cooked to order, but the sauce can be prepared to the point where you add the coconut milk. If you do cook the mussels in advance, they will keep in the fridge for about 24 hours. Reheat them very gently in the sauce for 1-2 minutes, rather than pouring the sauce straight over the top.

Mussels with red curry sauce

TO SERVE 4

1 tsp Marigold Swiss vegetable bouillon powder

150ml boiling water

2 tbsp groundnut oil

1 large stick celery, finely chopped

1 large carrot, peeled and finely chopped

2 shallots, peeled and finely chopped

2 large cloves of garlic, peeled, crushed and finely chopped

1 crisp, sharp eating apple, peeled, cored and finely diced

50g Thai red curry paste

1 scant tbsp tomato purée

about 1.5kg fresh mussels, cleaned

half a (400ml) can of coconut milk

a small handful of fresh coriander leaves, chopped

12 large basil leaves, finely shredded

YOU WILL NEED

a very large saucepan, with lid

Combine the Marigold powder and boiling water, and set aside.

Heat the oil in a medium-sized sauté pan (or wide, shallow saucepan) over a low-to-medium heat. Tip in the celery, carrot, shallots and garlic, and gently fry for about 10 minutes, stirring occasionally, until the vegetables start to soften. Add the diced apple to the pan, and cook for a further 10 minutes, still stirring occasionally.

Turn up the heat to medium, and stir in the curry paste and tomato purée. Cook for 1 minute, remove the pan from the heat and pour in the Marigold stock. Remove from the heat and leave to one side.

Put the mussels into a very large saucepan over a high heat, clamp on the lid, and cook for 3-4 minutes. Shake the pan occasionally, using a thick oven cloth to keep the lid in place. As soon as the mussels have opened, remove the saucepan from the heat and leave to one side for 2-3 minutes, uncovered. Drain the mussels, reserving 150ml of the juices. Discard any closed mussels, and empty half-shells, but keep the mussels (still in their shells) warm, with a piece of clingfilm loosely draped over the top. (This will prevent them drying out.)

Add the reserved mussel stock to the sauce, and bring the contents to the boil over a high heat, uncovered. Reduce the heat, and simmer for 5 minutes. Pour the sauce into a liquidiser, and whizz until smooth. Return the sauce to the same pan over a medium heat, pour in just under 200ml coconut milk, and simmer for about 2 minutes. The sauce should be the consistency of double cream so, if necessary, pour in a little more coconut milk. Finally, stir in the coriander and basil.

Quickly divide the mussels between four warmed bowls, and pour over the sauce. Serve immediately.

Wintry main courses

Even though most of us sit around in offices all day, and have molly-coddling central-heating at home, there's still an atavistic belief that we must stoke up during winter. Well, you'll find lots of cocklewarming recipes here, not to mention more cuddly meat dishes than in the rest of the book put together. But as cod, sole, scallops and mussels are all at their best now, there are quite a few fish recipes, too – but only fish from northern waters. There's not a tilapia in the southern hemisphere that can touch our Atlantic fish for flavour.

The first time I ever ate a twice-cooked soufflé was at Le Gavroche in London, where the low-cost ingredients of their soufflé Suissesse – cheese, eggs and milk – were transformed into a fabulous, soaring, airy puff that was only surpassed by the stratospheric cost. My version of their recipe is not quite as feather-light but it still tastes very good and, more importantly, it's so reliable you could make it for a dinner party without any qualms.

Because the soufflé is so full of flavour it would also make an excellent vegetarian meal served with a tomato salad and some chewy bread. You can also substitute other vegetables for the spinach, but they must be cooked and moisture-free: the flavour should also be quite intense in relation to the quantity.

The first stage of the recipe can be finished up to 36 hours in advance, so it gives you plenty of time to sort out any problems – though there's no earthly reason why anything *should* go wrong. As soufflés go, this one is as good-natured as you'll find.

Twice-baked spinach and parmesan soufflé

TO SERVE 4 PEOPLE
250g leaf spinach, trimmed, rinsed and drained
a few scrapings of nutmeg
350ml full-cream milk
1 shallot, peeled and coarsely chopped
1 bay leaf, fresh or dried
40g unsalted butter
40g self-raising flour
3 large free-range eggs, separated
100g finely grated parmesan
a kettle of boiling water
150ml whipping or double cream

YOU WILL NEED
a wok; 4 (300ml) ramekins or straight-sided oven-proof bowls, well-buttered; a large roasting tin; 4 small buttered gratin dishes

Preheat the oven to 170°C (fan), 190°C (conventional), gas mark 5 for the first stage; and to 190°C (fan), 210°C (conventional), gas mark 6 1/2 for the final cooking.

Put the wok over a high heat, then toss in the spinach and a pinch of sea salt. Using a couple of big forks or tongs, keep turning the leaves until they have wilted but are still dark green – it shouldn't take more than 2-3 minutes. Drain the spinach in a colander, spreading it out as much as possible. Leave to cool.

Now, use your hands to squeeze out every drop of water, then pile the spinach into the centre of a clean tea-towel, gather up the corners and twist hard, until the spinach is forced into a tight ball. When all the water has drained off, tip the dry spinach on to a board, and chop it finely. Season with plenty of pepper and some freshly grated nutmeg. Leave to one side.

Put the milk, shallot, bay leaf and a little nutmeg in a largish saucepan over a low-to-medium flame. Bring to a gentle simmer, then take the pan off the heat and leave to infuse for 20 minutes. Strain the milk into a jug, discarding the seasonings.

Wash the saucepan then return it to a medium heat. Put in the butter and as soon as it has melted, whisk in the flour. Leave this roux to cook for 1 minute, then pour on the flavoured milk and whisk thoroughly, getting right into the corners of the pan. Still whisking,

'If you thought making a soufflé was difficult, think again: this one's a veritable pussy cat'

bring the sauce to the boil. Keep whisking for 2 minutes after the sauce has thickened dramatically, then take the saucepan off the heat and leave to cool, stirring from time to time.

Meanwhile, beat the egg yolks in one bowl, and whisk the egg whites into peaks that just hold their shape in another – you don't want the peaks to be excessively firm and shiny, but they must stand up.

When the sauce has cooled, scrape it into a fairly large bowl and beat in the egg yolks, chopped spinach, a little over half the grated parmesan and some salt and pepper. Using a large metal spoon, put about a fifth of the whisked egg whites into the bowl and gently fold them in. Now fold in the rest of the egg whites, trying to preserve as much airy lightness as possible.

Divide the soufflé mixture between the buttered ramekins and place them in the roasting tin. Slide the tin on to a middle shelf of the oven then carefully pour in a kettle of boiling water, to come about halfway up the sides of the ramekins. Cook the soufflés for about 20 minutes, or until slightly puffed up, and golden tinged. Remove them from the oven (and the roasting tin) and leave to cool. The soufflés will keep in the fridge, clingfilmed, for up to 36 hours.

To finish cooking the soufflés, first bring them to room temperature. Run a palette knife around the edge of each soufflé to release it. Tip the soufflés, upside down, into the gratin dishes. Sprinkle the remaining parmesan over the top, then drizzle over the cream. Put the dishes on to a baking tray, and cook for 12-15 minutes, or until the soufflés are puffed up and golden brown. Serve immediately.

When I owned the Fox and Goose Inn at Fressingfield (fondly referred to as the F&G by our regulars, and as the Effing G by my husband), we couldn't believe the number of customers who ordered the same thing each time they came: one woman ate Peking-style duck followed by sticky toffee pudding every fortnight for three years. I shouldn't sneer, though. On rare visits to The Ivy I always have steak tartare and chips; at the Sugar Club, seared scallops with chilli jam and crème fraîche; and whenever I eat at my new restaurant, The Trinity, seized cod with saffron mash (which we brought with us from the F&G). It was while pondering on how well starch and fish go together in general – think of mushy peas – that I came up with the idea of using crushed cannellini beans as a partner for the cod.

The bean purée can be made up to 24 hours ahead, though it will stiffen up considerably in the fridge; when you warm it through, add a touch more stock to let it down. The cod must be cooked to order.

Seized cod with white bean and parsley purée

TO SERVE 4

about 5 tbsp extra-virgin olive oil

3 cloves of garlic, crushed, peeled and finely chopped

2 shallots, peeled and finely chopped

2 (425g) tins cannellini beans, drained and rinsed

a large handful of fresh flat-leaf parsley, including stalks, roughly chopped

2 tsp Marigold Swiss vegetable bouillon powder

8 tbsp boiling hot water

8 pieces of cod fillet (about 85g each), skinned

a little plain flour

the juice of half a lemon

YOU WILL NEED

a large sauté pan (or wide-based saucepan); a large heavy frying pan

For the purée, heat the sauté pan over a low-to-medium flame. Pour in 2 tablespoons of oil, then stir in the chopped garlic and shallots. Fry them for 4-5 minutes, or until softened and lightly coloured.

Now turn up the heat a little, and stir in the beans, parsley, Marigold powder and hot water. Season with salt and pepper and cook for 2- 3 minutes, stirring vigorously. As soon as it is piping hot, scrape everything into a food processor. Whizz for 1-2 minutes, until the beans have reduced to a thick, smoothish purée. Taste, adjust the seasoning and keep warm.

In the meantime, season the cod fillets with salt and pepper, then dust them with a little plain flour, and lightly oil them.

Heat the frying pan over a very high flame. Pour in 2 tablespoons of olive oil, and wait until it is very hot. Put in the cod fillets and cook for about 2 minutes. Don't be tempted to peer, poke and generally fiddle with the cod or it will a) steam rather than sear, and b) stick to the pan so you lose all the lovely crust. Turn the fillets and cook for a further 3-4 minutes, or until the flakes of fish have turned from translucent to opaque, and the outside is golden-black.

To serve, divide the hot bean purée among 4 warmed plates and perch the pieces of cod on top. Finally, sprinkle on a little lemon juice – don't go mad – before eating immediately.

'Whichever type of scallops you buy, this is not going to be a cheap, everyday recipe – it's one to save for high days and holidays'

It will come as no surprise to anyone who is a devotee of bitter-sweet orange marmalade that Seville oranges, gently simmered with spices and vinegar, make a sparkling, assertive chutney, which goes particularly well with oily fishes such as grilled salmon, and with smoked meats such as venison and duck. It's also really good as a contrast to the rich, sweet succulence of griddled scallops. One possible snag is that Seville oranges are only in season for about six weeks, from mid-January to the end of February. They do freeze well, though, so bung some in the freezer if you get a chance.

The scallops I'm suggesting you use for this recipe are the big, juicy molluscs that come in those petrol company-logo, saucer-sized shells. (And, what about this for a priceless bit of info gleaned from *The Oxford Companion to Food*: as a result of seeing the famous Shell Company logo festooned all over their country, Thai people have dropped their traditional name for scallops, 'hoy phat' and started calling them 'hoy shell' instead. How long before thoroughbred race horses are known as Ferraris, I wonder.)

Anyway, the tiddy little queen scallops, called queenies or quins, will not do for this recipe. In fact, I think queen scallops are almost always a waste of time, except when they're mixed in with other seafood and their fragile appeal is well and truly disguised. It's true, though, that large scallops (pectin maximus) are hideously expensive. If you buy diver-caught scallops the price is even higher, but they are much cleaner and, because human divers do not disturb the sea bed in the same monstrous way as mechanical dredgers, more ecologically friendly. Whichever type you buy, this is not going to be a cheap, everyday recipe – it's one to save for high days and holidays. (Or, of course, for occasions when there's just you, your loved one, a spot of good old-fashioned greed, and a bottle of Gewurztraminer.)

Chefs have long decided that scallops only require the briefest of cooking, albeit at very high temperature. I am entirely at one with this philosophy, but there's no denying it does produce a scallop that's crisp and golden on the outside, while still being slightly rare in the middle. I love them like this – indeed, I adore scallops raw as long as they're thinly sliced – but I do know people (my sister, Dru, for one) who can't bear the translucent, firm-jelly-like consistency, and much prefer them cooked to an opaque stiffness. Fine, but unless you want them to end up like bouncy bullets, please ignore any instructions to cook scallops for 12-15 minutes, as I've seen one supermarket suggest.

The chutney should be made at least 3 days in advance and, of course, will stay fine for months. The scallops must be cooked to order.

Griddled scallops with Seville orange chutney

TO SERVE 4

**16 large scallops,
cleaned and trimmed**

a little plain flour

a little groundnut oil

**FOR THE CHUTNEY
(makes about 500g)**

3 Seville oranges

**2 smallish red onions,
peeled and finely chopped**

**2 large Bramleys, peeled,
cored and roughly chopped**

the juice of 1 lemon

**1 heaped tsp
white mustard seeds**

**a thumb-sized knob of root
ginger, peeled and finely grated**

50ml balsamic vinegar

100ml red wine vinegar

225g white sugar

YOU WILL NEED

**1 or 2 warm, sterilised jam
jars; a cast-iron griddle or a
large heavy frying pan**

Two rotten jobs to start, then the rest is a doddle. Firstly, remove the zest from the oranges (this is one instance where a knife might be more useful than a zester to tackle the bumpy Seville skins, especially if the oranges have been frozen), chop it roughly and put it into a fairly large mixing bowl.

Second, quarter the oranges and remove (and discard) the 10 zillion pips. With a small sharp knife, carefully tease the pip-free segments from the pith, trying to retain as much juice as possible. Put these messy-looking segments into the bowl with the rind and roughly tear them apart. Now add the onion, apple, lemon juice, mustard seeds, ginger and some salt. Mix everything together thoroughly.

Put a largish saucepan on a medium heat, pour in the vinegars and stir in the sugar. Bring the contents gently to the boil, stirring at the beginning to dissolve the sugar. Tip in the orange mixture and stir again. Reduce the heat to low, and simmer the oranges gently for about 90 minutes, uncovered. The oranges should have reduced to a thick, shiny, marmalade-coloured gloop. Remove the saucepan from the heat, leave the chutney to cool for 15 minutes, then pour it carefully (it will be very hot) into the clean jars, and seal immediately. Try to resist using the chutney for at least 3 days while it matures.

To cook the scallops, heat the griddle pan over a very high heat until it is shimmeringly hot. While it is heating, season the scallops, dust them very lightly with flour, and smear them equally lightly with a drop or two of oil. Put the scallops into the griddle pan, and sear them for 2 minutes – without touching, poking or fiddling with them. Turn, and cook for another minute; they should have a glistening, golden-brown crust, and the flesh should be plump and stiff, but not tough. Remove the scallops from the pan immediately. (If you are using the corals, lightly oil and flour them as you did the white meat, but only cook them for about 1 minute on each side.)

Serve the scallops with the chutney, and a handful of salad leaves.

'Like a good cappuccino, the butter is light and airy, but with real body underpinning the froth'

Back in the dim and distant past when we owned Hintlesham Hall, our then head chef, Robert Mabey, had a way of turning garlic butter into something really special. Robert is now the chef/proprietor of Regatta in Aldeburgh (and married to my beautiful niece). This is his recipe for garlic butter, although being a spontaneous person he's apt to tweak it as often as the wind blows (which is almost all the time on the east coast). Like a good cappuccino, the butter is light and airy, but with real body underpinning the froth. Quite marvellous, especially with mussels and, of course, scallops.

You will have too much butter for this recipe, but it's impractical to make less. The excess will keep for at least a week in the fridge, or for several weeks in the freezer.

Scallops with whipped garlic butter

TO SERVE 4
16 large scallops, cleaned and trimmed
a little plain flour
a little groundnut oil

FOR THE GARLIC BUTTER
6 cloves of garlic, peeled and crushed
100ml groundnut oil
250g unsalted butter, softened
a pinch of Marigold Swiss vegetable bouillon powder
a large handful of flat-leaf parsley, chopped
a few fresh tarragon leaves, chopped

YOU WILL NEED
a food processor with cake-making bowl and whisk attachment; a cast-iron griddle pan, or large heavy frying pan; 4 small gratin dishes

Preheat the grill to high just before cooking the scallops.

To make the butter, whizz the garlic and oil in a liquidiser until it's smooth. Put the butter in the cake-making bowl of a food processor, pour in the garlicky oil and add the Marigold powder, parsley, tarragon and plenty of black pepper. Turn the machine on and whisk for several minutes, or until the butter has tripled in volume and is fluffy. Scrape it on to a sheet of clingfilm, and twist it into a fat sausage shape. Refrigerate, but bring it to room temperature before using.

Heat the griddle pan over a very high heat until it is shimmeringly hot. Meanwhile, season the scallops, dust them very lightly with flour, and smear them equally lightly with a drop or two of oil. Add the scallops, and sear them for 2 minutes – without touching, poking or fiddling with them. Turn, and cook for another minute; the surface should be a glistening, golden-brown crust, and the flesh plump and stiff but not tough. Remove the scallops from the pan immediately. (If you are using the corals, lightly oil and flour them as you did the white meat, but only cook them for about 1 minute each side.)

Cut 16 thin slices from the butter. Divide the scallops among the gratin dishes (or scallop shells), and place the butter on top. Put under the grill until the butter starts to melt, then serve immediately.

Inspiration for 'new' recipes comes from all quarters. Although Simon Hopkinson, the food writer and erstwhile head chef at Bibendum (of which he is still a partner), thought up the idea of infusing mashed potatoes with saffron, he freely admits his inspiration came from Fredy Girardet, whose eponymous (and sadly defunct) Swiss restaurant was probably the best in Europe. There the mashed potato was whipped with olive oil and cream to create a silken purée smoother than an entire nursery of babies' bottoms.

In Simon's recipe, the subtle, slightly tannic flavour of the saffron turns the mash into something even more sophisticated. Combined with a white fish, such as cod, brill or hake, it is quite superb. At the Fox and Goose, we used to cook the potatoes from scratch in a large quantity of saffron-infused fish stock, but I think this version is less demanding on normal domestic resources. Brendan Ansbro (my brilliant head chef then – and now, at my hotel, the Crown & Castle), who trained with Simon for a short stint, decided to add the final dusting of gremolata: it could seem an unnecessary complication, but it works, and is well worth the extra effort.

By all means prepare the basic mash up to 24 hours in advance, using floury potatoes such as King Edwards or Maris Piper, and without adding any cream, milk or butter. Refrigerate the mash, then finish it off to order. The gremolata and cod both need last minute (but very short) attention.

Cod with saffron mash and gremolata

TO SERVE 4
8 small pieces of cod fillet (about 85g each), skinned
a little plain flour
a little olive oil

FOR THE MASH
a big pinch of saffron threads
8 tbsp extra-virgin olive oil
3 cloves of garlic, peeled, crushed and finely chopped
150ml fish stock
150ml double cream
500g cooked potatoes, mashed

FOR THE GREMOLATA
3 tbsp finely chopped flat-leaf parsley leaves
1 tsp very finely grated or chopped lemon zest
1 small clove of garlic, very finely chopped

YOU WILL NEED
a large heavy frying pan (preferably not non-stick)

Mix the gremolata ingredients together, clingfilm, and set aside.

To make the mash, first toast the saffron in a dry pan for 30 seconds over a medium heat. Set aside. Now gently heat 3 tablespoons of the olive oil in a largish saucepan over a low heat, and cook the garlic for a few minutes without colouring it. Add half the fish stock and the saffron, bring to the boil, then leave to infuse for 10 minutes off the heat. Add the cream, mashed potatoes and the remaining oil, and beat over a low flame until the potatoes are piping hot. The mash should be quite sloppy, so add more fish stock, if necessary. Season with salt and pepper, cover, and set aside in a warm place.

Heat the frying pan over a very high flame. Meanwhile season the cod fillets, dust them lightly with flour, then oil them just as lightly. When the pan is searingly hot, put in the cod and cook it for 2 minutes, without disturbing. Turn the pieces, and cook for a further 3-4 minutes, until the cod is black-gold on the outside and just opaque in the middle. Remove the pan from the heat.

Quickly spoon the mash on to four warmed dinner plates, put the cod on top, then sprinkle with a pinch or two of gremolata – don't go mad, it's very powerful. Finally, swish a thin cordon of extra-virgin olive oil (or Collona lemon oil) on the cod, and serve.

Doubtless there is a very good scientific reason why mussels and aniseed have such an affinity, but as organolepsy is not my specialist subject – and I'm damned sure it's not yours either – I couldn't tell you why. I am happy simply to sit back and slurp my way through a bowl of these beautifully sweet, cider-coloured molluscs as they swish around in a fabulously tasty, creamy broth. When you've finished checking the dictionary, you might like to do the same.

The recipe can be part-prepared up to 8 hours in advance. Take it to the point where the vegetables have been softened, and make sure the mussels are clean, then keep everything refrigerated. If you are cooking this from scratch, it only takes about 30 minutes from start to finish.

Mussel and fennel broth

TO SERVE 4

3 tbsp extra-virgin olive oil

2 large shallots, peeled and finely chopped

2 large cloves of garlic, peeled, crushed and finely chopped

1 leek, trimmed, washed and finely diced

half a large bulb of fennel, outer layer and root discarded, the rest finely diced

300ml dry white wine

3kg fresh mussels, cleaned

50ml Pernod or Ricard (but not a sweet aniseed liqueur)

a large handful of flat-leaf parsley, coarsely chopped

about 300ml whipping cream

YOU WILL NEED

a very large saucepan, with lid

Heat the oil in the saucepan over a low-to-medium heat. Add the shallots, garlic, leek and fennel, and cook for 10-15 minutes, stirring frequently, until the vegetables have softened. Reduce the heat if they show any sign of colouring.

As soon as the vegetables are soft, turn up the heat and pour in the wine, swiftly followed by the mussels. Put on the lid and cook for 4-5 minutes. Shake the pan energetically once or twice, using a thick oven cloth to keep the lid clamped on. As soon as the mussels have opened, remove the pan from the heat and leave it to one side for a few minutes, uncovered.

You now need to separate the mussels from their juices. I use a wire spider to lift them out of the pan, but if you haven't got one of these fantastically useful tools, then drain the mussels into a big colander, making sure you catch all the liquid in another saucepan.

At this point you will also need to decide whether you've got the time and energy to remove one of the empty shells from each mussel. It's not essential – just nice. Either way, keep the mussels warm, with a piece of clingfilm draped over the top to prevent them drying out.

Add the Pernod and parsley to the reserved mussel juices and bring the broth to the boil over a high heat. Pour in the cream, bring back to the boil, and bubble for 3-4 minutes, uncovered and without stirring, until the broth has thickened a little, and the colour has turned from bone-white to honey-white. Season with black pepper, then taste, and some salt if it's needed.

Return the mussels to the pan, and toss them gently in the broth. Scoop them out and divide them between four warmed bowls, then pour over the broth. Serve immediately with chunks of French bread, and soup spoons to lap up the liquor.

A million years ago, or maybe only 20, there was an extraordinary place just outside Bedford, called Milton Ernest hotel. The proprietors (advertising people, I believe) were as odd but stylish as the huge Victorian gothic building, designed by the architect William Butterfield. I remember many things with fondness, including the genuinely freshly squeezed orange juice (then an unheard-of luxury), the Château Talbot 1970, and this main course. It was fantastically simple: just a handful of fresh bay leaves, a few cloves of garlic, and a cluster of huge, pink, whiskery Mediterranean prawns, all wallowing in a great puddle of piping hot oil and butter, with loads of crusty baguette to mop up the juices. You could track the dish by the wonderful smell (I refuse to say aroma, but why does 'smell' have such awful connotations) that wafted its way from kitchen to table. In the way cooks do, I've added a little chilli, as well as some big black juicy flat mushrooms, but essentially this is the same simple dish.

The type of prawns you use is important. During the Seventies and Eighties we called them Mediterranean prawns, but nowadays you're more likely to find them basking under the name of crevettes or Madagascan prawns. This is because very little fish (or hardly any that is exported) comes from the Mediterranean any more. While you could economise and use whole Greenland pink prawns (the ones that are sold by the pint – and please don't tell me it's 50cl now), avoid using tiger prawns, whether they are cooked or uncooked: they simply don't have the right flavour or texture for this recipe.

This is a start-to-finish swoop, taking about 15 minutes in total.

Crevettes with flat mushrooms and garlic

TO SERVE 4

12 tbsp extra-virgin olive oil

4 very large flat mushrooms (preferably chestnut), wiped

3 tsp mushroom ketchup (optional)

30g unsalted butter

6 cloves of garlic, peeled and crushed

1 red chilli, deseeded and finely chopped

8-10 fresh bay leaves

20 large cooked Madagascan prawns/crevettes

YOU WILL NEED

a very, very large frying pan

Place the frying pan over a medium heat and when it is hot pour in 3 tablespoons of the oil. Leave for 1 minute, then put the mushrooms into the pan, gill-sides down, and season with salt and pepper. Fry for about 5 minutes. Turn the mushrooms over, add another 3 tablespoons of oil and, if desired, trickle over the ketchup. Fry the mushrooms for a further 3-5 minutes, or until they have softened and the juices are just starting to weep. Remove them from the pan and keep warm.

Using the same frying pan, heat the remaining 6 tablespoons of oil, and the butter, over a moderate flame. When the fat has stopped sizzling, put in the garlic, chilli and bay leaves, and fry for about 3 minutes, stirring once or twice. Now turn up the heat, throw in the prawns and season with salt and freshly ground black pepper. Fry the prawns for about 3 minutes until piping hot, tossing them from time to time. (They don't need cooking per se, just warming through in the garlicky oil.)

Serve immediately, dividing the prawns and mushrooms among the plates, with a share of all the buttery juices and seasonings from the pan. Eat with good, scrunchy, chewy bread to mop up the juices.

'This is fantastically simple: a cluster of huge pink, whiskery Mediterranean prawns, all wallowing in a great puddle of piping hot oil and butter'

I've always loved the late Jane Grigson's cookbooks because they are packed with arcane and interesting information about the historical, cultural and sociological aspects of food. Which is a pretentious way of saying that she wrote riveting stories about the hows and whys of food, and the way it's cooked. She could also write a mean recipe. During my early married life the only cookbook that really gave all the low-down on fish was her incredibly useful *Fish Cookery* – Rick Stein and Keith Floyd were then mere tadpoles in the bouillabaisse of cookery writers.

As she says, the combination of fried sole and strips of pancake sounds unlikely, but tastes sensational. I've had the temerity to play with her original recipe over the years, adding saffron to the pancakes. I also keep the fillets of sole whole, but if you prefer to cut them into finger-sized goujons (okay, okay, that's tautology), be my guest. One thing that mustn't be altered, though, is Mrs Grigson's admonition to use clarified butter for frying the sole, if you want sweet-smelling, golden fish.

The pancake batter should be made at least 30 minutes, and up to 24 hours, in advance and kept refrigerated. It is better if the pancakes are not cooked more than a few hours ahead, and the fish must be cooked at the last minute.

Dover sole meunière with saffron pancakes

TO SERVE 4
4 small or 3 large Dover soles, filleted and skinned
a little plain flour
115g unsalted butter, clarified
a large handful of flat-leaf parsley leaves, chopped

FOR THE PANCAKES
30g unsalted butter, plus a scrap
a pinch of saffron threads
55g plain flour
1 large free-range egg
75ml water
75ml milk, plus 2 tbsp extra

YOU WILL NEED
a very large non-stick frying pan

Make the pancake batter: to add flavour, first melt the 30g of unsalted butter in a little saucepan, and cook for a couple of minutes until it starts to froth, then changes to a nutty-smelling golden brown. Don't leave it any longer or you'll end up with burnt butter, which ain't at all nice. Leave the butter to cool for a few minutes, then pour it into a blender.

Rinse out and dry the saucepan. Put in the saffron threads and 'toast' for 1 minute over a medium-to-high heat. Add the 2 tablespoons of milk and bring to the boil, whisking constantly. Remove the pan and leave the milk to infuse for 10 minutes. Now put the rest of the pancake ingredients into the blender, add the saffron-infused milk, and whizz until the batter is smooth. Leave it to stand for at least 30 minutes.

To cook the pancakes, very lightly butter a non-stick frying pan (size immaterial), then place it over a medium flame. When the pan is hot, pour in just enough batter to thinly cover the base of the pan when you swirl it around. Cook the pancake for about 2 minutes, and when the underside is a light golden-brown, flip it over. Continue cooking for another minute or so, until the underside is mottled with

'The combination of fried sole and strips of pancake sounds unlikely, but tastes sensational'

brown blisters. The first pancake is nearly always a disaster while you make adjustments to heat and quantities – discard it, and don't worry about it.

As the pancakes are ready, remove them from the pan and leave them to cool. Roll each one up like a rug, and slice it into thin strips, so it looks a bit like tagliatelle. Leave the strips to one side.

To prevent the sole curling up, lightly score the sides where you can still see traces of white skin. Dust the fillets sparingly with flour seasoned with salt and pepper.

Heat the clarified butter in a large non-stick frying pan over a medium flame, and when it's hot, arrange the fillets in a single, uncrowded layer. (You will almost certainly need to fry the sole in two batches.) Fry the fillets for 2-3 minutes, then turn them and fry for a further 1-2 minutes until cooked. Transfer the fillets to a warm serving dish and continue to keep warm.

Reserve the buttery frying pan, and throw in the pancake strips. Quickly warm them through, tossing all the time. Finally, stir in the parsley, add some seasoning, then pour the entire contents of the pan over the fillets of sole. Serve immediately.

In Italian, fritto misto simply means 'mixed fry', and is one of my favourite dishes. A Venetian fritto misto will normally consist of scampi, squid, prawns, mussels and whitebait, but in Turin I once ate a traditional guts-and-garters version comprising veal sweetbreads, kidneys and brains, with the most astonishing sweet cream fritters – a taste experience akin to eating fish and chips with deep-fried Mars bars.

If you're fortunate enough to be able to buy ultra-spanking-fresh fish – which almost by definition excludes any fish bought in a supermarket – it will only require a light flouring before being deep-fried. Otherwise, I think it's better to use this batter.

Because the deep-fat frying needs last minute and constant attention, fritto misto is a dish I'd recommend serving only to close friends or family. If you are using a wok or saucepan, you will need to let the fat heat up in between batches. Keep the fish warm as it emerges from the oil, although in very casual company you might prefer to serve the fritto misto straight from the fryer.

Fritto misto

TO SERVE 4

about 500g fresh mussels, cleaned

about 200g small or medium-sized squid, cleaned and trimmed

about 500g firm white fish fillets (cod, sole, monkfish), skinned, and cut into fingers

4 large raw tiger prawns, shelled, but with tails still on

about 200g whitebait (fresh, or frozen and defrosted)

1 lemon, quartered lengthways, the pips removed

FOR THE BATTER

2 large free-range eggs

4 rounded tbsp plain flour

2 tbsp dry white wine

YOU WILL NEED

a deep-fat fryer, or a large wok or saucepan half-filled with groundnut oil; a large dish lined with 2 layers of kitchen paper

Preheat the oil in the deep-fat fryer to 190°C; place the wok or saucepan over a moderate-to-high heat.

Prepare all the fish and shellfish. Pile the mussels in a large saucepan, add a splash of water, and place over a high heat, covered. Cook the mussels for 4-5 minutes, shaking the pan occasionally, while holding the lid on with a thick oven cloth. The moment the mussels have opened, take the pan off the heat and remove the lid. As soon as they are cool enough to handle, pick out the mussels and put them to one side. Discard any mussels that remain closed.

Slice the squid sacs into 1cm thick rings. Leave to one side.

To make the batter, whisk all the ingredients together in a deep bowl, and season generously. The batter should be a thick-but-pourable liquid, so you might need either a little more flour or wine.

Fry the white fish first. Dip the pieces into the batter, shake off the excess, and plunge the fish into the oil. Cook for 3-4 minutes until golden, then remove the fish, and put in the paper-lined dish to drain.

Fry the whitebait next. Coat them all at once in the batter, then scoop them out with a spider (or slotted spoon), draining off any excess batter. Drop them into the oil, separating any that cling together, and fry for 2-3 minutes, until golden brown. Now fry the prawns in the same way and, finally, the squid and mussels, both of which will only require about 1 minute in the oil.

Serve the fritto misto as quickly as possible, with a wedge of lemon to squeeze over the fish.

There's no doubt it's a bit of a palaver making a good steak and kidney pie, but the end result is really worth it: crisp, buttery, crumbly pastry; thick, brown, savoury gravy; tender chunks of meat, and rich nuggets of kidney; it might sound like some bullshit adspeak, but that's how wonderful steak and kidney pie can be, if you're prepared to make your own.

As there is nothing quite as gruesome as wobbly bits in a stew, the first essential is to trim the meat of fat and sinew to within an inch of its life, and remove every scrap of the white central core from the kidney. That dog who's eyeing you up so piteously will appreciate the bouncy stuff far more than your family. I always use top rump, which is quite lean anyway, but chuck or blade are a good choice, too.

The other essential is to brown the meat properly. If you overcrowd the pan the meat will steam rather than fry, but if you leave it too empty the fat will burn in a trice. Every chunk of meat should have its own-sized space all around it – for this recipe you will probably have to fry the meat in three to four batches. Another good trick is to sear the kidneys on a very high heat for just a minute or two, then leave all the juices to drain out before carrying on with the cooking. It's the smell of kidneys that so many people detest, and this is a good way to obviate that particular problem.

Ideally, the steak and kidney part should be made 24 hours before you finish the pie. Not only will the meat have a chance to cool properly before you put on the pastry (thus avoiding a slumped crust), but you can easily skim off, and discard, the layer of fat on top. An uncooked pie can be kept in the fridge for a few hours before it's baked, but once it's cooked, the pie should be eaten as soon as possible.

Steak and kidney pie

TO SERVE 6

FOR THE STEAK AND KIDNEY
about 1kg (trimmed weight) British top rump
about 350g (trimmed weight) ox kidney
250g flat mushrooms, wiped
about 3 tbsp groundnut oil
about 100g unsalted butter
1 large Spanish onion, peeled and thickly chopped
70g plain flour
600ml off-the-boil water
1 tbsp Marigold Swiss vegetable bouillon powder
1 large bay leaf, fresh or dried

FOR THE PASTRY
250g plain flour
140g cold unsalted butter, roughly cubed
1 large free-range egg yolk
4 tbsp cold water
1 small egg whisked with 1 tbsp milk for the egg wash

Preheat the oven to 140°C (fan), 160°C (conventional), gas mark 3 to cook the meat; and to 180°C (fan), 200°C (conventional), gas mark 6 for baking the pie.

Cut the beef into large bite-sized chunks. The individual lobes of the kidney are more or less bite-sized anyway, but cut up any bigger bits. Chop the mushrooms (including the stalks) into bite-sized chunks. Leave to one side.

Place a large non-stick frying pan over a high heat, and when it is hot, pour in a tablespoon of oil. After 30 seconds, throw in the kidneys and toss them around for about 1 minute, until they are barely coloured on all sides. Immediately tip them into a large strainer or colander, and leave the juices to drain out.

Wipe out the frying pan, and return it to a medium heat, adding 25g butter and 1 tablespoon of oil. Put in the chopped onion and fry for about 10 minutes, stirring occasionally, until it is soft and slightly golden on the edges. Transfer the onion to the casserole, using a slotted spoon so that the fat drains back into the frying pan. Reserve the pan.

YOU WILL NEED
a large casserole, with lid; a
30cm-long traditional enamel
pie dish; a pie-raiser

Tip the flour into a large plastic bag and season it very generously with salt and pepper. Throw in the beef and shake until every chunk is lightly covered. Return the frying pan to a high heat, adding a little more oil and butter as necessary. Shake any excess flour from the beef, then fry the chunks until golden-brown on all sides. When they are ready, transfer them to the casserole. You will probably need to brown the meat in 3-4 batches.

Now put the mushrooms into the same pan, tossing them almost constantly for about 2 minutes, or until they just start to wilt. Transfer them to the casserole along with the drained kidneys, hot water, Marigold powder, the bay leaf and any flour left in the bag. Stir the contents well then put the lid on and place the casserole in the oven. Cook for 80-90 minutes, or until the meat is tender, and the sauce has thickened. Remove and chill the stew, preferably overnight, then skim off the fat and discard it.

To make the pastry, whizz the flour and a pinch of salt together for a few seconds in a food processor, then add the butter and whizz until the mixture looks like coarse breadcrumbs. Whisk the egg yolk and water together and pour it into the flour mixture. Process again until the pastry has collected in a ball around the spindle. Wrap the pastry in clingfilm and leave it to rest in the fridge for up to 48 hours.

Butter the rim of the pie dish, and the shoulders of the pie raiser. Return the pastry to (cool) room temperature, then roll it out thinly on a well-floured surface. Invert the pie dish on to the pastry and use it as a guide to cut out the lid, adding 1cm all round. Leave the pastry lid to one side. From the remaining pastry cut out a 5-7cm-deep pastry collar to line the rim and a little way down the sides of the pie dish. Seal any joins with a little cold water.

Put the pie raiser in the middle of the dish, then spoon the steak and kidney around it. Don't let the mixture rise above the top of the dish or the gravy will bubble out. (Reserve any excess gravy, and heat it separately in a small pan.)

Brush the pastry collar with a little water, then put on the pastry lid, pinching the edges firmly to seal them. Make 4 neat slashes in the lid, then brush the pastry with the egg wash. Bake the pie for 30-35 minutes, turning the heat down 10-20 degrees after about 20 minutes. The finished pie should be golden-brown, bubbling-hot – and fabulous.

A couple of years ago I had to write an article about a mildly eccentric but very clever and sweet man who grows cobnuts on a beautiful farm in Kent, in concert with the most outrageously prestigious collection of Bösendorfer pianos. I also had to dream up some recipes for the cobnuts. Nutty puddings were easy, but I floundered around a bit with the savoury recipes, trying to avoid any hint of those smock-and-sandal, nut-roast horrors. Fortunately, nuts crop up a lot in Spanish cooking, and it was in one of my favourite cookbooks, *Catalan Cuisine* by Colman Andrews, that I found the basis for the following recipe.

I like the sauce to be slightly rough (texturally rough, that is, not dodgy rough), but if you haven't got a pestle and mortar to pulverise the nuts and garlic, a food processor will do: use the pulse button so the nuts retain some texture.

This is not a dish I'd advise making in advance, but as it only takes about 25 minutes from start to finish, it's not so very taxing.

Fried chicken with hazelnut sauce

TO SERVE 2

2 tbsp olive oil

2 large cloves of garlic, peeled and crushed

30g shelled hazelnuts, toasted

2 free-range chicken breasts, skinned and boned

1 large shallot, peeled and finely chopped

100ml dry white wine

1 medium tomato, deseeded, cored and coarsely chopped

a little hot water

a few sprigs of flat-leaf parsley, finely chopped

YOU WILL NEED

a large pestle and mortar

You will be using the same pan throughout the recipe, so don't absent-mindedly dump it into the sink halfway through.

Pour the olive oil into a medium-sized frying pan and heat it over a medium flame. Add the garlic and fry it for about 3 minutes, stirring occasionally, until the cloves are lightly gilded. Scoop out the garlic (reserving the pan and its oil) and put it in the mortar with the toasted hazelnuts. Grind to a grainy paste and leave to one side.

Season the chicken breasts with salt and pepper, then fry them in the garlicky oil over a medium heat for 10-15 minutes, turning once, until they are cooked through and golden brown. Remove the chicken from the pan. Cover it with foil and keep it warm while you finish the sauce.

Fry the shallot in the frying pan over a low-to-medium heat for 5-6 minutes until soft, stirring occasionally. Turn up the heat and pour in the wine. Scrape up all the bits from the bottom of the pan, and let the wine bubble furiously for a couple of minutes, until reduced to about 2 tablespoons.

Reduce the heat, add the chopped tomato and season with a little salt and quite a lot of black pepper. Carry on cooking for about 1 minute, then add the nut mixture and stir vigorously. The sauce will now be extremely thick, so stir in a couple of tablespoons of hot water to let it down. Finally, add the chopped parsley.

Place a chicken breast on each plate, spoon over the sauce and serve immediately, with some crunchy roast or sauté potatoes and a lively watercress, spinach or rocket salad.

Catalan Cuisine

by Colman Andrews, published by Grub Street

I can't tell you how good this book is. Full of anecdote and history, it's a truly interesting insight into genuine regional Spanish cooking. Some of the recipes are fairly esoteric, but most are eminently doable. I suppose it shouldn't come as a surprise that a country as rich in culture as Spain has such a marvellously varied cuisine, but for those who think Spanish cooking is confined to paella and tortilla, this book is a real eye-opener. I love it.

Despite having turned into the restaurant cliché of the last decade, confit of duck is light years better than the Eighties equivalent – aiguillettes de canard. Remember it? Thin and bloody slices of tasteless duck breast arranged in a fan – and not a shard of crispy skin in sight. Quite the opposite of a confit, in which the duck is cooked until the magnificently rich and flavoursome meat is nearly falling off the bone. What's more, the skin – the best part of the entire bird – is dry, crispy and swooningly good. The women of south-west France knew what they were doing when they potted up their fat ducks to see them through the winter.

Duck confit is at its best cooked in copious quantities of duck fat. You can buy duck (or goose) fat from a good butcher, specialist grocer or even in the smart section of some supermarkets. Or you could accumulate it yourself from previous whole-duck roastings, filtering each batch of fat and storing it in the fridge until needed. As a last resort, top up the duck fat with lard, but it shouldn't represent more than about 30 per cent of the total fat – it's essence of duck that's required, not pig.

The whole point of duck confit is that it can be made a few months ahead, as long as it's kept buried in its fat in a tightly sealed container in the fridge. Leave to mature for at least 2 days, anyway. The pearl barley stew can be made up to 24 hours ahead, and refrigerated – don't add the butter until after it has been gently reheated. If you find there's too much, the rest can be added to a vegetable soup.

Confit of duck with pearl barley stew

TO SERVE 4

FOR THE CONFIT
40g coarse sea salt
a few sprigs fresh thyme or marjoram
a few fresh bay leaves, torn
6-8 cloves of garlic, peeled and heavily crushed
2 tbsp olive oil
4 (280-350g) meaty duck legs, preferably Barbary or Rouen
about 700g duck or goose fat and/or lard, melted

Preheat the oven to 110°C (fan), 130°C (conventional), gas mark 3/4 for the initial cooking; and to 210°C (fan), 230°C (conventional), gas mark 8 for the second stage.

To make the confit, combine all the salt and seasonings (but not the fats) in the dish. Rub the duck with the seasoning mixture, then put it in the fridge, clingfilmed. After 24 hours, turn the duck legs over, rub in the mixture again, and leave for a further 24 hours. Now carefully scrape off all the seasonings, especially any residual salt. Reserve the herbs and garlic, but discard any liquid. Wash the dish to re-use later.

Place the frying pan over a fairly high heat. When it is hot, pour in the oil and when that is hot, put in the duck legs, skin-side down. Cook them for 3-4 minutes, until the skin is golden brown, then turn them and cook for another few minutes.

Transfer the duck and any fat from the pan to the dish, laying the legs skin-side up. Scatter on the reserved seasonings and pour on enough melted fat to barely cover the duck. Put the duck in the oven, and gently cook for 2 hours, or until the meat is completely tender and nearly falling off the bone.

FOR THE PEARL BARLEY

150g pearl barley

1 tbsp Marigold Swiss vegetable bouillon powder

2 tbsp olive oil

1 large onion, peeled and cut into tiny dice

1 stick celery, cut into tiny dice

2 large cloves of garlic, peeled, crushed and finely chopped

2 carrots, peeled and cut into tiny dice

a handful of flat-leaf parsley, chopped

30g unsalted butter

YOU WILL NEED

a non-reactive ovenproof dish large enough to take the duck in a single layer; a large heavy frying pan (preferably not non-stick); a large plastic storage container or kilner jar

Allow the duck to cool for 30 minutes, then put it in a plastic storage container – or glass kilner jar, if you want to be very smart. Carefully pour the cooking fat through a sieve into a jug, then into the container. Make sure the legs are completely covered with fat, then secure the container and store the confit in the fridge.

When you are ready to cook the duck, bring the legs to room temperature and scrape off most of the fat. Place them skin-side down in a roasting tin and cook in the very hot oven for 4-5 minutes. Drain off the melted fat (reserving it for a later use), turn the legs, and cook them for a further 4-5 minutes. By this time the duck skin should be as dry and crisp as an autumn leaf. Serve immediately with the pearl barley stew.

To prepare the pearl barley, follow the instructions on the packet, but add 1 tablespoon of Marigold powder and enough water to cover by about 5-6cm. Simmer gently for 50-60 minutes, with the lid on, or until the barley is tender but not pappy. (The last packet I bought suggested a much longer cooking time, but the barley would have been wrecked.)

In the meantime, heat a frying pan over a low-to-medium heat and pour in the oil. When it is hot, throw in the onion, celery, garlic and carrots and gently fry for about 15 minutes, stirring frequently, until the vegetables are soft but not squishy. Remove the pan from the heat and leave to one side.

When the pearl barley is tender, drain it, reserving 200ml of the cooking liquid and discarding the rest. (Or, if it has all been absorbed, make up 200ml stock with hot water and a teaspoon of Marigold.)

As soon as the duck goes into the oven for the final cooking, put the pearl barley, reserved stock and parsley into the frying pan with the vegetables, and stir thoroughly. Place the frying pan over a low-to-medium flame, season with salt and pepper, and gently reheat. When the stew is hot, remove the pan and stir in the butter. Serve immediately, with the duck.

Why do we never see Betty actually making her famous hotpot in *Coronation Street*? If it comes to that, we rarely see anyone eating it, either, unlike Roy's fry-ups. I'd be interested to know if Betty browns the lamb first. It's not the traditional Lancastrian way of making a hotpot, but the result is much tastier. In fact, for something so plain, boring and deeply untrendy the result is gorgeously, guzzlingly wonderful.

Although hotpot is not quick in the sense that it's ready to eat within minutes, it only takes about half an hour to prepare – and that's the part that matters. Do make sure every single bit of extraneous fat (and skin) is trimmed off the lamb chops. Unless it's well frazzled, lamb fat really doesn't taste very nice. Use the widest possible casserole, too, so there's lots of scrunchy potato topping.

The hotpot can be prepared several hours ahead, up to the point where you top it with the potatoes. Once the potatoes are sliced, they need to be cooked immediately or they go brown. Although a cooked hotpot can be reheated, I don't think it's as good as when freshly made.

Not Betty's hotpot

TO SERVE 4
40-60g dripping or lard
2 heaped tbsp plain flour
12 thickish, best end of neck lamb chops, trimmed of skin and fat
4 lamb's kidneys, cores discarded, and cut into bite-sized chunks
2 large onions, peeled and thickly sliced
100g medium-sized mushrooms, quartered
1 bay leaf, fresh or dried
about 1kg potatoes (eg Maris Piper), sliced as thickly as a Jaffa cake
2 tsp Marigold Swiss vegetable bouillon powder
425ml off-the-boil water
a walnut-sized knob of butter

YOU WILL NEED
a very large non-stick frying pan; a very large shallow casserole, with lid

Preheat the oven to 150°C (fan), 170°C (conventional), gas mark 3½.

Place the frying pan over a medium-to-high flame. After a couple of minutes, put in 40g dripping or lard and leave it to melt and heat up.

In the meantime, tip the flour into a large plastic bag and grind in plenty of salt and pepper. Shake the lamb chops in the flour, a few at a time, then put them in the hot frying pan. Sear them for about 2 minutes each side, turning only once, until golden brown. (If the fat burns, wipe out the pan and heat some more lard.) Transfer the chops to the casserole, packing them in evenly and tightly.

Throw the kidneys into the same frying pan, and toss the chunks around for 1 minute, until just sealed on the outside. Transfer the kidneys to a colander and leave them to drain, discarding any juices.

Lower the heat and fry the onions in the same pan for about 15 minutes until soft and slightly golden, stirring occasionally. Tip in any remaining flour, and stir it around for 30 seconds until it has been absorbed.

Pack the onions, mushrooms and kidneys around the meat. Tuck in the bay leaf and season well. Cover the casserole with overlapping slices of potato, then pour in the Marigold dissolved in the hot water.

Season the potatoes, dot them with scraps of butter, place the lid on the casserole and put it in the oven for 2 hours. Remove the lid and turn the oven up to 170°C (fan), 190°C (conventional), gas mark 5 and cook for a further 30 minutes until the potatoes are edged golden-brown. Serve the hotpot with lots of tender greens.

'I'd be interested to know if Betty from *'Coronation Street'* browns the lamb for her hotpot first. It's not the traditional Lancastrian way of doing it, but the result is much tastier. And for something so plain and deeply untrendy, the result is gorgeously, guzzlingly wonderful'

Wintry puddings

It reduces me to near apoplexy when I pick up a restaurant menu in February and see fresh apricots on it. Not only are they utterly tasteless, but there is a vast array of more appropriate produce available. Here at home, we have the finest apples and pears in the world. Elsewhere, lemons, oranges, lychees, dates, mangoes and pineapple – to name a few – are all at their very best. And what about all the wintry store cupboard ingredients? Coffee, nuts, chocolate, dried fruit, sweet spices, stem ginger, honey, liqueurs...

This Seville orange version of Sussex Pond pudding is a slightly sophisticated take on the original homely pudding. But if you haven't got any Seville oranges, use a whole, pierced lemon, in the traditional way. I strongly advise you not to replace the beef suet with vegetarian suet, though: a Christmas or two ago, I ruined an entire batch of mincemeat by using this horrible stuff.

Suet pastry doesn't stand up to being made in advance, but as the pudding takes 4 hours to cook, you are ahead of yourself anyway. And, don't be put off by the long instructions – this is definitely one of those easier-to-do-than-describe recipes.

Seville Pond pudding

TO SERVE 4
1 Seville orange
225g self-raising flour
115g grated beef suet
a pinch bicarbonate of soda
75ml cold water
75ml milk, plus a little extra
175g unsalted butter, roughly chopped
175g natural demerara sugar
55g dark muscovado sugar
a kettle of boiling water

YOU WILL NEED
a 1.4-litre pudding basin, lavishly buttered;
a very large saucepan, with lid

Half-fill a small saucepan with water and bring it to the boil. Drop in the orange and simmer it for 15 minutes, uncovered. Discard the water, fill the pan again with fresh water, bring it to the boil and simmer the orange for a further 15 minutes. Drain off the water, and leave the orange to cool.

Combine the flour, suet and bicarbonate of soda in a mixing bowl, then pour in most of the cold water and milk to make a very soft but not sticky dough. If it is too dry add a bit more liquid, but go very gently as it only takes a teaspoon to make the dough too sloppy.

On a well-floured surface, and with a well-floured rolling pin, roll the dough out to the thickness of a piece of Wilton or Axminster carpet – but definitely not shag-pile. Upturn the pudding basin, place it lightly over one corner of the pastry, and cut round this template to make a lid. Put the circle of pastry to one side. Drape the remaining dough into the basin and press out the folds to line the interior. Do this as evenly as you can, but bear in mind you are not trying to achieve a Marco Pierre White standard of pâtisserie – patches and joins are fine as long as the lining is well sealed. Leave 1cm of the dough hanging over the edge of the basin.

Now put half the butter, and half the sugars into the lined basin. Although the classic Sussex Pond recipe calls for a whole lemon, there are too many pips for comfort in a Seville orange, so cut the (unpeeled) orange into quarters and remove as many seeds as possible, trying not to lose any juice. Put the orange quarters into the basin and cover with the remaining butter and sugar.

'I suppose there might be a more comforting and scrumptious winter pudding than Sussex Pond, with its golden suet crust and core of molten sugar and lemon, but I am very hard pressed to think of one'

Place the pastry lid on top of the basin, and crimp it together with the lining to make a tight seal. Cut a piece of foil large enough to reach halfway down the outside of the basin, make a pleat in the middle, and cover the top of the pudding. Now stand the basin on another piece of foil and bring it up to fold over the top, pressing it firmly into place to make a really good water-tight seal. Tie a piece of string around the lip of the basin to keep the foil secure, and if you are very clever, make a handle too. (Too tricky for me.)

Stand the basin in the large saucepan, and pour in boiling water to reach halfway up the sides. Put the lid on the pan, bring the water to the boil, then reduce the heat to a lively simmer and cook the pudding for 4 hours, replenishing the water from the kettle as necessary.

When the pudding is ready, remove the foil, and either serve the pudding directly from the basin or, if you're feeling brave, turn it out into a shallow bowl. Either way, make sure each person has their fair share of flaky suet crust, a wedge of bitter orange, and a good ladle of the piping hot, buttery, citrus juices. A good dowsing of thick cream wouldn't go amiss either.

Apart from tasting good, bananas make an ideal impromptu pudding when your partner complains that you aren't looking after him properly. (Or is that just mine?) I love banana fritters with lime syrup, banana custard, Chinese-style toffee bananas, banana trifle – in fact, bananas any old how will do me. For this recipe, either serve the bananas as they come, or with a scoop of vanilla or ginger ice-cream, if you have any in the freezer.

Everything happens a bit quickly once you get going, so do read the recipe through first if you don't want to be hunting for the can opener while the bananas burn.

Butter-fried bananas
with orange and coconut syrup

TO SERVE 2
a scrap of unsalted butter
2 tbsp natural caster sugar
2 large firm bananas, peeled and cut diagonally into three
50ml fresh orange juice
50ml coconut milk
1 tsp toasted sesame seeds
a squeeze of lemon juice (optional)

Melt the butter in a medium-sized, non-stick frying pan over a medium heat. As soon it has melted, sprinkle the caster sugar evenly over the base of the pan and watch it like a traffic warden guarding a meter which has only seconds to expire. After about 2 minutes, when the sugar begins to bubble and starts to look like a Callard & Bowser Creme Toffee, stir it briskly, then toss in the bananas.

Turn the bananas in the caramel as it continues to brown, stirring all the time. After about 30 seconds when the caramel is thick, bubbling and golden brown, pour in the orange juice. Stir frantically for about 30 seconds, and then tip in the coconut milk. Stir briskly for another minute while the sauce bubbles away.

Remove the pan from the heat and divide the bananas between two plates. Taste the sauce and squeeze in a little lemon juice if you think it's a mite too sweet – it very much depends on how sharp the orange is. Pour the sauce over the bananas, sprinkle with the sesame seeds and serve immediately.

'There aren't many people who turn their noses up at a hot banana pudding, and this is one of the best'

Biting into a gorgeous-looking fruit tart and discovering there's only air between the fruit and the pastry is almost as miserable as finding your Easter egg is hollow. A smear of fruit purée is one step better, but a proper fruit tart should have a layer of sweet crème pâtissière lining the pastry. That's what separates a tarte aux pommes française from an English apple tart.

My entrée into French apple tart-making was courtesy of Robert Carrier in his original *Great Dishes of the World*. But true to form, I've tinkered with it over the years, replacing the cookers with dessert apples (because they hold their shape better), and changing the alcohol from kirsch to Triple-Sec (for no particular reason, except I like it).

You can make any fruit tart in much the same way as this, but if you are using strawberries, raspberries or other soft fruits, they will not need the final grilling, and the glaze should be made from redcurrant jelly, rather than apricot jam.

You can cook the crème pâtissière and the pastry case up to 24 hours ahead, but don't assemble and finish the tart until 2-8 hours before it's needed. The tart will still be OK after 36 hours but the pastry will get soggier as time goes by.

French apple tart

TO SERVE 8-plus

FOR THE PASTRY
225g plain flour
1 rounded tsp icing sugar
1 level tbsp caster sugar
a pinch of fine sea salt
140g cold unsalted butter, roughly chopped
1 large free-range egg yolk
3 tbsp ice-cold water

FOR THE CRÈME PÂTISSIÈRE (pastry cream)
3 rounded tbsp cornflour
115g caster sugar
425ml full cream milk
5 large free-range egg yolks, well-beaten
2 tbsp Triple-Sec (or rum, kirsch, Cointreau)

Preheat the oven to 170°C (fan), 190°C (conventional), gas mark 5 for the pastry; preheat the grill to finish the apple tart.

First, make the pastry: whizz the flour, sugars and salt together for a few seconds in a food processor, then add the butter and whizz again, until the mixture looks like coarse breadcrumbs. Whisk the egg yolk and water together and pour into the flour mixture. Process again until the pastry has collected in a ball around the spindle. Form the pastry into a thick rectangular shape, wrap it in clingfilm and leave to rest in the fridge for a minimum of 30 minutes, or up to 2 days.

Take out the pastry, let it return to (cool) room temperature, then roll it out thinly. Line the tin – making sure you don't stretch the pastry – and trim the edges. Put the pastry case back in the fridge and chill for at least 30 minutes.

To make the crème pâtissière, sieve the cornflour into a medium-sized saucepan then mix in the sugar. Pour in the milk, whisk until the mixture is smooth, then put the saucepan on to a high heat. Whisking throughout the process, bring the mixture to the boil until it thickens dramatically, then cook for exactly 1 minute.

Remove the saucepan from the heat, whisk in the egg yolks, then return the saucepan to a low-to-medium heat. Still whisking, simmer the pastry cream for 3 minutes, then plunge the base of the saucepan into ice-cold water. Carry on whisking for a couple of minutes, then

FOR THE FILLING AND GLAZE

4-6 large Cox's apples (or other
well-flavoured dessert apple)

3 heaped tbsp runny apricot
jam (eg Bonne Maman)

1 tbsp Triple-Sec (or other
alcohol, as above)

YOU WILL NEED

a heavy, non-stick baking tray or
Swiss roll tin, measuring
roughly 38cm x 25cm x 2cm
deep, lightly buttered;
ceramic baking (or dried) beans

leave the pastry cream to cool thoroughly, stirring occasionally to keep the cream smooth. When it's cool, stir in the Triple-Sec.

Line the pastry with a piece of foil large enough to tuck over the edges of the tin, then weigh it down with baking (or dried) beans. Cook the pastry for about 15 minutes on the middle shelf of the oven until it no longer looks raw. Remove the foil and beans, reserving the foil, and continue to cook for 5-6 minutes until the pastry is an even pale-honey colour. Remove the tin from the oven, and leave to cool.

Spread the cold pastry cream evenly over the bottom of the cooked pastry case in a thick layer – you might not need all of it. (If you made the pastry cream well in advance, and it has set too solidly, give it a whizz in the food processor to restore its spreadability.)

Peel, core and slice the apples into slices about 1/2cm thick. Starting at one end of the tin and working in a line downwards, cover the pastry cream with the apples, overlapping each slice with the next.

Place the tin on top of the reserved foil and then curl the foil over the edges of the pastry to protect it from burning. Slide the tart on to a shelf about a hand's length below the elements, and grill for 5-10 minutes, or until the edges of the apple are well toasted. Remove the tart and leave it to one side to cool.

In the meantime, put the Triple-Sec and apricot jam (without any bits of fruit, if possible) in a small saucepan over a medium heat, stir well, then heat until the jam starts to bubble. Remove the pan and brush this glaze over the apples as quickly as possible. Leave the tart to cool for two hours before serving.

'This needs no accompaniment, other than an occasional sigh of bliss'

Lemon meringue pie is one of the most perfect puddings in existence. Well, it would be if it hadn't been bastardised into gloopy, over-sweetened, mealy-pastried yuk by frozen food manufacturers – a good example of an all-time great suffering sadly from commercial exploitation. Anyway, it's time to put lemon meringue pie back on its pedestal. I've noticed that a number of English cookbooks suggest nothing more than a basic lemon curd for this pie but I think it is imperative that the filling should have a slightly jelly-like consistency. So I follow the American lead, and add cornflour. Apart from that, all a great lemon meringue pie needs is good buttery pastry, and a soft, marshmallow-cloud of toasted meringue.

There are three stages to making a lemon meringue pie, the first two of which – pastry case and lemon filling – can be made up to 48 hours in advance. The final baking should take place 1-4 hours before serving. NB you will need 4 eggs in total – the yolks for the filling, and the whites for the meringue.

Lemon meringue pie

FOR THE PASTRY

225g plain flour

1 rounded tsp icing sugar

1 level tbsp caster sugar

a pinch of fine sea salt

140g cold unsalted butter,
roughly chopped

1 large free-range egg yolk

3 tbsp ice-cold water

FOR THE LEMON FILLING

4 large free-range egg yolks

the zest of 2 large lemons, in
strips, or roughly chopped

125ml fresh lemon juice
(about 2-3 lemons)

110g caster sugar

3 heaped tbsp cornflour

225ml cold water

85g unsalted butter,
roughly chopped

FOR THE MERINGUE

4 large free-range egg whites

115g caster sugar

YOU WILL NEED

a 23cm diameter x 5cm deep,
loose-bottomed
tart tin, buttered

Preheat the oven to 170°C (fan), 190°C (conventional), gas mark 5 to bake both the pastry case, and to finish the pie.

First, make the pastry: whizz the flour, sugars and salt together for a few seconds in a food processor, then add the butter and whizz again, until the mixture looks like coarse breadcrumbs. Whisk the egg yolk and water together and pour it into the flour mixture. Process until the pastry has collected in a ball around the spindle. Form the pastry into a thick disc, wrap it in clingfilm and leave to rest in the fridge for a minimum of 30 minutes, and up to 2 days.

Take out the pastry, return to (cool) room temperature, then roll it out thinly. Line the tin – making sure you don't stretch the pastry – then trim the edges. Put the pastry case back in the fridge and chill for at least 30 minutes. Line the chilled pastry case with foil and pour in baking (or dried) beans to weigh it down. Bake for 15 minutes, remove the foil and beans, and carry on baking for 5-6 minutes. When it is ready, the pastry should look crisp and dry, but blond rather than brown. Leave the pastry case to cool in the tin.

To make the lemon filling, whisk the egg yolks then pour them into a medium-sized saucepan, and add the lemon zest and juice. Set the pan aside. Combine the caster sugar, cornflour and a pinch of salt in a medium-sized bowl, then gradually whisk in the water to make a smooth mixture. Pour this into the saucepan, and whisk thoroughly. Put the saucepan over a medium-to-high heat and bring the mixture to the boil, whisking all the time. When it has thickened dramatically, carry on cooking for 30 seconds, then remove the pan from the heat and beat in the butter. Quickly dunk the bottom of the pan into ice-cold water and let the filling cool for a few minutes, whisking frequently. Once it is tepid, you can leave it to cool completely, with just the occasional stir to prevent a skin forming.

Whisk the egg whites in a grease-free bowl until they stand in peaks and don't fall out of the bowl if you turn it upside down. Whisk in the sugar, a tablespoon at a time, until the peaks have transformed into very shiny, firm hillocks. Spoon the lemon filling into the pastry case, pushing the mixture right up to the sides, because it tends to shrink away during baking. Spread the meringue over the filling, taking it right to the edges. Swirl the meringue into little peaks with a fork, then put the pie into the oven for 10-15 minutes, or until the surface is a perfect sea of undulating pinky-brown and white waves.

Allow the pie to cool in the tin for 30 minutes, then transfer it (still on its metal base) to a flat serving plate.

A glorified version of a Margaret Costa recipe, and an excellent way to rustle up a quick hot pudding, this is as easy to prepare for one as for six. I suggest using panettone because I always seem to have loads left over from Christmas – I'm a sucker for the shiny boxes and wrappings – and, well wrapped up, it keeps for ages. But you can always use good-quality bread or brioche, if you prefer. The plums should be ripe enough for the stones to be easily removed without having to halve them. As they cook, the juices meld into the crisping panettone, and the resulting combination of hot soft fruit, sugary juices and crisp almonds is quite delectable. This is another pudding where thick, cold, double cream or crème fraîche is almost mandatory.

You can stone the plums a few hours in advance, but don't proceed with the recipe until it is nearly time to cook and serve it.

Baked plums on panettone

TO SERVE 1
6-8 ripe Victoria plums
about 55g dark muscovado sugar
about 1 tbsp flaked almonds
30g unsalted butter, softened
1 doorstep slice of panettone
30g caster sugar

YOU WILL NEED
a heavy baking tray

Preheat the oven to 180°C (fan), 200°C (conventional), gas mark 6.

Cut a small slit in the side of each plum and extract the stone, trying to keep the plums as intact as possible. Put a little pinch of muscovado sugar in each cavity, then plant a small clump of flaked almonds a little way into the sugar. Once the plums are filled leave them to one side.

Spread half the softened butter thickly over the panettone, then sprinkle half the caster sugar over the butter. Put the plums on top, almond-side up, and sprinkle with the remaining caster sugar, and any muscovado sugar you might have left over. Transfer to the baking tray.

Put the baking tray in the oven, and cook for 25-35 minutes: it depends on how ripe the plums are, but the pudding is ready when the plums have just started to wilt. Eat as soon as decently possible.

Four Seasons Cookery Book

by Margaret Costa, republished by Grub Street

Not many recipe books have stood the test of time as well as Margaret Costa's Four Seasons Cookery Book, first published in 1970. Back then she was the owner (with her husband, Bill Lacy) of one of London's most esteemed restaurants. Most importantly, she really understood about good, honest food – and how not to bugger it around. When I was first married, I read her wise words as avidly as I plundered her delightful recipes and, despite having three copies of the book, was delighted when Four Seasons was rescued and reprinted a couple of years ago. A cookbook to read, use and treasure.

I speak the truth: of all the fruits that make the best pies, crumbles or cobblers, damsons are the most sublime. The juices are almost indescribably beautiful – gloriously, deeply purple, like a bishop's robes; the flavour is a complex amalgam of sweet, tannic, plummy sharpness; and the aroma is heady beyond belief. With soft, crumbling, ground almond cobbles (nothing more than elaborate scones) plumped on top, damson cobbler is a seriously swoonable pudding.

I am normally assiduous about removing the stones and pits from fruit destined for pies and puddings, but here it really is a non-starter. Damson stones stick to the flesh like a fox terrier to a bone, and only cooking dislodges them – perhaps I should try the same trick with Jessie. So this is one instance when everyone will have to do a lot of tinker-tailoring – just remember to warn people in advance.

The cobbles need to be cooked as soon as they're made, so this isn't a pudding to part-make in advance. It will reheat quite well, but won't be quite as wonderful as when served fresh and hot from the oven.

Damson and almond cobbler

TO SERVE 6-plus
1kg damsons, washed and de-stalked
85g white caster sugar
85g light muscovado sugar, plus 1 tbsp
115g plain flour
100g ground almonds
3 level tsp baking powder
a pinch of fine sea salt
85g cold unsalted butter, roughly chopped
175ml buttermilk (or full cream milk mixed with 1 tsp lemon juice)
2-3 drops real almond essence or extract
15g flaked almonds

YOU WILL NEED
a 1.2-litre, about 25cm diameter ovenproof dish, buttered

Preheat the oven to 200°C (fan), 220°C (conventional), gas mark 7.

Pile the washed and drained damsons into the dish, levelling the surface as best you can, then sprinkle with the white and brown sugars. Leave to one side while you make the scone mixture.

Combine the flour, ground almonds, baking powder and a pinch of salt in a food processor, and whizz for a few seconds. Add the butter and whizz for a few more seconds, until the mixture looks like coarse breadcrumbs. Pour in the buttermilk (or the milk and lemon juice) and 2 or 3 drops of almond essence – be careful, it's potent stuff. Process again, until the mixture forms a soft, claggy mass. Remove the blades, scraping any mixture on them back into the bowl.

Using a tablespoon and your fingers, dollop tangerine-sized heaps of the mixture on top of the damsons – there should be enough to make eight little cobbles, seven round the edge and one in the middle. Finish with a scattering of flaked almonds and the remaining tablespoon of muscovado.

Put the dish on the middle shelf of the oven, and cook for 25-30 minutes until the cobbles have risen and are golden brown, and the damson juices are bubbling. Remove the cobbler and leave it to cool for about 10 minutes, then serve with lashings of thick cream (Jersey if at all possible), crème fraîche or custard.

Let's face it, cheesecake can be awful. I am thinking about those claggy, ultra-sweet ones, with a neon-red glaze like a tart's lipstick. On the other hand, baked cheesecakes made with real curd cheese can be triumphant. One of my sisters, Drusilla, makes the best cheesecake in the world, but this pumpkin one I've come up with isn't bad. What's more this recipe has not been subtly sabotaged in the transition from donor to recipient (Oh come on, sis, why can I *never* make your cheesecake recipe work!)

I am told that canned pumpkin is a good substitute for fresh pumpkin, but it seems a shame not to use the real thing when it's in season. Anyway, I like the idea of using a traditional pumpkin for something more than a stupid lantern. As for the praline, although it's tempting to use the seeds from the pumpkin, I'd recommend buying them separately as they're much meatier.

Without the praline topping, the cheesecake will keep for a good 3 days in the fridge. But as the praline will start to deliquesce after a few hours in the cold (which, in plain English, means the caramel will start to soften and weep), don't finish the cheesecake until you are nearly ready to serve it.

Pumpkin cheesecake with pumpkin seed and maple praline

TO SERVE 8-plus

FOR THE BISCUIT BASE
140g amaretti biscuits
85g unsalted butter, melted

FOR THE FILLING
450g pumpkin flesh
(or one 425g tin)
4 large free-range eggs
2 (200g) packets
Philadelphia cream cheese
1 (250g) tub ricotta cheese
115g light muscovado sugar
the grated zest of 1 orange
15g cornflour

Preheat the oven to 180°C (fan), 200°C (conventional), gas mark 6.

Whizz the amaretti in a food processor until they are the texture of coarse sand, then turn the crumbs out into a bowl and mix them thoroughly with the melted butter. Press this mixture evenly into the base of the tin and a little way up the sides. Leave to one side.

Cut the fresh pumpkin into large chunks and put them in the middle of a double sheet of foil. Make a loose but tightly sealed parcel, place it on a baking sheet and cook in the preheated oven for 30-35 minutes, or until the pumpkin is very soft. Unwrap the parcel and leave the pumpkin to cool completely. Leave the oven on.

Crack the eggs into the food processor and whizz for a few seconds. Add the cooled (or tinned) pumpkin and the remaining filling ingredients. Whizz again, until the mixture is completely smooth.

Pour the pumpkin mixture into the biscuit-lined cake tin. Place the tin on the un-oiled baking sheet and put it on the middle shelf of the oven. Cook for 15 minutes, then reduce the heat to 100°C (fan), 120°C (conventional), gas mark 1/2, and cook for a further 50-60 minutes, or until the cheesecake is firm to the touch. Turn off the oven but leave the cheesecake inside for 30 minutes before removing it. Cool it in the tin, then transfer to the fridge to chill thoroughly.

'Baked cheesecakes made with real curd cheese can be triumphant – and I like the idea of using a traditional pumpkin for something more than a stupid lantern'

FOR THE PRALINE
55g pumpkin seeds
100ml real maple syrup

YOU WILL NEED
a 23cm diameter springform cake tin, well oiled with groundnut (or hazelnut) oil; 2 baking sheets, one of them well-oiled (but not completely blotto)

For the praline, tip the pumpkin seeds into a large frying pan and place it over a high heat for 1 minute, shaking frequently. Pour in the maple syrup and leave it to bubble for about 3 minutes, or until it has darkened and thickened considerably. To test, spoon up a small dollop and plunge it into a bowl of ice-cold water – if it hardens immediately, the praline is ready; if it's still bendy, cook it for a little longer.

Pour the pumpkin seed praline on to the oiled baking sheet as evenly as you can, and allow it to cool thoroughly. To finish, tip the praline into a food processor and pulse until it has reduced to coarse crumbs about the size of Grape-nuts (or seal the praline in a thick plastic bag and bash it with a rolling pin).

Run a palette knife around the edge of the cheesecake, and gently remove the sides of the tin. Transfer the cheesecake to a serving dish, and scatter the praline over the top. (You may not need it all – use any left over to fold into some vanilla ice-cream for another occasion.) If you're feeling very slim, you can dribble a little more maple syrup on top, too.

There can be few people alive who won't like this cake: it's got all the taste and texture you could want: sweet, crisp but chewy meringue; toasted, knobbly nuts; intensely rich, slightly sharp fruit; and, soft, luscious cream. Stacked three layers high, it looks absolutely spectacular – just right for a celebration.

As with many puddings, I think this cake is best served a few hours after it's assembled, but you can make the meringue layers up to 48 hours ahead and keep them wrapped in foil. You will need to soak the apricots for 8 hours. Once broached, the cake will keep in the fridge for about 2 days, but will get softer and stickier as the hours go by.

Hazelnut and apricot meringue cake

TO SERVE 8-plus

FOR THE FILLING
250g unsulphured dried apricots
3-4 tbsp amaretto liqueur
300ml whipping or double cream
1 heaped tbsp natural icing sugar

FOR THE MERINGUE LAYERS
280g natural caster sugar
1 rounded tsp cornflour
a pinch of ground cloves
5 large free-range egg whites
100g hazelnuts, toasted and chopped fairly coarsely

YOU WILL NEED
the loose bases of 3 cake tins measuring 23cm diameter, lined, with the edges very lightly oiled with groundnut (or hazelnut) oil, or 3 baking sheets lined with non-stick baking parchment

Preheat the oven to 120°C (fan), 140°C (conventional), gas mark 1.

Soak the apricots for about 8 hours in 2 tablespoons of amaretto, plus just enough warm water to cover them. Drain the plumped-up apricots thoroughly, stone them if necessary, then whizz them in a food processor with 1 tablespoon of amaretto until smooth. If the purée will take a little more amaretto without becoming too sloppy, add another tablespoon. Leave the purée to one side.

To make the meringue, sift the sugar, cornflour and ground cloves together. Whisk the egg whites in a clean, grease-free bowl until they form stiff glossy peaks, then whisk in a large tablespoon of the sugar mixture. Using a large metal spoon, carefully fold in the rest – about a fifth at a time. Try to retain as much air in the mixture as possible.

Most experts will tell you to line some baking sheets with parchment, and then draw neat circles on which to spread the meringue. I find it far easier to line appropriate-sized cake tin bases, because the shape's already there, and they take up much less space in the oven.

Spread the meringue evenly on to the cake tin bottoms, leaving a 1/2cm gap round the edge for the meringue to expand. Now sprinkle the nuts over each layer – don't worry if some spill over the edges.

Slide the meringue layers into the oven and cook them for 60 minutes. Switch off the oven and leave them for another hour, without opening the door. Remove the meringues from the oven, and leave to cool completely.

Meanwhile, whip the cream with the icing sugar into soft peaks.

To assemble the cake, gently peel off the parchment from the meringues, then place the first layer on to a serving plate, nut side down. Spread with half the apricot purée, then half the whipped cream. Place the next layer on top, nut side down, and spread with the remaining apricot and cream. Place the final layer on top, this time nut side up. Press down very, very gently to meld the layers. Leave in a cool place until required.

I can't tell you how good this dessert is, except I just have. Quite unlike the thin, lacy numbers we eat on Shrove Tuesday, these pancakes are small, wodgy and stuffed with fresh coconut – tropical Scotch pancakes. They have an intriguing slightly chewy texture, and are more than moreish served fresh from the pan with a dribbling dollop of nutty rum-and-maple butter on top.

I have specified freshly grated coconut, which is nothing like as esoteric as it might seem. Simply pierce the coconut, drain off the juice (and drink it), throw the coconut on a cement floor (or crack it open with a hammer round the 'fault' line), and separate the flesh from the shell. Peel off the hard, brown skin with a sharp knife, then grate the flesh in a processor, using the fine grating blade. If you don't want to do this (and it doesn't take long), use desiccated coconut soaked in a little water and patted dry.

The pancakes can be made 24 hours in advance, and the butter up to a week. Wrap the pancakes in a foil parcel, and warm them gently in a low oven. Bring the butter to room temperature before serving.

Coconut pancakes with maple, pecan and rum butter

TO SERVE 4

FOR THE PANCAKES
100g self-raising flour
half a rounded tsp baking powder
55g natural caster sugar
1 large free-range egg
175ml milk
115g fresh coconut, peeled and finely grated
1 tbsp dark rum

FOR THE BUTTER
115g natural caster sugar
115g unsalted butter, softened
2 tbsp real maple syrup
2 tbsp dark rum
30g pecans, chopped roughly

To make the pancake batter, put the flour, baking powder and sugar into a food processor and whizz for a few seconds to combine. Add the egg and the milk and whizz until completely smooth, stopping to scrape down the sides once or twice. Finally, tip in the coconut and the rum, whizz for a couple of seconds, then leave the batter to rest for 20 minutes.

To make the butter, put the sugar and butter into a food processor and whizz for about 3 minutes until the mixture is completely soft and smooth. Add the maple syrup, rum and chopped pecans, and pulse once or twice to combine them – don't overprocess. Scrape the butter into a bowl, and keep in the fridge until required.

Lightly butter a large non-stick frying pan, and put it over a medium flame. Spoon in a large tablespoon of batter, spreading it out into a circle about 10cm in diameter. Remember the pancakes expand a little while they are cooking so how many you can make at one time depends on the size of your frying pan – normally, I'd say three.

Cook the pancakes gently for about 3 minutes, then lift up an edge to check the underside is golden brown before turning over and cooking for a further 3 minutes or so. (You might need to ditch the first pancake while you make heat adjustments.)

Serve the pancakes straightaway with a good knob of the rum butter melting on top.

'The filling of slightly warm mincemeat and cold ice-cream is a real tooth-trembler'

I 'invented' this pudding for a Christmas feature in Sainsbury's *The Magazine* many years ago. The idea of deep-frying ice-cream is not new – the Victorians did it – but I've never seen this particular combination before. It's a stunning way of using up any jars of mincemeat left over at Christmas; the crisp brown parcels not only look terrific, but the filling of slightly warm mincemeat and cold ice-cream is a real tooth-trembler.

Although the parcels need to be fried to order, you can prepare them in advance and store them in the freezer; bring them out for 10 minutes prior to frying them.

Deep-fried mincemeat and ice-cream parcels

TO MAKE 12 PARCELS
1 (400g) packet authentic Greek filo pastry (defrosted)
about 400g mincemeat, preferably home-made
about 500ml top-quality vanilla ice-cream
a little caster sugar

YOU WILL NEED
a deep-fat fryer, or a large wok or saucepan half-filled with groundnut oil; an oiled baking sheet

Preheat the oil in the deep-fat fryer to 190°C; place the wok or pan over a moderate-to-high heat.

Put the baking sheet in the freezer. Unfold the sheets of pastry, then immediately cover them with a clean damp tea towel so they don't dry out. Cut out (about) 30cm squares as you need them, bearing in mind that in this recipe speed is more important than precision.

Place a square of filo on the work surface. Spoon 1 tablespoon of mincemeat about 5cm in from the front right-hand corner, then dollop a tablespoon of ice-cream on top. Starting from the same corner, roll the pastry over twice, working away from you. Now fold in the right-hand flap and roll again; fold in the left-hand flap and roll again. The packet should now look like an open envelope. Dab a spot of ice-cream on to the point of the triangular flap, and continue rolling until the parcel is sealed. As you complete the parcels transfer them to the baking sheet in the freezer.

Fry the parcels for about 2 minutes in the preheated oil, turning them halfway through. When they are golden-brown, remove the parcels from the oil and leave them to drain on a pad of kitchen paper. Serve immediately with a little caster sugar sprinkled on top.

As a restaurateur, I know coffee-flavoured puddings aren't as popular as chocolate ones. I have a theory that this is because people don't want to end the meal with a double dose of coffee. Personally, I'd forgo liquid coffee any day for coffee granita, the ice-cold shards of bitter-sweet espresso biting through a sumptuous slick of Jersey cream. Not just coffee granita, either, but coffee eclairs, coffee (walnut) cake, coffee ice-cream, or this rich, aromatic coffee, rum and cardamom trifle.

Now the trouble with a magnificent-looking, family-sized trifle is that the whole thing collapses into an unsightly slurry of cream and custard as soon as the first spoonful is removed. So although it's a bit more of a hassle I prefer to make trifle in individual glasses. As a general rule, you'll need fewer trifle sponges, pro rata, for a small trifle than for a large one.

The custard can be made 48 hours in advance and kept refrigerated; the whole ensemble should be made at least an hour in advance, and will keep for 24 hours as long as it, too, is refrigerated.

Coffee, rum and cardamom trifle

TO SERVE 6
about 6 trifle sponges
8-10 tbsp dark rum
about 300ml whipping cream
1 heaped tbsp natural
caster sugar
8-10 green cardamom pods
1/4 tsp cinnamon powder
a small handful of toasted,
flaked almonds

FOR THE CUSTARD
425ml full cream milk
150ml whipping or
double cream
8 large free-range egg yolks
115g natural caster sugar
1 level tbsp cornflour
1 heaped tbsp good-quality
coffee granules

YOU WILL NEED
6 (300-350ml) glass bowls
or squat tumblers;
a pestle and mortar

First make the custard. Heat the milk and cream in a saucepan until just below simmering point. Meanwhile, whizz the egg yolks, sugar and cornflour together in a food processor until the mixture is thick, creamy and paler than when you started. Take the milk off the heat, pour it on to the egg mixture, and pulse for just long enough to blend – the custard should not be too aerated and bubbly.

Quickly, but thoroughly, rinse out the milk pan, and pour the custard back in. Return the saucepan to a medium-to-high heat and bring the contents to the boil, whisking almost continuously. Still whisking, reduce the heat and simmer the thickened custard for one minute. Tip in the coffee granules, and stir for a few seconds until dissolved. Remove the pan from the heat and plunge the base into ice-cold water. Continue whisking for 2-3 minutes until the custard has cooled a little, then leave it to cool completely, stirring occasionally.

Arrange the trifle sponges in the bottom of the glasses, breaking them up to fit (I like a fairly thick layer but it's up to you). Sprinkle the rum evenly over the sponges. Again, the quantity is up to you, but the sponges should be fairly damp. Leave to soak for at least 30 minutes.

Whip the cream and sugar into soft peaks. Put the cardamom pods in a mortar, and pound them lightly. Remove and discard the husks, then grind the little seeds into a fine powder. Now gently fold the ground cardamom and cinnamon powder into the whipped cream.

To assemble the trifle, spoon the cold custard over the trifle sponges in a thick layer, then top with the whipped cream. Finish with a scattering of toasted almonds.

Oh, those Seventies dinner parties. The ones that took a week of planning, two days shopping and another two days cooking. By the time Saturday night came, the hostess (we were always women) was as dead as a Game Boy's battery on Boxing Day. I don't miss those dinners one bit, but I'm pleased this (actually quite fast) pudding has survived in my culinary repertoire. I first had hot fruit salad at Lacy's (the London restaurant owned by Margaret Costa and her husband), and the combination of cool rum-soused fruits and warm crackle-sugared cream is as devilishly good now as it was then.

Any fruits will do, but I particularly like this tropical selection. It probably doesn't need saying but the fruit must be completely free of skin, peel, pith and seeds. The lime syrup is my own addition, and can be omitted, but it helps to keep the bananas from browning, as well as adding to the general flavour. The quantity here is enough for 8, but you could make a smaller amount, especially if you were to cheat and use a bowl of Marks & Spencer's prepared fruit salad – if it hasn't been delisted, the pineapple, mango and passion fruit selection is ace.

The syrup can be made aeons in advance. The fruit salad, with the exception of the bananas, can also be made surprisingly well in advance – up to 48 hours, as long as it's refrigerated – which just leaves a few minutes to whip the cream and put the fruit salads under the grill.

Hot fruit salad brûlée

TO SERVE 8
150ml hot water
115g white sugar
the finely grated zest and juice of 1 large lime
3-4 tbsp dark rum
2 oranges, cut into skin-free segments
1 large mango, cut into chunks
1/2 large pineapple, cut into small chunks
2 large bananas, sliced
4 passion fruit, pulp and seeds
300ml whipping cream, whipped into soft peaks
8 tbsp light muscovado sugar

YOU WILL NEED
8 ovenproof bowls or ramekins, 10cm diameter x 7cm deep; a heavy baking tray

Preheat the grill to brûlée the fruit salads.

First, make the lime syrup. Put the water and sugar into a small, heavy saucepan over a medium heat and, stirring almost constantly, bring the liquid to the boil. Bubble for 5 minutes, then add the lime juice and zest. Remove the saucepan from the heat and leave the syrup to cool. Stored in a screw-top jar in the fridge, the syrup will keep for nigh-on eternity.

When you are ready to use it, pour the lime syrup and the rum into a large mixing bowl, add the fruits and mix well.

Arrange the serving bowls on the baking tray and spoon fruit salad into each, leaving about 3cm headroom for the whipped cream. Flop the cream on top of the fruit, making sure it doesn't rise above the level of the bowls, then sprinkle thickly with the muscovado sugar.

Quickly slide the baking tray under the very hot grill. Don't go away. After about 1 minute the sugar will bubble, darken and start to sink into the cream. Remove the bowls immediately, and transfer each one to a cold under-plate. Serve immediately, with a warning that the bowls are very hot.

The original idea for this recipe came from Elizabeth David's *French Country Cooking*; she called it Saint Emilion au chocolat. Feeling bold and brave one day at the Fox and Goose, my erstwhile Suffolk restaurant, we tampered with it a little – highly audacious since Elizabeth David's repertoire is considered something of a culinary Eucharist.

Not only did we replace the macaroons with ginger biscuits, but I also renamed the recipe – for the very prosaic reason that for much of the Eighties, every Tom, Dick and Harry of a restaurateur had chocolate Saint Emilion on his menu. Pavé translates as 'slab' or 'paving stone', which I readily admit lacks charm, but is nonetheless descriptive of the solid, rich, suede-smooth texture.

As long as you buy very good-quality chocolate, the flavour of this pavé could not be more deeply, darkly intense. I like to use a combination of chocolates, one with about 55 per cent cocoa solids, the other about 70 per cent. Mixing the two seems to give the right depth of flavour, and a satisfying balance between sweetness and bitterness.

I've suggested using rather Christmassy stem ginger for this recipe (in fact, it's a perfect pud to have on standby over the holiday), but the pavé is excellent with (drained) bottled cherries buried in the chocolate, too. You could also use reconstituted dried apricots or prunes, with equal success.

The pavé freezes beautifully, indeed it can be served almost straight from the freezer – give it 15 minutes or so to soften a little. Otherwise, it will keep for several days in the fridge, clingfilmed.

Chocolate and stem ginger pavé

TO SERVE 8-plus
about 225g ginger biscuits
350g unsalted butter, softened
300g (55 per cent cocoa solids) dark chocolate
100g (70 per cent cocoa solids) dark chocolate
225ml full cream milk
140g caster sugar
2 large free-range egg yolks
1 jar (about 350g) stem ginger, drained (reserve the syrup to drizzle over ice-cream)

YOU WILL NEED
a 25cm diameter x 5cm deep loose-bottomed tart tin; a baking sheet

To make the base, first whizz the ginger biscuits in a food processor until reduced to fairly fine crumbs. Melt 115g of the butter in a small saucepan over a low heat, then stir in the biscuit crumbs. Line the base of the tin with this mixture, pushing it as far up the sides as you can. Put the tin on the baking sheet and leave it to one side.

Break the chocolate into squares, and put it into a medium-sized saucepan with the milk. Place the saucepan over a very low heat, and melt the chocolate. Remove the saucepan from the heat, whisk the milk and chocolate together, and leave it to cool.

In the meantime, whizz the remaining butter with the caster sugar in a food processor until the mixture is very pale, then add the egg yolks and whizz again. Scrape the cool chocolate mixture into the processor and whizz until everything is thoroughly combined.

Cut the knobs of stem ginger in half and arrange them on the biscuit base, then pour over the chocolate mixture. Put the tin (on its baking sheet) in the freezer for 2 hours, or until the chocolate has set firmly.

'On our mildly intoxicated, dank-dark meander back to the hotel, we came upon an apparently respectable elderly American out walking his shih-tzu. Soon after we had accepted the offer of a digestif at his flat, I realised I had the supporting role in a parody of a Thomas Mann novella'

The most heavenly Christmas dinner I've ever eaten was at the Fenice restaurant in Venice about 20 years ago (sadly, it is no longer anything to write home about). I started with the blackest squid-ink risotto, followed by a cluster of the freshest, sweetest grilled scampi and finished with a divine zuppa inglese. Mind you, it wasn't just the perfect dinner that made the evening so memorable. On our mildly intoxicated, dank-dark meander back to the hotel, we came upon an apparently respectable elderly American out walking his shih-tzu. Soon after we had accepted the offer of a digestif at his flat, I realised I had the supporting role in a parody of a Graham Greene/Thomas Mann novella. Still, I think my husband was quite flattered.

This is my approximation of that original Venetian zuppe inglese, although I've used trifle sponges and amaretto, rather than the traditional sponge cake and Alchermes liqueur.

The trifle sponge and chocolate cream stage of the recipe must be made at least 6, and up to 24 hours in advance: finish the pudding with the meringue topping 2-8 hours before it is required. The zuppa will then keep for about 2 days in the fridge, although it won't be quite as good as when eaten the same day.

Chocolate zuppa inglese

TO SERVE 6-plus

4 large free-range eggs, separated

175g natural caster sugar

2 level tbsp cornflour

400ml full cream milk

70g (at least 65 per cent cocoa solids) dark chocolate

100ml whipping or double cream, whipped into soft peaks

1½ boxes of trifle sponges (10-12 pieces)

6-8 tbsp amaretto liqueur

YOU WILL NEED

a 1 litre oven-to-table dish, at least 8cm deep

Preheat the oven to 170°C (fan), 190°C (conventional), gas mark 5 just before making the meringue.

Discard one of the egg whites, reserving the remaining three for the meringue, and lightly beat the four egg yolks. Leave them to one side.

To make the pastry cream, put 90g of the caster sugar and the cornflour in a smallish saucepan, then very thoroughly whisk in the milk. Put the saucepan on a medium heat and bring the mixture to the boil, whisking almost constantly. Once it has thickened, carrying on cooking for another minute, then remove the saucepan from the heat and whisk in the egg yolks.

Return the saucepan to the heat for a further 2 minutes, still whisking. Remove the pan from the heat, plunge the base into ice-cold water, and continue to whisk for 1-2 minutes. Leave to cool thoroughly, stirring occasionally.

Melt the chocolate in a bowl suspended over hot water that's just on the cusp of a simmer. (Or you could use a double saucepan, microwave or the warming plate of an Aga.) Stir the melted chocolate into the pastry cream, and leave the mixture to one side. Once it's completely cold, fold in the whipped cream.

Cut the trifle sponges in half horizontally to make lots of thin slices – it's easiest to do this while they are all joined together. Spread a thin layer of the chocolate cream on the bottom of the dish. Cover it with a layer of trifle sponges, using scraps to fill in any gaps, and then sprinkle the sponges with about 2 tablespoons of amaretto. Repeat the layers twice more, then cover the dish with clingfilm and refrigerate it for a minimum of 6, and up to 24 hours.

Whisk the reserved egg whites into stiff peaks in a large, grease-free bowl. With a large spoon, carefully fold in the remaining caster sugar, a third at a time, keeping as much air in the meringue as possible. Cover the sponge and chocolate cream base with the meringue, flicking the surface into little waves.

Put the dish on to a high shelf in the oven and cook for 10-15 minutes until the top has risen and is golden brown. Remove the dish and leave it for 2 hours in a cool place, though not the refrigerator unless absolutely necessary.

It might seem a pretty obvious thing to say, but if you don't put flavour into food at the beginning, you won't get any out at the end. Trying to conjure a big taste out of thin air is as fruitless as alchemy. But when it comes to bread and butter pudding, a certain timidity of flavour is part of its exquisite delight – that, and the fragile, trembling texture. My recipe honours this tradition, but if you want a more defined yet still intriguing flavour use a really characterful honey, such as lavender, heather or orange blossom. And don't forget, you must use good-quality bread – not pre-sliced, bargain-basement, fluff-and-air stuff.

Bread and butter pudding is best eaten about 30 minutes after it's emerged from the oven, when it's still warm and puffy. If it helps, you can prepare the dry ingredients, and make up the custard mixture in advance, but don't cook the pudding until an hour or so before you want to serve it.

Bread and butter pudding with honey

TO SERVE 8-plus

4 medium-thick slices of top-quality white bread, the crusts removed

about 55g unsalted butter, softened

400ml full cream milk

1 (284ml) carton double or whipping cream

50g natural caster sugar, plus a tbsp or so more

3 generous tbsp thick honey

a small pinch of ground cinnamon

5 large eggs, well beaten

1 (200g) packet Merchant Gourmet Mi-cuit plums, stoned and halved (optional)

YOU WILL NEED

a 1.5 litre ovenproof dish, buttered

Preheat the oven to 140°C (fan), 160°C (conventional), gas mark 3.

Thickly butter the bread, then cut the slices in half, diagonally, and leave them to one side.

Heat the milk, cream, 50g sugar, honey and cinnamon in a medium-sized saucepan to just below simmering point. Pour the milk mixture on to the beaten eggs and stir gently to combine. Leave to one side.

Strew the halved plums in the bottom of the dish, if desired. Place the buttered pieces of bread on top, in slightly overlapping layers, long edge down and point upwards. Gently pour the egg-and-milk custard through a sieve (to trap the froth and any white threads) into the dish. Press the pieces of bread firmly into the liquid – they will try to float – and leave them to saturate for about 10 minutes.

Slide the dish on to the middle shelf of the oven. Bake the pudding for about 30 minutes, then take it out and quickly sprinkle a tablespoon or so of sugar over the bread. Put the dish back in the oven and cook for a further 15-20 minutes or until the top is golden brown and puffed up, and the custard has set but still shivers very slightly when you gently shake the dish.

Remove the pudding from the oven and leave it for about 30 minutes at (warm) room temperature before serving. Although it's hard to believe, an extra slosh of ice-cold double cream is magnificent with bread and butter pudding.

'A rich, creamy pudding with an alluring hint of cardamom and rosewater'

I found the basis for this rice pudding in the *Independent Cookbook*, written by the late and exceptionally talented Jeremy Round. (I am pleased to say, the book is soon to be reprinted.) Using double cream as well as milk, my version is quite a bit richer than the original, but retains the alluring, subtle hint of exoticism lent by the cardamom and rosewater. The only thing I've never quite made my mind up about is the pistachio nuts. Sometimes I think they're an unnecessary addition, sometimes I like them stirred in, and sometimes I prefer them sprinkled on top. Would that all decisions were so difficult.

The rice pudding can be eaten hot, tepid or cold, according to taste, and will keep for at least 3 days in the fridge. Don't add the pistachios until you are ready to serve it.

Afghan rice pudding with cardamom, rosewater and pistachios

TO SERVE 6
115g round pudding rice
568ml cold water
1 (284ml) carton double cream, preferably Jersey
300ml full cream milk
4 green cardamom pods
115g natural caster sugar
2 tsp rosewater
about 30g unsalted raw pistachios, chopped finely

YOU WILL NEED
a pestle and mortar

Put the rice in a sieve and wash it thoroughly under cold running water. Transfer the rice to a medium-sized saucepan and pour in the cold water. Cover the pan and bring the contents to a boil over a medium heat. Reduce the temperature, remove the lid, and simmer the contents until the water has virtually evaporated, stirring frequently to prevent the rice sticking to the bottom of the pan.

Once the rice has absorbed the water, stir in the cream and milk. Bring the mixture back to the boil, then reduce the heat again. Simmer gently for about 25 minutes, uncovered and stirring frequently until the rice pudding has thickened to the texture of sloppy porridge.

In the meantime, gently crush the cardamom pods in a mortar, remove and discard the husks, and crush the remaining black seeds to a fine powder. Now add the sugar and cardamom seeds to the rice pudding, and cook for a further 2-3 minutes. Remove the pan from the heat and stir in the rosewater. Stir in, or sprinkle the pistachios on top of each portion of rice pudding, according to your mood.

I adore Lebanese food, whether it's the hot, puffy bread, the smoky, sultry aubergine purée called mutabbal, or the juicy chunks of grilled chicken that glisten with creamy garlic sauce. I can even nibble on deep-fried lamb's brains, not to mention balls, without gagging.

But, oh dear, those Lebanese restaurant puddings. To the uninitiated, the huge array of golden brown sticky-sweet pastries looks seriously inviting, but one bite and you realise they're all mouth and no trousers. Conversely, this home-made baklava with its (inauthentic) marzipan filling is as moist and fragrant as it is crisp and nutty.

The baklava will be good to eat for about 24 hours after it's made, but keep it in a cool place rather than the refrigerator.

Marzipan baklava

TO SERVE 8-plus
1 (400g) packet authentic Greek filo pastry (defrosted)
175g unsalted butter, clarified and melted
150g unsalted raw pistachios, roughly chopped

FOR THE FRANGIPANE
100g natural caster sugar
85g unsalted butter, softened
55g plain flour
150g ground almonds
2 large free-range eggs
4-6 drops almond essence
1 tbsp rosewater

FOR THE SYRUP
500g granulated sugar
275ml hot water
the juice of half a lemon
1 tbsp rosewater

YOU WILL NEED
a baking dish, about 35cm x 24cm, lightly oiled; a sugar thermometer would be useful, but is not essential

Preheat the oven to 150°C (fan), 170°C (conventional), gas mark 3 1/2.

To make the frangipane, combine all the ingredients in a food processor and whizz for a minute or two, until the mixture is quite smooth. Leave to one side.

Before you start to make the syrup, have the lemon juice and rosewater ready. Put the sugar and water into a medium-sized saucepan and place it over a low-to-medium heat. Stir frequently until the sugar has completely dissolved. Now turn up the heat and let the syrup boil vigorously for about 5 minutes, uncovered, and without stirring. When it reaches 105°C (or the syrup just clings to the back of a spoon in a uncoloured but viscous film), add the lemon juice and rosewater. Continue to boil for another 30 seconds, then remove the pan from the heat and leave the syrup to cool completely.

Unroll the filo pastry sheets and cover them with a clean damp tea towel to stop them drying out. I've allowed enough pastry to accommodate the fact that filo comes in wildly differing sizes (depending on the manufacturer), and that some of the sheets are often irredeemably stuck together. Depending on the size, you might want to double the sheets over, or add another half. It is important to remember that the baklava should be light and airy, so float the sheets of pastry one on top of the other – don't press them down.

Drape two sheets of filo in the bottom of the baking dish. Trickle a good tablespoon of clarified butter over the pastry – tilting the dish to spread it around – then sprinkle on a handful of chopped pistachios. Repeat this sequence until there are between 6 and 8 layers of filo in the dish. Stop at this point, and spread the frangipane lightly over the last sheet.

Continue to float another 6-8 layers of filo on top of the frangipane, remembering to trickle on the butter and sprinkle the pistachio nuts every second layer, including the last and final layer. (Any excess butter can be refrigerated and used at a later date.)

With a very sharp knife, cut through the baklava diagonally to make large diamond shapes – the cuts don't have to go all the way through. Put the baklava into the oven on the middle shelf, and bake for 30 minutes. Reduce the heat to 110°C (fan), 130°C (conventional), gas mark 1, and continue cooking for a further 45 minutes, or until the pastry is crisp and a uniform dark-honey colour.

Remove the baklava from the oven and immediately pour the cold syrup over the entire surface. Leave the baklava to cool before serving, with cream.

Wintry lunches

As I spend most days working on my own, lunch tends to be confined to a sandwich (Philly and cucumber, or smoked ham and mustard); a bowl of Japanese rice (with smoked mackerel or trout, soy and sansho); or an avocado (with lemon juice and black pepper). But now and again someone does tip up for lunch, and then I'm quite happy to make a bit of an effort although I still like to keep the meal to a pretty casual, one-plate affair. All these recipes are stuffed with flavour, but stay on the informal side of the entertaining street.

Not being a vindaloo warrior, I've always been a little wary of Mexican food, which seems to be wantonly brazen about the use of bottom-searingly-hot chillies and raw onion. Knock the heat back a bit, though, and there's absolutely nothing wrong with the central American habit of combining warm, spicy flavours with cold, creamy ones. This recipe stays well away from the molten lava school of cooking, and I defy even the most bloodthirsty of carnivores to notice the absence of meat.

The bean filling for the tortillas can be made up to 48 hours in advance, and kept in the fridge. Reheat it over a low flame before assembling the tortillas, which should themselves have been warmed in a foil packet in a low oven. Don't make the salsa until the last minute.

Burritos with spicy beans and avocado salsa

TO SERVE 4

1 tbsp groundnut oil

1 large onion, peeled and cut into medium dice

3 cloves of garlic, peeled, crushed and finely chopped

1 red pepper, deseeded and cut into medium dice

1 tsp ground cumin

1 tsp ground allspice

1/2 tsp hot chilli powder

1 bay leaf, fresh or dried

1 (420g) can pinto beans, drained and rinsed

1 (420g) can organic baked beans, the tin rinsed out with 15ml cold water

1 packet of soft, flour tortillas

FOR THE SALSA

1 large, ripe Hass avocado, peeled and cut into medium dice

1 red chilli, deseeded and finely chopped

1 large tomato, deseeded and chopped into medium dice

1 shallot, peeled and finely chopped

a handful of fresh coriander leaves, roughly chopped

a squeeze of fresh lime juice

about 200g natural Greek yoghurt

Preheat the oven to 120°C (fan), 140°C (conventional), gas mark 1 to heat the tortillas.

To make the salsa, mix the avocado, chilli, tomato, shallot and coriander together, then season with salt and pepper and add a squeeze of lime juice to taste; the salsa should be quite sharp and spiky to offset the richness of the tortillas. Put the salsa in one bowl, and the yoghurt in the other, and leave them in the fridge.

For the beans, place a large frying pan over a medium heat, and pour in the oil. When it is hot, tip in the onion, garlic and pepper. Fry the vegetables for 5-6 minutes, stirring occasionally, until slightly softened, then add the cumin, allspice and chilli powder. Stir thoroughly and cook for another 2 minutes, stirring frequently.

Now put in the bay leaf, beans and the rinsing liquid from the can. (I recommend Whole Earth baked beans because – apart from being organic – they taste of something other than sweet red glop.) Simmer for 15 minutes, stirring occasionally to prevent the beans sticking, until the mixture is thick and gooey. Season with salt and pepper.

Meanwhile, wrap the tortillas in foil and warm in the oven for about 15 minutes. To assemble the burritos, trickle about 3 tablespoons of bean mixture down the centre of each warmed tortilla, before rolling them up like rugs. Let everyone help themselves to the yoghurt and the salsa to dollop on top of the burritos.

I actually prefer to use casarecce pasta (which looks like small pieces of twisted corrugated iron – without the rust) for macaroni cheese, because it has a brilliant shape for capturing creamy sauces. I know macaroni cheese is regarded as a simple, family supper dish, but it creates mountains of messy pots and pans. One way to reduce the washing-up is to add cold rather than hot milk to the roux: as long as you whisk the sauce constantly, it won't go lumpy. As for the cheese, I like to use a combination of a strong tasting cheddar (for general oomph), a mild gruyère (for fruity sweetness), and a little parmesan (for salty, nutty highlights). This gives a full-bodied, complex flavour that tastes so bloody delicious I wouldn't be embarrassed serving it to the Queen, should she fancy roughing it one day.

Macaroni cheese can be made up to 48 hours ahead but you must make the sauce more liquid than normal because it stiffens up dramatically when refrigerated, and no amount of gentle reheating will return it to its original creamy consistency.

Macaroni con brio

TO SERVE 6-plus
225g mature cheddar, grated
115g gruyère, grated
85g parmesan, finely grated
about 55g fresh white breadcrumbs
55g unsalted butter, plus a little more
40g plain flour
about 700ml full cream milk
150ml double cream
about 10 gratings of nutmeg
about 500g casarecce (or similar tubular pasta)
about 250g cherry tomatoes, stalks removed

YOU WILL NEED
a 23cm x 30cm ovenproof dish, buttered

Preheat the oven to 200°C (fan), 220°C (conventional), gas mark 7.

Mix the cheeses together in a bowl, then scoop out about a quarter of the quantity and mix it with the breadcrumbs in a separate dish.

To make the sauce, melt the butter in a large saucepan over a medium heat, and whisk in the flour to make a smooth paste. Cook this roux for 1 minute, then whisk in the milk, making sure you get right into the corners of the pan. Bring the sauce to the boil, whisking almost continuously. Once the sauce has thickened, reduce the heat and allow it to simmer very gently for about 20 minutes, whisking occasionally. Finally whisk in the double cream, season with salt, pepper and nutmeg, and leave for 5 minutes over a very low heat.

Tip in the grated cheese (not the breadcrumb mixture) and whisk until the sauce is once again completely smooth. The sauce should be thick and creamy, but distinctly pourable. If it looks too thick and wodgy, add a little more milk (and quite a bit more if you are intending to reheat the macaroni cheese).

In the meantime, cook the pasta according to the instructions on the packet, then drain, and run it briefly under cold water.

Thoroughly mix the sauce and drained pasta – in the same saucepan if it's big enough – and gently stir in the tomatoes. Pour the macaroni cheese into the ovenproof dish, smooth the surface, and scatter the breadcrumb mixture evenly over the top. Dot with little scraps of butter, then slide the dish into the hot oven for 15 minutes, or until the crust is golden-brown, and the sauce is bubbling hot.

'If I could only have one dish from the diverse and fantastic repertoire of Italian cooking, it would have to be risotto. Not only are the classic flavourings – asparagus, porcini, saffron and cuttlefish - all to die for, but risotto is also amenable to a little experimentation. However, that does not include resorting to using bottles of risotto sauce – an idea as ludicrous as ready-cooked omelettes or packets of grated cheese.

'When I consider what was laughingly served under the guise of risotto in my childhood, it's something of a miracle that it has become one of my very favourite foods'

This is the first of about four risottos in this book – and, while we're on the subject, I know that a number of risottos should be referred to properly as risotti, but my editor quite rightly feels this is taking authenticity a pluralisation too far. Being a timid creature, I can only agree with her.

Conversations with my peers reassure me that I'm not alone in having been brought up to think risotto was an orange-hued mess of long grain rice and tinned tomatoes, liberally larded with lumps of cold ham, bacon or chicken, and any other faintly edible detritus gleaned from the back of the fridge – pace, Mum.

To be fair, it was impossible to cook a proper risotto in Britain until really quite recently even if, theoretically, you knew what should go into it. Arborio rice was not freely available (never mind carnaroli or vialone nano), and most British housewives had to rely on long grain (aka patna) rice for anything from a pilaf to a paella – which is a bit like expecting a duffle coat to double up as a pashmina. There's no excuse for not making risotto correctly nowadays, though. All it takes is a bit of time (in which you can chat, or simply dream), a handful or two of carnaroli rice, some good stock gently smiling on the back of the stove, and a few choice morsels to add colour, texture and flavour.

This recipe came about when I was trying to think of something slightly different to do with butternut squash, that sunset-orange, densely-fleshed vegetable, which (along with spaghetti squash and acorn squash) seems to have put paid to our traditional green marrow. (And for which I still have a lingering affection when lightly steamed and strewed with fresh herbs and lemon juice, or – dare I admit – napped with a creamy cheese sauce.) I like the combination of the sweetish, nutty squash and the sweetish, gooey garlic with the slightly bitter oregano; and the rice provides a good foil to these potent flavours.

I have suggested preparing the roast vegetables and the oregano purée before cooking the risotto but experienced cooks could probably handle the two stages simultaneously, with the vegetables going in to roast just prior to making the risotto.

You can prepare all the vegetables in advance, but don't cook the rice until it's needed.

Roast butternut squash, garlic and oregano risotto

TO SERVE 4

4 tbsp fruity
extra-virgin olive oil

3 bushy sprigs of fresh oregano

half a large butternut squash,
peeled, halved,
deseeded, and cut into
small-bite-sized chunks

1 whole head of garlic,
separated into *unpeeled* cloves

4 rounded tsp Marigold Swiss
vegetable bouillon powder

1 litre boiling water

40g unsalted butter

2 shallots, peeled and
finely chopped

1 mild red chilli, deseeded and
finely chopped

300g carnaroli (or arborio) rice

100ml dry white wine

YOU WILL NEED

a small roasting tin;
a pestle and mortar;
a fairly large sauté pan or
a wide, shallow saucepan

Preheat the oven to 180°C (fan), 200°C (conventional), gas mark 6.

Pour half the olive oil into a small roasting tin and throw in 1 sprig of oregano, the squash and garlic. Season with salt and pepper, and toss the vegetables in the oil. Put the tin in the oven and roast for about 25 minutes, turning the vegetables halfway through.

When the vegetables are tender and lightly browned, remove them from the oven. Discard the oregano, and remove the skin from the garlic, keeping the cloves intact. Leave the vegetables in the pan.

Meanwhile, strip the leaves from the remaining oregano stalks. Mix them with the remaining oil, and reduce them to a purée in a pestle and mortar or in a mini food processor – there's not enough quantity for a normal-sized liquidiser or food processor. Leave to one side.

Combine the Marigold powder and boiling water in a medium-sized saucepan, and keep this stock gently simmering over a low heat.

Melt the butter in the sauté pan over a low-to-medium flame, and fry the chopped shallots and chilli for 5-10 minutes, or until soft and barely coloured. Tip in the rice, and cook for 2 minutes, stirring until all the grains are glistening. Turn up the heat, pour in the wine, and let it bubble up for 1 minute, stirring once or twice, before reducing the heat again. Start adding the hot stock, a ladle or two at a time. Adjust the heat to keep the risotto at a simmer, adding just enough liquid to bathe the rice, not drown it, and stirring almost constantly. As the stock is absorbed add a little more. Continue with this routine for about 20 minutes.

At this point, start testing the rice by biting into a grain. When it's ready the grains should be tender – neither gritty, nor soggy - and the risotto should have a wettish, porridgey look – not dry like a pilaf. (Carnaroli rice normally takes 25-30 minutes, and arborio 20-25 minutes.) If you run out of stock before the rice has cooked, add a little hot water.

When the risotto is just about ready, scrape in the vegetables and the oregano purée. Stir very gently so the squash doesn't get squished, and, if necessary, add a touch more stock to loosen the risotto. As soon as the squash is hot, and the rice tender, remove the pan from the heat. Serve immediately.

Named after a region in France rather than the smart London hotel, this omelette looks more complicated than it is because all the ingredients are cooked from scratch. But if you're harbouring any cold, cooked peas, ham or potatoes in the fridge, you can reduce the cooking time significantly – it's undoubtedly what the Savoyards would do. Whether the ingredients are secondhand or brand-new, there's only one word to describe this omelette, and it's a word (along with delicious) that I strive officiously to avoid – tasty. Very tasty, in fact. And perfect for a fireside supper with some good chums and a video.

All the ingredients can be prepared in advance, but the omelette itself must be cooked at the last minute

Savoy omelette with peas, pepperoni and potatoes

TO SERVE 4

7 tbsp groundnut oil

1 large thickly-cut slice of white bread, crust removed, cut into small cubes

30g unsalted butter

1 large onion, chopped into medium dice

2 cloves of garlic, peeled, crushed and finely chopped

about 500g potatoes, peeled and cut into small cubes

about 100g thinly sliced pepperoni

about 115g frozen peas, defrosted

a small handful of parsley, finely chopped

12 large free-range eggs, lightly beaten

55g gruyère, grated

100ml double cream

YOU WILL NEED

a 28cm diameter, fairly deep, non-stick frying pan

Preheat the grill after the potatoes have been cooked.

A warning about size: most people (especially men) have a hugely inflated idea of size but if the cubes of potato are too big, they will burn before they cook. In this instance, small means no bigger than the size of a sugar cube.

Pour 3 tablespoons of oil into the frying pan and heat it over a fairly high flame. Tip in the cubes of bread and toss them for about 3 minutes, until they are lightly gilded on all sides. Don't over-brown them as they will be going under the grill later on. Remove the croûtons, and drain them on a pad of kitchen paper.

Wipe out the frying pan, put in another tablespoon of oil and half the butter, and reheat the pan over a medium flame. Tip in the onion and garlic and fry for about 15 minutes, until the onion has softened and is just starting to brown on the edges. Remove it with a slotted spoon, draining as much oil as possible back into the pan. Leave the onion and garlic to one side.

Replace the frying pan, turn up the heat and add the remaining butter and oil. Throw in the potatoes and fry them for about 15 minutes, turning the chunks frequently, until they are evenly browned and tender in the middle. If they start to brown too quickly, reduce the heat. Season the potatoes with salt, before scooping them out. Discard any remaining oil from the pan, but *don't* wipe it out.

Mix the onion, garlic, potatoes, pepperoni, peas and parsley in with the beaten eggs, and season generously with salt and pepper.

Return the frying pan to a very high heat, pour in the egg mixture and cook it as you would a normal French omelette, drawing all the

'Tasty. Very tasty, in fact. And perfect for a fireside supper with some good chums and a video'

cooked egg in from the sides and bottom of the pan with a fork, and letting the raw egg flow in to take its place. (The pepperoni tends to clump up so make sure it is evenly distributed.) When only the centre of the omelette is still a little liquid, remove the pan from the heat.

Strew the croûtons and grated gruyère on top of the omelette, then trickle over the cream. Slide the pan (but not the handle) under the hot grill, and cook the omelette for 3-4 minutes, or until the cheese has melted and the top is golden. Serve the omelette as soon as possible, cut into moist, creamy wedges.

Every afternoon Jessie and Jack (mother and son, wire fox terriers) come with me to see the chickens, one of us with the intention of feeding them, and two of us with the intention of eating them. Fortunately, homo sapiens always wins: a dish of corn is scattered in front of a few appreciative Black Rocks and Marans and, with luck, a few eggs are collected from the nesting boxes.

I can imagine how nauseating this rustic scene might appear but until you've dipped a chunk of buttered bread into the pert, plump, saffron-yellow yolk of a really fresh, genuinely free-range egg, you won't know what you're missing. It's the quality of the eggs that transforms something as pedestrian-sounding as an omelette into a sublime but simple meal, redolent of a time when the countryside was green and lush thanks to manure and manual labour, rather than slug pellets and subsidies.

I found this recipe in Elizabeth David's evocative *French Provincial Cooking* many years ago. I like to add a few croûtons to what is already a blissful recipe, but it's a lot quicker to make it without them.

Remember, it should take less than a minute to cook an omelette, which means the heat must be very high. For this omelette, with its additions, I'll give you 2 minutes max – very generous.

Omelette Molière with parmesan and gruyère

TO SERVE 1
3 large free-range eggs, lightly beaten
a knob of unsalted butter
1 tbsp gruyère, cut into tiny dice
1 heaped tbsp finely grated parmesan
1 tbsp double cream
a small handful of tiny croûtons (optional)

YOU WILL NEED
a heavy 20cm diameter omelette pan

Season the eggs fairly generously with salt and pepper. Put the omelette pan on to a very high heat, and after a minute throw in a good knob of butter. Swirl the butter in the pan while it heats up, and as soon as the sizzling subsides, pour in the eggs.

As the curds set, draw them into the middle of the pan with a fork, and let the liquid egg flow in to take their place. As soon as the centre is a pile of moist folds, and there is only a little liquid egg left on the surface, remove the pan from the heat.

Quickly scatter the gruyère, three-quarters of the parmesan and the croûtons (if you're using them) over the omelette. Dribble on the cream, and continue to cook the omelette for a further 30 seconds.

Using a palette knife, flip the edge of the omelette nearest your hand into the middle. Slide the side farthest away from you on to the warmed plate, and then gently tip the first folded side over it to form a nice fat roll.

Spear a tiny scrap of butter on the tip of a knife and smooth it over the omelette, then sprinkle it with the remaining parmesan. Eat immediately with some crusty, chewy bread.

Potatoes and cheese make a devastatingly good partnership. What might seem odd about this recipe is the combination of potatoes with pastry. But the older I get the more I like starch with starch. I can barely eat pasta without a chunk of bread in one hand – somehow the combination works. As for the cheese, although I've used lovely smelly livarot (whose bark is much worse than its bite), you could use époisses, munster, pont l'Eveque or taleggio to equally good effect.

You can make the tart up to 24 hours in advance, but try to keep it in a cool place other than the fridge, as the texture of the filling becomes rather solid if it is too cold. A better idea is to bake the pastry case in advance, leaving just 30-40 minutes for the final assembly and cooking. The tart is at its most magnificent eaten about 20 minutes after it emerges from the oven.

Livarot, rocket and potato tart

TO SERVE 4-plus
30g unsalted butter
2 tbsp olive oil
1 large Spanish onion, peeled and roughly chopped
2 cloves of garlic, peeled, crushed and finely chopped
4 shallots, peeled and halved (or split into natural sections)
50g rocket, stalks removed and leaves roughly torn
1 whole livarot, chopped into bite-sized chunks, the rind discarded
250g small new potatoes, cooked and peeled
2 large free-range eggs, plus 1 egg yolk
225ml double cream
about 10 scrapings of nutmeg

FOR THE PASTRY
225g plain flour
1 level tbsp icing sugar
a pinch of fine sea salt
140g cold unsalted butter, roughly chopped
1 large free-range egg yolk
3 tbsp ice-cold water

YOU WILL NEED
a 23cm diameter, loose-bottomed tart tin, lightly buttered; ceramic baking (or dried) beans

Preheat the oven to 170°C (fan), 190°C (conventional), gas mark 5.

First, make the pastry: whizz the flour, icing sugar and salt together for a few seconds in a food processor, add the butter and whizz again, until the mixture looks like coarse breadcrumbs. Whisk the egg yolk and water together and pour into the flour mixture. Process again until the pastry has collected in a ball around the spindle. Form the pastry into a thick disc, wrap in clingfilm and leave to rest in the fridge for a minimum of 30 minutes, and up to 2 days.

Take out the pastry and return it to (cool) room temperature, then roll it out thinly. Line the tin – making sure you don't stretch the pastry – then trim the edges. Return the pastry case to the fridge and chill for at least 30 minutes. Now line the pastry with foil, pour in the baking beans and cook for 12-15 minutes. Remove the foil and beans, and continue to bake for another 5-6 minutes. The pastry should look dry, but blond rather than brown. Remove the tin and leave the pastry case to cool in it. Keep the oven on.

In the meantime, melt the butter and olive oil in a medium-sized frying pan over a low-to-medium heat. Tip in the onion, garlic and shallots, and fry them gently for about 15 minutes until soft, stirring occasionally. Put in the rocket and toss it for 1 minute, or until the leaves start to wilt. Take the pan off the heat. When the onion mixture has cooled thoroughly, strew it in the bottom of the pastry case, arranging the chunks of livarot and potatoes on top.

Whisk the eggs (and yolk) and cream together, season with plenty of salt, pepper and grated nutmeg, then pour the mixture into the pastry case. Slide the tin on to the middle shelf of the oven, and bake the tart for 25-30 minutes, or until the custard has set to a shivery firmness. Remove the tart from the oven and leave it to cool a little.

'I love the way the tender, puffy base mops up the black, herby mushroom juices, and the contrast between the pungent onion and cool, creamy mascarpone is inspired'

Jeremy Lee is big, handsome, Scottish and frighteningly articulate. He trained with two of the best chefs in Britain – Simon Hopkinson and Alastair Little – and cooks the kind of food at the Blueprint Café that you actually want to eat, rather than admire. Bursting with flavour, style and vitality, it's neither cutting-edge nor zany, just intelligent, and brilliantly good.

One day when I ate there, this pizza was on the menu. I love the way the tender, puffy base mops up the black, herby mushroom juices, and the pungent onion and cool, creamy mascarpone is inspired – unlike those ghastly, supermarket chicken tikka and glacé cherry jobs, which are merely demented.

This is my homely version of Jeremy's pizza. If you don't want to make your own dough, you could cheat and use a packet of pizza dough or ciabatta mix. But please don't waste your time, or these good ingredients, on those ready-made pizza bases which are nothing more than edible chipboard.

Flat mushroom, red onion and mascarpone pizza

TO SERVE 4-plus

4 tbsp extra-virgin olive oil

2 red onions, peeled and cut into 8-10 thick wedges

2 large cloves of garlic, peeled, crushed and finely chopped

about 350g flat mushrooms, wiped with a damp cloth and cut into quarters, or sixths, depending on size

the leaves of 2 bushy sprigs of fresh thyme

1 heaped tbsp finely grated parmesan

1 (250g) tub mascarpone

FOR THE DOUGH

500g strong white organic bread flour, plus a handful

1 level tsp fine sea salt

1 level tbsp natural caster sugar

1 (7g) packet fast-action dried yeast

about 2 tbsp light, extra-virgin olive oil

1 large free-range egg

300ml lukewarm water

YOU WILL NEED

a 35cm x 25cm heavy, non-stick baking tray, lightly oiled

Preheat the oven to 220°C (fan), 240°C (conventional), gas mark 9/10 just prior to cooking the pizza.

To make the dough, thoroughly combine the flour, salt, sugar and yeast in a large non-reactive bowl, and add two tablespoons of oil. Whisk the egg and water together, and pour this on to the flour mixture. Using one hand, mix the ingredients thoroughly into a horrible, sticky lump. Turn this mess out on to a well-floured surface, and start to knead it with both hands: sod the door bell.

To knead, push the lump down and away with the heel of one hand, curl the far side back towards you with the fingers of the other hand, then push down and away with the other hand, then curl back again, trying to establish a rhythm. Don't worry if all you are doing is slapping, pushing and punching – it will have the same effect in the end. Continue kneading for 5 minutes, or until the dough is silky, loose and only marginally sticky. (Add a drop more water if it is too tight and dry.)

Wash out the bowl, dry it thoroughly and oil it generously. Put in the dough, cover it with clingfilm and leave it in a warm place (the airing cupboard would be good) for 2 hours, or until it has doubled in size.

Transfer the puffy, aerated mass of dough on to a floured work surface and bash it down again for about 30 seconds. You can now roll it out to the size of the baking tray. Actually I adopt a rather unconventional half-rolling, half-dangling technique, suspending the dough in mid-air and pulling it around, sideways, longways and turning it top to toe. Spread the dough on the baking tray, drape clingfilm over it and leave it to rise for another hour, in a warm place.

Meanwhile, heat the olive oil in a large frying pan over a medium flame, and fry the onions and garlic for 5-6 minutes, stirring frequently, until the garlic is a light nutty-brown. Some of the onion wedges will break up, but that's okay. Now put the mushrooms in the frying pan and toss them around until all the chunks are well-coated with oil. Season fairly generously with salt, then fry for 3-5 minutes, stirring occasionally. When the mushrooms have just started to wilt, stir in the thyme leaves, season with black pepper, then pull the pan off the heat and leave to cool.

Once the dough has risen again on the baking tray, spread the onion-and-mushroom mixture over the surface, leaving a 3cm border, and making sure the mushrooms and onions are evenly dispersed.

Slide the baking tray into the oven and cook the pizza for 12-15 minutes or until the edges are puffy and well-browned. Remove the pizza from the oven, sprinkle with parmesan, then cut it into slices, and dollop some mascarpone on each piece. Serve immediately.

There aren't many people who can resist pancakes. Whether they're warm, fragile crêpes dusted with sugar and sprinkled with tart lemon juice, or plump little pancakes swirled with sour cream and caviar – they are divine. These savoury pancakes, stuffed with molten cheese and sweet ham, are no exception.

I'm actually slightly surprised that I haven't put fontina in my list of favourite foods, but then again the number of cheeses I love is longer than the queue for Space Mountain. I'm also slightly surprised that fontina is stocked in some supermarkets, as it's really quite an esoteric cheese, made in the Valle d'Aosta, high in the Italian alps. Looking not unlike the famous raclette, fontina is an unpasteurised, firm, cow's milk cheese with a fabulously complex, lingering flavour – all at once earthy, fruity and aromatic. Just as importantly fontina melts into a perfect, smooth, creamy mass. It's the close-knit contrast between the taste and textures of the various layers of pancake, ham, cheese sauce, sour cream, and more cheese – toasted this time – that makes this dish taste so good.

The recipe looks a bit fiddly, but the béchamel sauce and the pancake batter can be prepared up to 24 hours ahead. Even starting from scratch it only takes about 45 minutes from start to finish.

Ham and fontina pancakes

TO SERVE 4
8 slices (60-80g) top-quality lean ham
about 300ml sour cream
70g fontina, grated

FOR THE BATTER
15g unsalted butter
175g plain flour
3 large free-range eggs
500ml full cream milk

FOR THE BECHAMEL SAUCE
40g unsalted butter
40g plain flour
350-400ml full cream milk
a few scrapings of nutmeg
70g fontina, grated

YOU WILL NEED
a shallow ovenproof dish, well-buttered, and large enough to contain 8 rolled pancakes in a single layer

Preheat the oven to 190°C (fan), 210°C (conventional), gas mark 6^1/$_2$.

Make the pancake batter first as it needs to rest for at least 30 minutes: to add flavour, melt the butter in a little saucepan and cook it for a couple of minutes until it starts to froth, then changes to a nutty-smelling, golden brown. Don't leave it any longer or you'll end up with burnt butter. Leave it to cool for a few minutes, then pour it into a food processor or blender. Add the flour, eggs and milk, and whizz until the batter is smooth. Season with salt and pepper.

To make the sauce, melt the butter in a medium-sized saucepan over a medium heat, then whisk in the flour. Cook this roux for 1 minute, then whisk in 350ml of the milk, making sure you get right into the corners of the pan. Bring the sauce to the boil, whisking almost constantly. Once the sauce has thickened dramatically, reduce the heat and allow it to simmer very gently for about 15 minutes, whisking frequently. The sauce needs to be very thick but if it looks too much like plastic grouting, add a little more milk.

Remove the pan from the heat, stir in the grated fontina, and season well with salt, pepper and nutmeg. Leave to cool, stirring occasionally.

To cook the pancakes, very lightly butter a large non-stick frying pan and place it over a medium heat. When the pan is hot, pour in just enough batter to thinly cover the base of the pan when you swirl it around. Cook for about 2 minutes. When the underside is traced

'Wouldn't it be great if all the Bank Holidays were changed into pancake days: even that nonsensical Labour Day would have some point then'

a light golden brown, flip the pancake over. Continue cooking for another minute or so, until the underside is dotted with brown blisters. The first pancake is nearly always a disaster, while you make adjustments to heat and quantities – don't worry about it. As the pancakes cook, stack them on a large plate. This quantity of batter makes about 10 pancakes, but you'll only need 8 – the rest are the cook's perks.

Place a pancake, blistered side-up, on the work surface. Smear it with one-eighth of the sauce, leaving a wide border. Cover the sauced area with some ham, then season with freshly ground black paper. Tuck in the side of the pancake nearest to you, then roll the pancake up like a rug. Repeat with all 8 pancakes.

Arrange the pancakes side-by-side in the buttered dish. Finally, trickle the sour cream over the pancakes and scatter the grated cheese over the top. Season again with salt and pepper. Put the dish on the top shelf of the oven, and cook for 15-20 minutes, until the cheese has melted and is dappled with colour, and the pancakes are hot. Serve the pancakes with a dressed green salad, or a tomato salad.

Bread, mushrooms and cheese – it's an unexceptional but completely satisfactory combination. Actually, I use bread twice in this recipe, everyday white breadcrumbs in the stuffing, and open-textured Italian ciabatta for the crisp crostini. The warm, melting, slightly smoky, golden scamorza (smoked mozzarella) completes the textural hedonism. If you can't find scamorza, substitute any oozing, faintly pongy cheese.

This is not a meal that can be made in advance, apart from the vegetable preparation; but it only takes about 30 minutes anyway.

Stuffed mushroom crostini with smoked mozzarella

TO SERVE 2
50g unsalted butter
1 large shallot, peeled and finely chopped
2 cloves of garlic, peeled, crushed and finely chopped
4 large flat mushrooms, wiped with a damp cloth
50g fresh, fine white breadcrumbs
a large handful of flat-leaf parsley, chopped
2 large fresh sage leaves, finely chopped
a few scrapings of whole nutmeg
1 baked ciabatta
a few tbsp extra-virgin olive oil
1 (about 185g) pkt scamorza, cut into 4 thick slices

YOU WILL NEED
a heavy baking tray, lightly oiled

Preheat the oven to 190°C (fan), 210°C (conventional), gas mark 6½.

Melt the butter in a small non-stick frying pan over a low-to-medium flame. Tip in the chopped shallot and garlic, and fry gently for 3-4 minutes until soft, stirring occasionally. Leave to one side.

In the meantime, remove the stalks from the mushrooms, and chop them fairly finely. Put the chopped stalks in a bowl with the breadcrumbs, parsley and sage. Scrape the entire contents of the frying pan, melted butter included, into the bowl and season with nutmeg and a generous amount of salt and pepper. Mix everything together thoroughly, and leave to one side.

Divide the ciabatta into thirds, reserving one third for later use. Cut each piece in half horizontally so you have 4 slices just a little larger than the mushrooms. Drizzle olive oil generously over the ciabatta, and put the slices on the baking tray, crumb-side up.

Now lay a mushroom, gill-side up, on each piece of ciabatta. Fill the mushrooms with the stuffing, patting it gently into place and disregarding any little bits that fall off on to the bread.

Slide the baking tray on to the middle shelf of the oven, and cook for 15-20 minutes, or until both the topping and ciabatta are slightly golden. Remove the tray from the oven, and put a slice of scamorza on top of each mushroom. Quickly return the mushrooms to the oven, and cook for a further 3-5 minutes, or until the cheese has started to melt. Serve immediately, with dressed salad leaves.

If ever a recipe incorporated all my favourite foods, this is it. Thick, buttery hollandaise sauce; spanking-fresh poached eggs with rich, molten yolks; moist, smoky flakes of haddock; and a soft toasted muffin. Gorgeous. The ingredients must be first-rate, though – unsalted butter, undyed smoked haddock, and eggs no more than a few days old.

With the exception of the poached eggs, this is not a recipe that can be prepared in advance, but as it only takes 15-20 minutes from start to finish, it's not exactly arduous.

Smoked haddock Bénédict

TO SERVE 2
2 undyed smoked haddock
fillets, about 175-200g each
4 large, very fresh,
free-range eggs
2 plain English muffins,
split and toasted

FOR THE HOLLANDAISE
175g unsalted butter
2 large free-range egg yolks
1 tbsp cider vinegar
(or a little less lemon juice)
1 heaped tbsp
chopped fresh tarragon

YOU WILL NEED
a baking tin large enough
to take the haddock in
a single layer

Preheat the oven to 180°C (fan), 200°C (conventional), gas mark 6.

Trim off and discard any tough edges from the haddock fillets, as well as any flappy thin bits, and remove the little line of bones near the thickest part. Don't remove the skin. Cut each fillet in half to make two pieces, one squarish, the other a triangular shape.

Pour 1cm of water into the baking tin, and put in the smoked haddock, skin side-down. Season with pepper. Cover the tin with foil and cook the fish for 10-15 minutes until the flesh is opaque. Drain the fillets on a pad of kitchen paper, then carefully remove and discard the skin. Cover the fish to prevent it drying out, and keep it warm.

In the meantime, make the hollandaise. Melt the butter in a small saucepan until it's just below bubbling point. Whizz the egg yolks and vinegar in a liquidiser for 1 minute. With the motor going, pour in the butter, first drop by drop, then a trickle, then a thin stream – as if you were making mayonnaise. Continue pouring, discarding the milky residue. Season, then add the chopped tarragon, and whizz for 2 seconds. Leave the sauce in the liquidiser with the lid on.

Bring 6cm of water to a simmer in a wide, shallow pan. Carefully break the eggs into the water, in a contained, downward action. Poach the eggs for 2-3 minutes, until the whites are set and the yolks are still soft. (To test, scoop one out with a draining spoon and gently prod it. The thick, white part should be set through, not wobbling around underneath the surface; the yolk, conversely, should be wobbling around underneath the filmy top layer.) Drain the eggs on a pad of kitchen paper, scissoring off any scruffy bits of white.

Working quickly, place two halves of toasted muffin on each plate, and top each with a chunk of haddock, followed by a poached egg. Give the hollandaise sauce a quick whizz, then spoon it over the eggs – this is called 'napping', in case you're interested. Eat at once.

If the paucity of sauce in this recipe frightens you, remember that pasta is not just a tasteless, bulky mass to be swamped with a sea of gunk, but a miracle of texture. Each shape has its own virtue – long, shiny strands coil around light, oily coatings; short, fat, slippery tubes suck up thicker, creamier sauces; and gaping, open ended trumpets entrap little morsels of meat or vegetables.

This classic clam sauce is slight, but full of flavour. I very much like the 'bianco' (white) version, but it's perfectly acceptable to add tomatoes, if you prefer: I suggest you stir a tin of chair de tomate in with the clams and parsley. I've used bottled clams (vongole al naturale) for this recipe, but if you see a basket of fresh clams at the fishmongers, then they must be your first choice. Steam them open with a little wine in a lidded saucepan over a high heat, just as you would for mussels. Make the wine and garlic sauce as per this recipe, and finish by piling the fresh clams, shells included, over the linguine.

Nothing can, or need be, prepared in advance – we're talking minutes here.

Linguine with clams, parsley and garlic

TO SERVE 4
500g dried linguine (or spaghetti)
1 tbsp extra-virgin olive oil
3 cloves of garlic, peeled, crushed and finely chopped
about 175ml dry white wine
2 bottles (150g each) vongole al naturale (without shells), the juices reserved
a very large handful of flat-leaf parsley, chopped

YOU WILL NEED
a really large pot for the pasta

As everything happens at breakneck speed, it's important to have all the ingredients ready.

Cook the linguine in masses of boiling water, taking a strand out and testing it towards the end of the recommended cooking time. The linguine should be slightly resistant, neither nutty in the middle, nor pasty. Drain the linguine, and run it under cold water, but reserve the cooking liquid and keep it at a slow simmer.

Pour the oil into a smallish frying pan, and place it over a low-to-medium heat. When it is hot, put in the garlic and fry it gently for 3-4 minutes, stirring occasionally, until very lightly coloured. Turn the heat up high, pour in the wine and clam juices and bubble them for about 3 minutes until they have reduced a little.

Meanwhile, put the linguine back into the simmering water, then immediately draw the pan off the heat. Leave to one side.

Tip the clams and parsley into the frying pan, and season generously with freshly ground black pepper and a little salt. Stir, then cook for 1 minute until the clams have heated through. Remove the pan from the heat, and leave it to one side while you drain the linguine, but not over-thoroughly – it's good to accompany the pasta with a spoonful or two of water as it acts as a lubricant.

Divide the linguine among the warmed plates, and spoon over the sauce. Eat with really good, chewy bread.

Wintry suppers

Cosy, cuddly and quick are all words that spring to mind when I think about wintry suppers – but then I suppose they could be applied equally well to nappy-changing. One of God's finest creations, pasta is always top of the list when I need to conjure up an easy, relaxed supper. But I'm just as fond of earthy beans and pulses – and bread, in any guise. And, in case you think I'm fixated with Italian food, two of the very best supper dishes – smoked haddock and haggis – hail from Scotland, a very chilly place.

There's vegetable soup, and there's fabulous, hunky, home-made Italian minestrone. Just like spaghetti, the more of this soup you eat, the more there is left. This is probably because each time you reheat it you'll find the broth has thickened and you'll need to add a bit more water. My mother, who is famous in our family for favouring a kill-by, rather than sell-by, date, had a pot of minestrone on the go from one end of the year to the next. We've not only lived to tell the tale, but still love minestrone.

Don't be put off by the huge list of ingredients. The method is as simple as kiss your hand. Remember to wash all the vegetables thoroughly; discard any particularly tough outer layers, inedible peel or skin; and, top, tail and discard root ends and hard cores where necessary.

This is a soup which positively thrives on being made in advance – days rather than hours. But, unlike dear Mama, do refrigerate it, and bring it to the boil every third day.

Mum's minestrone soup

TO SERVE 10-plus
3 tbsp extra-virgin olive oil
2 large Spanish onions, peeled and cut into medium dice
3 cloves of garlic, peeled, crushed and finely chopped
3 leeks, halved lengthways and sliced fairly finely
1 fennel bulb, cut into medium dice
4 celery stalks, cut into medium dice
4 medium carrots, cut into medium dice
3 heaped tbsp Marigold Swiss vegetable bouillon
4 litres water
about 500ml tomato passata
2 sprigs fresh thyme
about 100g small pasta (eg conchigliette)
1/4 Savoy cabbage, sliced fairly finely
4 medium courgettes, cut into medium dice
1 (400g) tin of chickpeas, rinsed and drained
1 (420g) tin of cannellini beans, rinsed and drained
a handful of parsley, chopped
a small handful of fresh basil leaves, torn

YOU WILL NEED
a huge (about 7 litre) saucepan, with lid

Pour the oil into the saucepan and heat it gently over a low-to-medium flame. Add the onions, garlic and leeks, stir thoroughly to coat all the pieces in oil, and leave them to cook for a few minutes. Throw in the fennel, celery and carrots, stir, and continue cooking gently for about 10 minutes, or until the vegetables have softened a little. Add the Marigold powder, water, passata and thyme, and bring the soup to the boil, with the lid on. Reduce the heat, and gently simmer for 35 minutes with the lid half on. Now put in the pasta, cabbage and courgettes, and bring the soup back to the boil. Add some more water if the soup is stupidly thick.

Again reduce the soup to a simmer, and continue to cook for a further 20 minutes. Now throw in the chickpeas and beans, and cook for a further 10-15 minutes. Taste the soup, and add some salt if necessary, together with black pepper and the chopped fresh herbs. The soup is ready when the broth has thickened, the vegetables have softened, and you can see both have formed a permanent alliance.

The minestrone can be served immediately, but I like it better when it has rested for a day. My husband likes lots of grated parmesan with it, but I think cheese spoils the complex flavours. Take your pick, but tough country bread for dipping and dunking is mandatory.

'My mother, who is famous in our family for favouring a kill-by rather than a sell-by date, had a pot of minestrone on the go from one end of the year to the next'

I had no intention of creating a vegan recipe when I came up with this combination, but vegan it is. Baffling. Of course, there's nothing to stop you adding a few strips of lean cooked pork, lamb or chicken if you think this is too zen-like; toss them in at the point where you add the soy sauce and sesame seeds. For the noodles, I've used the dark buckwheat ones that the Japanese call soba, and which they serve cold, with dashi broth and strips of toasted nori seaweed. It's a combination I love, but I can quite see it wouldn't be to everyone's taste – unless you're Japanese. It took me far longer to embrace the superior marrow-like things so prosaically named squash. But butternut and acorn squash, in particular, do have an intriguing sweet, nutty flavour.

The vegetables can be prepared a few hours in advance, and kept refrigerated, but the whole dish only takes about 20 minutes to make.

Buckwheat noodles with squash, soy and sesame seeds

TO SERVE 3

3 large carrots, peeled

1 bunch of slim spring onions, trimmed

1 butternut squash, peeled, quartered lengthways, and deseeded

about 300g buckwheat (soba) noodles

3 tbsp groundnut oil

1 large onion, peeled and finely sliced

2 cloves of garlic, peeled, crushed and finely chopped

1 red chilli, deseeded and finely chopped

a thumb-sized knob of root ginger, peeled and grated

4 tbsp dark soy

15g toasted sesame seeds

a small handful of fresh coriander leaves, chopped

YOU WILL NEED

a large wok or very large frying pan; a very large saucepan lid

Cut the carrots into very fine, diagonal slices, discarding the ends (not literally – they are perfect for nibbling). Slice the spring onions diagonally into thick chunks. Cut the butternut quarters crossways into fine slices – when you get to the bulbous part at the base, you'll need to halve each quarter again, so the pieces end up a uniform size.

Put a large pan of salted water on to boil, and cook the noodles according to the instructions on the packet.

Heat the oil in a wok over a fairly high heat, and throw in the onion and garlic. Fry for 4-5 minutes, stirring frequently, until they have softened, and are a little brown around the edges. Add the carrots, spring onions and chilli, and fry for a further 3 minutes, tossing occasionally. Now add the squash and grated ginger, toss everything together again, and place a lid on the wok – don't worry if it doesn't fit properly. Cook for a minute or two, toss again, then cook for a further couple of minutes until the squash is tender.

Stir in the soy sauce, sesame seeds and coriander. Finally, add the cooked, drained noodles, and toss thoroughly. Serve immediately, making sure everyone gets their fair share of vegetables.

Pumpkin tortelloni served with melted butter and parmesan is a classic Italian dish, but to make it at home you need fresh pasta. At its best, fresh pasta is silky, smooth, achingly tender and with a gossamer-like texture – not at all like the clumsy fresh pasta that's so often served in restaurants. The trouble is that to make perfect pasta, you first have to get the dough right, and then you have to push it through one of those mangle-like devices about a million times. I don't know about you, but I'd rather watch daytime television – if only to wonder at how infinitely little talent you need to host a show.

If you live in central London, you can buy ready-made pumpkin tortelloni from specialist Italian delis, such as the Lina Stores in Brewer Street. It was here that one of the helpful staff gave me a really good tip for livening up something bland or rich (like pumpkin tortelloni). 'Add some chopped chilli to the butter,' she said. It's a simple but effective idea, and I now put a little chilli in almost anything very creamy, especially vegetable gratins, to cut the richness.

As a compromise to buying or making your own tortelloni this recipe for sweet butternut squash (or pumpkin or acorn squash) tossed with ribbons of pappardelle is very satisfactory.

You can make the pesto a few hours ahead, but the squash and pasta will need cooking to order: the whole recipe takes about 30 minutes.

Pappardelle with squash and sage pesto

TO SERVE 4

1 large butternut squash (or other squash or pumpkin), peeled, deseeded and cut into bite-sized cubes

30g unsalted butter, roughly chopped

4 large fresh sage leaves

350g dried pappardelle

30g pinenuts, toasted

FOR THE PESTO

115g parmesan, finely grated

30g pinenuts

3 cloves of garlic, peeled and crushed

4 large fresh sage leaves

100ml extra-virgin olive oil

1 mild red chilli, deseeded and finely chopped

YOU WILL NEED

a baking tray

Preheat the oven to 180°C (fan), 200°C (conventional), gas mark 6.

Pile the squash on to a piece of foil big enough to fold into a roomy pouch. Add the butter and sage leaves, and season very liberally with salt and black pepper. Seal the packet, leaving plenty of headroom for the steam. Place the pouch on a baking tray, and bake for 20-25 minutes, or until the squash is just tender to the point of a knife.

In the meantime, make the pesto. Whizz the parmesan, pinenuts, garlic and sage in a food processor until they are very finely chopped. Slowly pour in the oil until the mixture is a soft, smooth, only-just-pourable purée. (You might not need all the oil.) Scrape the pesto out into a bowl, and stir in the finely chopped chilli. Leave to one side.

Cook the pappardelle according to the instructions on the packet, or until just tender. Drain, reserving a little of the cooking water.

When the squash is cooked, discard the sage leaves, and pour all the juices from the foil packet over the drained pappardelle. Toss until glistening and, if necessary, add a spoonful or two of the pasta water to moisten it. Divide the pasta evenly between four warmed plates, followed by the baked squash. Finally, spoon a dollop of pesto over the top, and sprinkle with the toasted pinenuts. Eat immediately.

Pasta with breadcrumbs sounds fairly unlikely, but the slippery noodles coupled with crunchy shards of bread taste great. Add sweet onions, salty anchovies and hot chilli, and you have a kind of lingual Turkish bath, sauna and blitz in one. It's important to use a robust country bread such as pugliese, sourdough or ciabatta for the crumbs, and to grate them into little tufts and shards, rather than the fine breadcrumbs you'd use to coat fish or chicken.

Although the linguine cooks quickly, the onions take up to 40 minutes slowly to caramelise, so this isn't an 'instant' supper. But there is nothing to stop you preparing the breadcrumbs and the onions up to 48 hours in advance; it will then take about 15 minutes to finish the dish.

Linguine with caramelised onions and fried breadcrumbs

TO SERVE 4

FOR THE BREADCRUMBS
4 tbsp olive oil
75g very coarse, fresh white breadcrumbs

FOR THE PASTA AND ONIONS
2 tbsp olive oil, plus a little more
30g unsalted butter
4 large cloves of garlic, peeled, crushed and finely chopped
1 large red chilli, deseeded and finely chopped
1 large shallot, peeled and finely chopped
2-3 (about 750g) Spanish onions, peeled, halved and sliced quite finely
50g anchovies, drained, chopped, the oil reserved
a handful of fresh basil leaves, finely torn
350g dried linguine (or spaghetti, strangozzi)

YOU WILL NEED
a very large non-stick frying pan

To fry the breadcrumbs, place a large non-stick frying pan over a medium-to-high flame and pour in the olive oil and the reserved anchovy oil from the pasta ingredients. When the oil is hot, throw in the breadcrumbs, stirring them thoroughly so they soak up all the oil. Fry for 4-5 minutes, or until light golden-brown, stirring constantly. Turn the fried crumbs out immediately into a bowl lined with kitchen paper (or they'll keep browning). Leave them to one side.

Wipe out the frying pan, return it to a low-to-medium flame and add the 2 tablespoons of olive oil and the butter. Throw in the garlic, chilli and shallot and fry for about 4 minutes, stirring occasionally, until slightly softened. Reduce the heat to low, tip in the onions and stir thoroughly. Leave the onions to cook for about 30 minutes, stirring occasionally, until they are very soft and slightly golden. Towards the end of the cooking time, put on a large saucepan of salted water, ready to cook the linguine.

Now turn the heat up high under the onions. Stirring almost constantly, fry for a further 5-6 minutes until the onions are dark golden – not burnt and frizzled, but just a really rich caramel colour. Remove the frying pan from the heat, and stir in the anchovies and basil. Season with black pepper, and a little salt if needed.

Drain the pasta, then toss it with a little swish of olive oil, and a spoonful or two of the cooking water. Divide among four warmed plates, then spoon a tangle of onions over the top, followed by a handful of the crunchy breadcrumbs (they do not need to be reheated). Serve immediately.

This is not a mere pasta dish, but a luxurious recipe calling for cream, parmesan and flat-leaf parsley, not to mention porcini, the most highly prized mushrooms in Europe.

Although they are at their most magnificent when fresh, there's no denying that the flavour of dried Italian porcini (known as ceps or penny-buns in England, and as *cèpes* in France) has the most incredible, earthy intensity. Add a few grams to any recipe calling for ordinary mushrooms, and it's like having the Ladysmith choir doing backing vocals for Westlife (or any Five, S57, Steps – who they? group). I am blessed with a good friend, Giuseppe Simonini, who lives and works on the edge of the New Forest; every Christmas he sends me a big jar of porcini that he has picked and dried himself, and every time I use them I think of him. So much better than a bottle of Chanel.

If you are desperate to save time, you could prepare the vegetable part of this recipe a few hours ahead. Otherwise, it will take about 30 minutes in total to make.

Casarecce with porcini and pinto beans

TO SERVE 6
10-15g dried porcini
3 tbsp olive oil
1 large onion, peeled and finely sliced
3 cloves of garlic, peeled, crushed and finely chopped
1 small fennel bulb, trimmed, cored and finely sliced
1 (420g) tin pinto (or borlotti) beans, drained
about 115g good-quality ham, cut into medium dice
500g casarecce (or any tubular pasta)
a small handful of finely grated parmesan
about 300ml whipping cream
a large handful of flat-leaf parsley, chopped

YOU WILL NEED
a large non-stick frying pan

Put the dried porcini in a small bowl, pour on boiling-hot water to barely cover, and leave the porcini to soak for 15 minutes.

In the meantime, pour the oil into the frying pan and heat it over a low-to-medium flame. Tip in the onion and garlic, and cook for 6-7 minutes, stirring frequently. Add the fennel and cook for another 7-8 minutes until the vegetables are soft and very lightly coloured. If they start to brown and frazzle, reduce the heat.

Scoop out the softened porcini and squeeze dry, reserving all the liquid. Chop the porcini roughly, then add to the frying pan together with the pinto beans, ham and the soaking liquid. Season with salt and pepper, then turn up the heat and bring the contents to a boil, stirring frequently.

Meanwhile, cook the casarecce according to the instructions on the packet, then drain, reserving some of the cooking water.

Add the parmesan and cream to the frying pan, and let the sauce bubble until it has thickened a little. Remove the pan from the heat, and combine the sauce with the drained pasta and the parsley. Toss until every strand is thoroughly coated in the sauce, adding some of the reserved water if the sauce is too stiff. Serve immediately.

There are a zillion Middle-Eastern recipes which major on dough, batter or pastry. Stuffed with any number of fillings, the resulting little savouries are fashioned into all sorts of shapes, which are then fried or baked. The single common denominator is that they all taste fantastic – well, in my limited experience they do, but then I've never eaten a sheep's eye and bum-fluff borek. If you're a poor soul who can't tolerate goat's cheese, feel free to use feta or mozzarella – even the herbs can be substituted for dill, chives or coriander. Don't mess with the borlotti beans though; their sweet, earthy flavour is essential.

Both the batter and the filling can be prepared up to 24 hours ahead, and kept refrigerated, but leave the frying to the last minute.

Borlotti bean and goat's cheese pasteles

TO SERVE 2

FOR THE PANCAKES
115g Stamp Collection
wheat-free all-purpose flour
2 large free-range eggs
1 tbsp groundnut oil
150ml cold water

FOR THE FILLING
1 tbsp olive oil
1 large shallot, peeled
and finely chopped
1 large clove of garlic, peeled,
crushed and finely chopped
1 (420g) tin borlotti beans,
rinsed and drained
a large handful of
flat-leaf parsley, chopped
about a dozen fresh
mint leaves, chopped
about 150g soft, rindless,
mild goat's cheese
groundnut oil

YOU WILL NEED
a large non-stick frying pan

First, make the pancake batter. Put the flour, eggs and oil into a food processor and season with salt. Pour in the water, and process until the batter is smooth, scraping down the sides of the bowl halfway through. It should be on the thin side of single cream so, if necessary, add another splash of water. Leave the batter to stand for at least 30 minutes. This flour absorbs more liquid than normal, so be prepared to let the batter down with a little more water before using it.

Heat the olive oil in a small frying pan over a medium flame, toss in the shallot and garlic and fry for 4-5 minutes, until softened and lightly coloured. Remove the pan from the heat and leave to cool, then tip everything into a bowl, with the beans and herbs. Season generously with salt and pepper, and leave to one side.

To cook the pancakes, very lightly oil a large non-stick frying pan, then place it over a medium flame. When the pan is hot, pour in enough batter to form a very thin layer over the base. Cook the pancake for 2-3 minutes then, as soon as it has started to colour underneath, flip it over with a palette knife. Cook for a further 2-3 minutes until the pancake is lightly coloured but still supple. The first pancake is nearly always a disaster while you make adjustments to heat and quantities – don't worry about it. As the pancakes are ready, transfer them to the work surface and start filling them.

Spoon a tablespoon (no more, or the pasteles will be over-filled) of the borlotti mixture on one edge of the pancake, followed by a slice of goat's cheese. Roll up the pancake, folding in the sides after one turn, and finishing with a neat, cylindrical packet. Repeat.

Put the frying pan over a fairly high flame, and pour in about 1cm of oil. When the oil is hot, fry the pasteles for 2-3 minutes each side until they are golden brown. You will probably need to do this in two batches. Drain the pasteles on a pad of kitchen paper, and serve immediately with a leaf salad.

'I'll bet he eats his supper naked in the bath'

No one makes food sound more delectable than Nigel Slater. Everything he cooks is fragrant, nutty, juicy, creamy, crisp, sizzling, sticky, warm, golden and generally luscious - I'll bet he eats his supper naked in the bath. Whenever I think of cheese, and all the gorgeous suppers you can make with it, Nigel's way of cooking, and eating, instantly springs to mind.

While bruschetta, at its simplest, is just a slice of ciabatta or pugliese toasted and rubbed with garlic, I've gone overboard on this one, piling the bread high with a gutsy, gooey mélange of parmesan, beans and herbs. It's about as inauthentically Italian as Gianni was in Eastenders: just in case you ever play a restaurateur again, carissimo, it's broo-sketta, not broo-shetta.

The recipe only takes 15 minutes from start to finish.

Italian beans on toast

TO SERVE 4
4 tbsp extra-virgin olive oil
2 sprigs fresh rosemary
2 large cloves of garlic, peeled, crushed and finely chopped
30g unsalted butter
140g parmesan, finely grated
1 (420g) tin cannellini beans, the liquid reserved
1 (420g) tin borlotti beans, drained, the liquid discarded
1 (50g) tin anchovies, drained chopped, the oil reserved
a large handful of flat-leaf parsley, chopped
1 baked ciabatta
a handful of fresh basil leaves, finely torn

YOU WILL NEED
a very large frying pan

Heat 2 tablespoons of the olive oil in the frying pan over a medium heat. Toss in the rosemary and stir it around for 2 minutes, then remove and discard. Add the garlic and fry it for 1 minute, stirring frequently. Now put the butter, parmesan, beans (including the reserved liquid), anchovies (but not their oil), and three-quarters of the parsley into the pan. Stir everything together, mashing about a quarter of the beans to thicken the juices. Reduce the heat to low-to-medium and gently cook for about 6 minutes, stirring occasionally, until the contents of the pan look a thick, gloopy – but nice – mess.

In the meantime, cut the 'heels' off the ciabatta and discard them, slice the loaf in half horizontally, then cut each half in two, to make four pieces. Toast the ciabatta, or for those with a solid top, press the cut sides straight on to the hot plate, to blacken them lightly. Immediately drizzle each piece with a mixture of the reserved anchovy oil and the remaining two tablespoons of olive oil.

Stir the basil and the remaining parsley into the bean mixture, and season it generously with black pepper, and sea salt to taste. Spoon the beans on to the ciabatta. Serve immediately.

When it turns seven o' clock, and the decision about what to cook for supper cannot be put off any longer, I doubt if haggis is the first thing that springs to mind. But haggis is really no more exotic (or sinister) than a packet of sausages, and this robust jumble of fried potatoes, onions, savoury bacon and sweet apple is gustatory proof. Of course, if any Scots are reading this, they will require no further persuasion, but for any timid Sassenachs, I can assure you that haggis is very unalarming – and I speak as someone who isn't even very keen on meat, never mind funny visceral Scottish-type meat. In fact, I positively like its mild, peppery flavour and rough, dryish texture. If you're still not convinced, I'll concede that chunks of (cooked) sausage would be fine instead.

Although the vegetables can be prepared in advance, the rest of the cooking must be done to order: it will take all of 20 minutes.

Haggis, potato, bacon and apple fry-up

TO SERVE 3

about 250g waxy potatoes (Charlotte, Anya), peeled, and cut into bite-sized chunks

1 haggis

2 tbsp groundnut oil

1 large Spanish onion, peeled and roughly chopped

2 cloves of garlic, peeled, crushed and finely chopped

85g bacon (streaky or back), cut into medium dice

1 large crisp apple, peeled, cored and cut into large dice

a small bundle of chives, chopped

Boil the potatoes in salted water until tender. Drain, and leave to one side. Cook the haggis according to the instructions on the packet.

In the meantime, heat the oil in a large non-stick frying pan over a low-to-medium heat, and fry the onion and garlic for about 5 minutes, or until slightly softened. Throw in the diced bacon and fry for another 5 minutes, stirring occasionally. Add the diced apple, season with salt and pepper, and cook for a further 4-5 minutes, stirring occasionally.

Turn up the heat. Tip the potatoes into the frying pan and gently toss them together with the onions and apples. Cook for a few minutes until everything looks slightly frazzled and golden-brown. Remove the pan from the heat and scatter over the chopped chives.

Serve immediately with the roughly sliced, piping-hot haggis, and a spot of mustard, if you like.

There's a reversal of the Jack Spratt rule in our house (albeit that I've ended up as the fat one). This is especially true when it comes to pasta, with my husband always plumping for a cream sauce while I prefer my pasta much more austerely dressed. This recipe definitely comes into the rich category, but the slightly bitter, verdant taste of the kale offsets the creaminess very effectively. You can, of course, substitute the kale for any other tannic-tasting greens; I imagine cavolo nero (if there's any left after the River Cafe has had its delivery) spring greens or spinach would be equally effective.

The recipe takes about 25 minutes; there is nothing that can really be prepared in advance.

Penne with kale, mascarpone and pancetta

TO SERVE 4

about 300g curly kale (or other greens)

2 tbsp extra-virgin olive oil

70g pancetta, cut into very small dice

3 cloves of garlic, peeled, crushed and finely chopped

about 15 scrapings of whole nutmeg

350g penne (or similarly robust tubular pasta)

1 (250g) tub mascarpone

about 300ml whipping or double cream

a large handful of finely grated parmesan

YOU WILL NEED

a large wok; a large saucepan lid

First, prepare the kale. Strip off the leaf part, discarding all the tough stalks and thick veins, and tearing any large leaves in half. Wash thoroughly, and drain.

Heat the oil in the wok over a low-to-medium heat. Throw in the pancetta and cook the cubes gently for 6-7 minutes, until they have shrivelled slightly and are faintly golden. Remove the pancetta and drain it on a pad of kitchen paper, reserving the wok and cooking oil.

Return the wok to the heat, and toss in the garlic. Fry it for 3 minutes, stirring occasionally, then add the damp kale – the wok will be very full. Using two big forks (or salad servers), toss the leaves for about 5 minutes until completely covered with the garlicky oil. Season generously with salt and pepper, and the nutmeg. Cover the wok with the lid (it doesn't matter if the lid sits directly on top of the kale, rather than the wok), and cook for another 7-8 minutes, stirring occasionally, until the kale is tender and wilted.

While the kale is cooking, cook the pasta according to the instructions on the packet, or until it is tender to the teeth. Reserve some of the cooking water.

As soon as the kale is ready, add the mascarpone, cream, parmesan and pancetta to the wok, and toss everything together. Raise the heat and bubble for 3-4 minutes, uncovered, until the sauce is about as thick as double cream, stirring occasionally. Check the seasoning, and adjust to taste.

Now tip the drained pasta into the wok and mix the sauce and pasta together. Add a little of the pasta cooking water, if necessary, to achieve the right coating consistency. Serve immediately.

Any cookery writer with a modicum of modesty will tell you that genuine invention is a rare thing. As far as recipes go, there is nothing that someone hasn't thought of already, whether it's from a culture halfway across the world, or the distant past. As far as new stuff goes, the best we writers can hope to do is to apply a different spin, using an idea from here and an ingredient from there.

If ever there was a case of recipe evolution, this is it. Starting with one of my favourite Japanese dishes, kake age (deep-fried tangles of shredded vegetables and, often, fish), I decided to try using strips of chicken, but with the usual soy dipping sauce. Not bad, but I thought it would be better with mussels. Then I decided I wanted the taste of Indian spices, but didn't like the idea of soy with the likes of cumin and coriander. So I changed the dip to a yoghurt one – albeit a pale pastiche of genuine raita. Quite a few steps from the original idea, it's turned out to be a success.

The mussels and veg can be prepared up to 24 hours ahead and kept refrigerated, leaving the frying to the last minute. The recipe only takes about 20 minutes, and is even quicker if you have a food processor.

Deep-fried mussel and vegetable tangles

TO SERVE 2

about 500g fresh mussels, cleaned

2 small courgettes, topped and tailed

1 large carrot, peeled

1 large leek, trimmed

2 cloves of garlic, peeled, crushed and finely chopped

a small handful of flat-leaf parsley, chopped

about 200g natural Greek yoghurt

FOR THE BATTER

1 large free-range egg

150ml cold water

140g plain flour

3 rounded tsp garam masala (or curry powder/paste)

a small handful of fresh coriander leaves, chopped

YOU WILL NEED

a deep-fat fryer, or a large wok or saucepan half-filled with groundnut oil

Preheat the oil in the deep-fat fryer to 180°C; place the wok or saucepan over a moderate-to-high heat.

Pile the mussels into a large saucepan, put on the lid, and place the pan over a very high heat. Cook for 3-4 minutes, shaking the pan from time to time, until all the mussels have opened. Remove the pan from the heat and leave the mussels to cool, uncovered. As soon as you can handle them, remove the mussels from the shells (discarding any that haven't opened), and put the meat to one side.

Julienne the courgettes and carrots in a food processor, or cut them by hand into fine, little finger-length strips. Cut the leek into fine strips by hand. Leave the vegetables to one side.

For the batter, whisk the egg and water together in a mixing bowl, and tip in the flour, garam masala (or curry powder/paste), coriander and a generous amount of salt. Continue to whisk until the batter is smooth. Mix in the mussels, vegetables and garlic really thoroughly – it's easiest to use your hands, even if it is a bit messy. Now scoop up a tangerine-sized clump of the mixture and plonk it into the fryer: it will spread out a bit, but there should be enough space to cook three tangles at a time. Fry for 3-4 minutes, turning halfway through, until the tangles are golden brown. Remove and drain on a pad of kitchen paper; keep warm while you cook the rest.

Stir the parsley into the yoghurt and season it with salt and black pepper. Divvy it out between the bowls, and serve it with the tangles.

Most traditional fish soups, including chowder, started off as a cheap way for fishermen to feed themselves and their families. Using the dregs of the day's catch, any other ingredients used in the soup would be equally inexpensive. Well, times change. You only have to think of bouillabaisse to see how a simple peasant dish can come up in the world. Even in the south of France (or perhaps I should say, especially), restaurants charge a fortune for a ruddy brew which includes luxury fish and shellfish – such as sea bass and langoustine – not to mention saffron.

Regardless of cost, I'm not sure I don't prefer our northern fish soups. Scotland has a particularly good repertoire, from mussel brose to partan bree (crab soup). Best of all is cullen skink, which sounds a bit like something a chap might put down his trousers, but is actually a wonderful broth of smoked haddock, onion, potato, butter and milk. This chowder owes a debt to cullen skink, but with the addition of the subtly subversive coriander and garlic, would be unrecognisable to Meg Merrilies. Chowder comes from the French *chaudière,* and the original ingredients included salt pork and clams, but nowadays any sort of fish goes – as well as the dreaded sweetcorn.

The chowder can be made 48 hours in advance – to the point where the parsley and cream go in – as long as it's refrigerated.

Smoked haddock chowder

TO SERVE 2
30g unsalted butter
1 large onion, peeled and cut into large dice
2 sticks celery, cut into medium dice
2 cloves of garlic, peeled, crushed and finely chopped
about 350g waxyish potatoes (eg Desirée), peeled and cut into large chunks
2 tsp Marigold Swiss vegetable bouillon powder
425ml cold water
250g undyed smoked haddock fillet, skinned, and cut into large chunks
75ml double cream or whipping cream
a small handful of flat-leaf parsley, roughly chopped
a handful of fresh coriander leaves, roughly chopped

Melt the butter in a large saucepan over a low heat. Throw in the onion, celery and garlic, and cook gently for about 10 minutes, without letting them colour, and stirring occasionally. Put in the potatoes, stir and leave to one side.

Meanwhile, combine the Marigold powder and water in another pan, and bring to the boil. Reduce the heat immediately, throw in the chunks of smoked haddock, and simmer them gently for 2 minutes. Scoop out the cooked fish and put it to one side, then drain the stock into the saucepan with the vegetables, and season with a little salt.

Simmer the vegetables in the stock, with the lid half on, for about 20 minutes, or until the potatoes are tender but not falling apart. Add the cream, parsley and coriander, bring the soup back to a strong simmer, and cook for 1 minute, uncovered. Now tip in the smoked haddock, and immediately remove the pan from the heat.

Season the chowder with ground black pepper, and taste to see if more salt is needed. Serve immediately, with some chewy chunks of brown bread for dunking.

'Not a new comedy double act, but traditional British food at its simplest and best – tender flakes of smoked haddock coupled with crisp bacon'

Oh my, are you in for a treat. Not just because this recipe tastes fabulous, but because it's so quick you'll be back from the kitchen and slumped in front of *The Bill* in the shake of a cat's tail. Actually, I'm not sure that's the right expression; you'd need plastic surgery if you tried shaking Archie's tail.

As with all simple recipes, the quality of the ingredients is utterly exposed: use only British, dry-cured, free-range bacon, and undyed smoked haddock, and you'll understand why ham and haddie, a traditional Scottish high tea, is so popular in our house. Nowt to do with hubby being a Scot, of course. (And when is the West Lothian issue going to be resolved?)

Ham and haddie

TO SERVE 2
2 undyed smoked haddock fillets, about 225g each
a splash of milk
30g unsalted butter
50ml double cream
4-6 rashers top-quality back bacon

YOU WILL NEED
a baking tin just large enough for the haddock to fit in a single layer

Preheat the grill.

Trim off any scraggy bits from the smoked haddock fillets. Pour in enough milk barely to cover the bottom of the baking tin. Put in the haddock, skin-side up, and dab 15g of butter on top of each piece.

Slide the baking tin under the grill, about a hand's length from the elements, and cook the haddock for 5-6 minutes. Remove the tin, and turn the haddock over with a fish slice: it should be almost cooked, and the milk reduced to a few milky-brown bubbles. Pour the cream over the fish, season with black pepper, then lie the bacon rashers on top of each piece of haddock: overlap the rashers if necessary, but make sure the fat is fully exposed to the heat.

Put the baking tin back under the grill and cook for a further 4-5 minutes, until the bacon fat is brown and crispy. (You don't need to turn the rashers.) Serve immediately, complete with the pan juices.

The credit for these excellent lamb patties goes to Brendan Ansbro, our head chef at the Trinity (the bistro at our hotel, the Crown and Castle) in Orford. They started as a way to use up the trimmings from the rumps of lamb, but progressed quickly from being a very popular staff supper to a slot on the menu itself. It is important to use lamb that's neither too lean (the patties will be dry), nor too fatty (they'll shrink to nothing). Personally, I'd eat them with a baked potato, but if you want to create something more glamorous, these roast vegetables provide a simple but sapid accompaniment.

The list of ingredients is long but all you have to do is swirl them together so it's not such a time-consuming recipe – in any case, the patties can be prepared up to 12 hours ahead.

Spiced lamb patties with roast vegetables

TO SERVE 4

FOR THE PATTIES

3 tbsp plain Greek yoghurt

a thumb-sized piece of root ginger, peeled and grated

3 cloves of garlic, peeled, crushed and finely chopped

1 red chilli, deseeded and finely chopped

1 heaped tsp ground cumin

12 cardamom pods, crushed, husks discarded, seeds pounded

1/2 tsp ground coriander

1 tbsp chopped fresh coriander

1.2kg coarsely-minced lamb

a little plain flour

olive oil

FOR THE ROAST VEGETABLES

4 large Maris Piper potatoes, peeled and cut into large-bite-sized chunks

about 300g cherry tomatoes

2 red onions, peeled, root left attached, and cut into eighths

1/2 level tsp ground cinnamon

3-4 sprigs fresh thyme

4 tbsp olive oil

TO SERVE

12 tbsp plain Greek yoghurt

3 tbsp chopped fresh coriander

YOU WILL NEED

a large roasting tin

Preheat the oven to 200°C (fan), 220°C (conventional), gas mark 7.

To make the patties, mix the yoghurt, ginger, garlic, chilli, spices and fresh coriander together in a large bowl. Season with plenty of freshly ground black pepper (but no salt at this stage), then tip in the minced lamb. Mix everything together very lightly, then fashion the lamb into 8 evenly-sized, not-too-plump patties – try not to compress the meat or the texture of the patties will be too dense. Put in the fridge.

Put the potatoes, tomatoes, onions, cinnamon, thyme sprigs and oil into the roasting tin 45 minutes before you want to eat. Toss them together thoroughly, and season. Roast the vegetables on a middle shelf for 30-40 minutes, turning them once. Lower the heat, if necessary, so the vegetables end up both tender and golden brown.

Depending on the size of your frying pan, you will have to cook the patties in two batches, keeping the first batch warm while you cook the second. If you can fry them all at once, start cooking them about 10 minutes before the vegetables are going to be ready, otherwise start about 20 minutes before.

Season the patties with salt, then flour them lightly on both sides. Place the frying pan over a fairly high flame and when it is hot pour in a thin film of oil. Leave for a minute, then put in the patties and fry them for about 4 minutes on each side: to ensure a good crust, resist the temptation to lift, fiddle with, or turn them more than once.

To serve, divide the roast vegetables and lamb patties among four warmed plates, then dollop some yoghurt on top, with a sprinkling of chopped coriander to finish. Serve immediately.

Summery starters

There's nothing better than sitting in the garden with a bunch of good friends, the sun blazing down, a few swallows darting and swooping high in the sky and the table laden with good food. (Not to mention a few bottles of wine chilling in a bucket.) Most of these starters are cool, fresh and jumping with vivid flavours – just right for launching a relaxed al fresco meal.

Over the years I've been served more horrible renditions of vichyssoise than I care to remember: I've had vichyssoise the texture of puréed carpet slippers, vichyssoise that tasted of fatty chicken stock, and vichyssoise the temperature of used bath water. All horrible, and, given that vichyssoise is only upmarket leek and potato soup, quite unnecessary. Let it here be known that the essential properties of a good vichyssoise are that the soup is a fine purée, no thicker than single cream; tastes only of leek and potatoes; and is chilled to within an inch of its life.

I'm normally loathe to tamper with classic recipes – especially when I've just been banging on about how to make them correctly – but in this instance I think my recasting of ordinary potatoes with sweet potatoes is a great success, but do use the terracotta-orange sweet potatoes rather than the purple-skinned ones: the chilli-spiked flavour is very pleasing, and the pale apricot colour very beautiful.

The soup can, and should, be made at least 12, and up to 48 hours in advance, and kept refrigerated.

Chilled sweet potato vichyssoise

TO SERVE 6-plus
3 tsp Marigold Swiss vegetable bouillon powder
1 litre water
1 Spanish onion, peeled and coarsely chopped
2 large leeks, trimmed, rinsed and chopped fairly finely
1 mild green chilli, deseeded and finely chopped
2 orange-fleshed sweet potatoes, peeled and cut into small cubes
1 (284ml) carton single cream
a small bundle of fresh chives
ground white pepper

YOU WILL NEED
chilled flat soup plates

Put the Marigold powder and water into a large saucepan, add all the vegetables, and season well with salt. Bring to the boil over a fairly high heat, with the lid on. As soon as the soup starts to bubble, reduce the heat and simmer for 20-25 minutes, half-covered, until all the vegetables are completely soft.

Cool the soup a little, then liquidise it to a very fine purée in 3 or 4 batches, as necessary.

If you are serving the soup within 12 hours or so, add the cream and chill the whole shebang at once. If the soup is for later, stir in the (very cold) cream just before serving. In both cases, season the soup with white pepper, and a little more salt if necessary. If the vichyssoise is too thick, dilute it to a thin cream with a little ice-cold water. Serve the soup with a sprinkling of chopped chives.

This cool, pistachio-green soup evokes a charming *Go-Between* nostalgia. In my mind's eye, I can see a family of aristocratic Edwardians lounging under a sun-dappled parasol, while a crocodile of servants bearing silver trays smooths its way across the striped lawn to a linen-napped table. An Edwardian sipping chilled cucumber soup would, of course, have had to do without the coconut milk. You, on the other hand, will have to do without the servants.

The soup can, and should, be made at least 12 hours, and up to 2 days ahead, and kept refrigerated.

Chilled cucumber and coconut milk soup

TO SERVE 4
1 very large cucumber
30g unsalted butter
2 small shallots, peeled and finely chopped
1 mild green chilli, deseeded and finely chopped
50ml dry white wine
2 rounded tsp Marigold Swiss vegetable bouillon stock
500ml water
150ml whipping or double cream
about 250ml coconut milk
1 tbsp of chopped fresh chives or tarragon

YOU WILL NEED
chilled flat soup plates

Peel the cucumber in alternate stripes, then halve lengthways, and deseed with a sharp teaspoon. Slice roughly into thinnish pieces and leave to one side.

Melt the butter in a large saucepan over a medium heat. Gently fry the shallots and chilli for about 5 minutes, until softened but not coloured. Throw in the cucumber and toss the pieces in the butter to coat them. Turn the heat up high and pour in the white wine, stirring constantly so the cucumber doesn't catch on the bottom of the pan. Bubble the wine madly for 45 seconds, then stir in the Marigold powder and water. Season with salt and pepper, reduce the heat, and gently simmer for 15-20 minutes, with the pan half-covered.

In the meantime, pour the cream and coconut milk into a small saucepan and bring to the boil over a high heat, uncovered. Boil for 3-4 minutes until it has thickened a little. Remove the soup from the heat, scrape in the cream mixture, and leave to cool.

Liquidise the soup until it is completely smooth, then chill very thoroughly. Adjust the seasoning, and if the soup is any thicker than single cream, stir in some ice-cold water. Serve with a sprinkling of chopped chives or tarragon.

Leeks are fabulous not only as a vegetable in their own right, but as an essential building-block to countless soups and stews. You can even use them as a cheaper, and less harsh, replacement for spring onions. (I much prefer shredded leeks to spring onions with Peking-style duck.)

For this cool, robust, but very pretty starter, the leeks must be as slim as copper piping – ideally 12 leeks to the kilo, but certainly no less than eight. If you can't find leeks this slender, then make something else.

The dressing and the leeks can be prepared up to 12 hours ahead, and refrigerated. Bring the salad to room temperature and add the other elements a couple of hours before serving.

Leek salad with tarragon, caper and parsley dressing

TO SERVE 4
about 1kg slim young leeks, trimmed
1 heaped tbsp capers, rinsed and chopped
3 anchovy fillets, finely chopped
2 large free-range eggs, hard-boiled, then chopped or sieved
a small handful of flat-leaf parsley leaves, chopped

FOR THE DRESSING
2 tbsp tarragon (or cider) vinegar
2 level tsp tarragon (or smooth German or Dijon) mustard
12 tbsp fruity extra-virgin olive oil
about 2 tbsp chopped fresh tarragon leaves

YOU WILL NEED
a serving dish large enough to take the leeks in a single layer

To make the dressing, whisk the vinegar and mustard together, and season. Then whisk in the olive oil to make a thick emulsion. Leave the dressing to one side, only whisking in the chopped tarragon at the last minute.

To clean the leeks, slice them lengthways down the middle without penetrating all the way through, then rinse them under cold running water. Bring a large saucepan of salted water to the boil, and cook the leeks for about 5 minutes, uncovered, until they are tender but not at all flabby. Drain off the water, then put the leeks on a clean, doubled-up tea towel and blot them as dry as you can with a second tea towel.

Arrange the leeks in the dish, season generously with salt and pepper, and pour over the dressing. Strew the chopped capers, anchovies, egg and parsley on top, and serve.

'The cool crisp cubes of juicy melon and salty fresh cheese taste perfect on a hot Mediterranean day'

If anything exemplifies the adage less is more, this stunningly simple recipe is it. In fact, it's not even a recipe in the sense that there's no measuring, weighing or cooking required. I first ate this dazzlingly fresh combination at the original London Sugar Club. Subsequently, I've found that it's a traditional Greek dish; it's not hard to imagine how reviving the cool, crisp cubes of juicy melon and salty fresh cheese would taste on a hot Mediterranean day. If you want to get the full effect, though, do use proper Greek or Cypriot feta, not the French-style one or any other pale pastiche of the real thing.

Prepare the melon and feta up to 12 hours in advance, and refrigerate separately, until required.

Feta and watermelon salad

TO SERVE 4

about 250g Greek or Cypriot
feta cheese

about a quarter
of a ripe watermelon

a little lemon juice

a little light, fruity
extra-virgin olive oil

Peel and cut the melon into large bite-sized chunks. If you've got the time and inclination, remove the seeds. (Or buy one of the seedless watermelons that have recently come on the market.)

Drain the feta, and cut it into similarly sized chunks. There should be rather more melon than there is cheese. Toss the feta and melon together – gently, so the cheese doesn't crumble too much and stain the melon – then sprinkle with a little lemon juice, and season with pepper. Divide the salad among the plates and dribble a little oil over each serving. Eat immediately – and thank God you're alive.

There's no doubt that it's recently been very fashionable to cook everything on a griddle. Unlike many food fads, though, I think this one might be here to stay – I hope so, because my store cupboard is already congested enough with the chicken brick, fondue set and waffle-maker.

English asparagus is the best in the world – tender, juicy and with an incomparable flavour. Although there is nothing to beat plainly boiled asparagus dripping with melted butter – except plainly boiled asparagus dripping with hollandaise sauce – asparagus takes to the griddle surprisingly well. The stems retain their moisture, and the flavour takes on an interesting nuttiness that's enhanced by the rich, sweetish, smoky sauce. (The sesame sauce is equally good with griddled chicken, by the way.) As an unusual but good-tempered starter this scores highly.

The sauce can be made up to 5 days in advance, but must be brought to room temperature before serving: if it's stiffened up too much, whisk in a little warm water. Serve the asparagus hot, warm or at room temperature, but don't refrigerate it or leave it hanging around for more than an hour or two, as the spears will start to shrivel up and look most unappetising.

Griddled asparagus with sesame sauce

TO SERVE 4
about 600g fresh asparagus,
medium to thick grade
about 2 tbsp groundnut oil

FOR THE SAUCE
1 medium clove of garlic,
peeled and crushed
2 tbsp light tahini
1 tbsp smooth
peanut butter
1 tbsp honey,
runny or set
4 tbsp groundnut oil
1 tbsp sake (or dry sherry)
1 tbsp mirin
1 tbsp white wine
1/2 tbsp dark soy sauce

YOU WILL NEED
a large griddle pan

Make the sauce first. Put all the ingredients in a liquidiser, and whizz for about 30 seconds. Scrape down the sides with a rubber spatula, then whizz again for another 15-20 seconds, until smooth. Pour the sauce into a bowl, and leave to one side.

Trim the asparagus spears, cutting off and discarding the woody ends. Toss the spears in a little oil, making sure each one is well-coated, then season them with salt.

Place the griddle on a very high heat. When it is extremely hot arrange the spears on it in a single layer – depending on the size of your griddle you might have to cook the asparagus in two batches. Turn the heat down to medium and cook the spears for 6-7 minutes, undisturbed. Using a pair of tongs, turn the spears and cook for a further 6-7 minutes, or until they are tender to the point of a knife, and lightly gilded.

Serve with a spoonful or two of the sesame sauce poured over the tips. Encourage everyone to use their fingers, rather than knives and forks, but supply lots of napkins.

If you are not familiar with girolles (also known as chanterelles), these are the apricot-coloured mushrooms with ribbed, flared undersides that crop up so often in classic French cuisine. With their elusive, slightly peppery flavour and creamy texture they marry beautifully with everything from sweetbreads, fish and chicken, to eggs and pasta. Quite a few British supermarkets and greengrocers are now stocking them, but you could always use the ubiquitous oyster mushroom instead – or any other mushroom if it comes to that; this is only a recipe, not a blueprint for a nuclear processing plant.

It is amazing how quickly mascarpone – the mild, Italian cream cheese – has established its place on the supermarket shelves. Along with French crème fraîche, it's difficult to remember how we did without it. But I can certainly live without the lacklustre low-fat or even zero-fat versions. As no one actually *needs* either of these dairy products and the whole point of them is their fabulous silky richness, it seems far better to eat the real thing – albeit only occasionally.

All the vegetables can be prepared in advance, but the cooking should be done at the last moment. If entertaining is the last thing on your mind, serve this as a really good supper for two people, instead.

Asparagus and girolles crostini

TO SERVE 4

about 350g fresh asparagus, medium to thick grade

about 125g fresh girolles

half a baked ciabatta loaf

1 tbsp extra-virgin olive oil

30g unsalted butter

1 medium red onion, peeled and thinly sliced

1 large clove of garlic, peeled, crushed and finely chopped

4 rounded tbsp full-fat mascarpone

2 heaped tbsp finely grated parmesan

a small bunch of flat-leaf parsley leaves, chopped

Trim the asparagus, cutting off and discarding the woody ends. Cut the spears diagonally into 3cm long pieces, keeping the tips whole.

All mushrooms need a wipe, but girolles tend to be particularly dirty, so clean them carefully with some damp kitchen paper. Cut off, and discard, the dirty tips of the stalks. Roughly chop the mushrooms, remaining stalks included, into bite-sized pieces.

Cut off and discard the ends of the ciabatta. Slice the bread in half lengthways, and half again crossways, to make four pieces. If you have an Aga, plonk the ciabatta straight on to the plate, cut side down, and blacken the surface slightly. Otherwise, toast the cut sides of the bread conventionally. Leave to one side.

Melt the oil and butter in a large frying pan over a low-to-medium heat. Throw in the onion and garlic, and fry for 7-8 minutes until soft and lightly coloured. Add the asparagus, season with salt, and cook for 8-10 minutes, stirring occasionally. Now add the girolles and gently toss until well-coated. Grind in some black pepper and continue to cook for 3 minutes, stirring occasionally.

Add the mascarpone, parmesan and parsley. Turn up the heat, and cook for about 2 minutes, stirring from time to time, until everything is piping hot and the sauce has thickened a little. Taste, and adjust the seasoning. Place the toasted ciabatta on warmed plates and spoon the asparagus mixture over the top. Serve immediately.

'The spinach, in particular, should be so young, fresh and springy, it could win the 100m hurdles'

I first ate this salad at Joe Allen's basement restaurant in Covent Garden, famous at the time for noise, razzmatazz and theatre stars. This was the place to get great American-Italian junk food, whether it was hamburgers, ribs and pasta or deep-fried onion rings, French fries and Caesar salad.

Because this salad is simple, the ingredients must be commensurately good – raw, bright spinach; crisp, salty shards of bacon; and, soft, smooth chunks of avocado. The spinach, in particular, should be so young, fresh and springy, it could win the 100m hurdles.

The dressing can be prepared 24 hours in advance, as can the croûtons and spinach leaves. Leave the final assembly to the last minute.

Spinach salad with avocado and pancetta

TO SERVE 6
about 225g young spinach leaves, trimmed, rinsed and dried
about 125g thinly-sliced pancetta (or streaky bacon)
2 ripe-but-firm Hass avocados
about 100g medium-sized chestnut mushrooms

FOR THE DRESSING
1 tbsp sherry vinegar
3 tbsp extra-virgin olive oil
3 tbsp walnut oil (or pumpkin seed oil)
2 tbsp whipping cream

To make the dressing, whisk the vinegar with salt and freshly ground black pepper. Pour the oils in slowly, and whisk to a thick emulsion. Finally, whisk in the cream. Leave to one side.

Cook the pancetta (or bacon) until crisp, then crumble it into bite-sized pieces. Cut the avocados in half, dig out and discard the stones, then peel off the skin and slice the flesh into bite-sized chunks. Wipe the mushrooms clean and slice them fairly thickly.

Pile the spinach leaves into a large bowl, season with salt and pepper, and pour in some of the dressing. Go easy, as you might not need it all; the surplus can be kept in the fridge for a later date. Toss the spinach leaves until they are well coated but not suffocating. Now gently toss in the avocado, mushrooms and pancetta, divide the salad among the plates, and serve immediately.

You might wonder why on earth I'm bothering to give you a hoary old recipe like this, but some things – actually, a lot of things – remain good whatever the current fashion dictates. You'd be surprised how many people are affectionately disposed towards egg mayonnaise but, like every simple dish, success hinges on the quality of the ingredients. For this recipe, free-range (and preferably organic) eggs are mandatory, as is proper home-made mayonnaise – Hellman's is fine for the odd sarnie but not for this.

As for the salty question of anchovies, well, you're going to get fed up with me saying it, but good-quality anchovies really don't taste like something Hannibal Lecter had for tea. If you're not convinced, substitute a bit of roasted red pepper, and write out a 100 times, I am a wimp, I am a wimp, I am a...

By all means boil the eggs and make the mayonnaise up to 12 hours in advance, but don't assemble the salad until the last minute – and make sure everything is at (cool) room temperature.

Old-fashioned egg mayonnaise

TO SERVE 4
6 large free-range eggs
a few handfuls of mixed salad leaves – watercress, rocket and Little Gem
12 anchovy fillets, split lengthways
a dusting of cayenne pepper

FOR THE MAYONNAISE
275ml groundnut oil
75ml light extra-virgin olive oil
2 large free-range egg yolks (or 1 whole egg and 1 yolk, if using a liquidiser)
1 rounded tsp smooth German or Dijon mustard
1-2 tbsp lemon juice
a little warm water

The eggs should be at room temperature, as should all the ingredients for the mayonnaise.

Carefully place the 6 eggs into a saucepan of strongly simmering water. Once the water has come back to the simmer, cook for 7-8 minutes, uncovered. Drain off the hot water, and run cold water over the eggs for about 2 minutes, to prevent OVPL – ovine visible panty line – that horrible grey edge around the yolk. Shell the eggs and leave them to one side.

You can either make the mayonnaise by hand with a mixing bowl and whisk, or in a liquidiser. First, mix the oils in a good pouring jug. Whisk or whizz the egg yolks and mustard together, then start adding the oil extremely slowly, either whisking constantly, or with the motor running continuously. Start with a very fine thread at first, then gradually increase to a thin stream as the mayonnaise starts to thicken. When the eggs have taken up about half the oil, add a tablespoon of lemon juice. Continue adding the oil very carefully, making sure it is all incorporated before more is added.

Season the mayonnaise with sea salt and black pepper, then taste it. Add more seasoning, and a little more lemon juice if it needs a bit more of a kick. The mayonnaise should now be a mound of glossy, stiff peaks; to convert it to the desired thick, smooth coating consistency, stir in 4-5 tablespoons of warm water.

Put a handful of salad leaves on each plate, then place three halves of egg, yolk side-down, on top. Coat these with mayonnaise, straddle each one with a cross of anchovy strips, then dust with a little cayenne pepper. Serve immediately, with buttered granary bread.

Normally I'm a great fan of buffalo milk mozzarella. It has a more pronounced yoghurty flavour than cow's milk mozzarella, which is a pleasant enough fresh cheese, but one that can be very mild. But in this instance there's no point in wasting money on buffalo milk mozzarella, because the cheese merely provides a benign, slightly chewy, milk-soft texture; the flavour is all in the basil-rich pesto, hot chilli, and savoury parma ham.

This is not so much a recipe, more an assembly job. It takes no talent, and hardly any time, but tastes bloody good. It's also the easiest recipe in the world to halve or double up. The assembled balls (sounds like a meeting of Lycra-clad male athletes) can be made up to 8 hours ahead, and refrigerated.

Fried mozzarella with pesto and chilli

TO SERVE 4
4 (about 100g) cow's milk mozzarella balls
about 4 tbsp hot chilli sauce
about 4 tbsp pesto (red or green)
4-6 slices parma ham
a little olive oil
a few handfuls of dressed salad leaves

Cut the balls of mozzarella in half, and spread one side with chilli sauce and the other with pesto. Clamp the two halves together and bind them up with a slice of parma ham. Make sure the re-assembled ball is completely covered with the ham, so use more than one slice if necessary.

Place a non-stick frying pan over a high heat. When it is hot, pour in a little oil. Now put the mozzarella balls in the pan and fry, turning them two or three times with a pair of tongs, until the parma ham is gorgeously brown, sticky and crisp, and the mozzarella has just started to weep. Serve immediately with a salad garnish. (They aren't very hot to begin with, and get cold quite quickly.)

'This is not so much a recipe, more an assembly job. It takes no talent, and hardly any time, but still tastes bloody good'

Salad with egg dressing was apparently a picnic favourite with the Royal Family in days of yore. Not so much of a picnic nowadays, being a Windsor. I've gone a step further and added bacon, the result being a pretty-as-a-picture, archetypally English salad that is a perfect way to start a summery meal. Oh, and it tastes all right, too. If you can't find Little Gem, use crisp-leafed cos or romaine; a soft, floppy lettuce won't do as the dressing is quite weighty and will bludgeon the leaves into sludge.

Both the dressing and the pancetta can be prepared up to 12 hours in advance, but don't finish the salad until moments before it's required.

Little Gem salad with egg and bacon dressing

TO SERVE 4

about 100g sliced pancetta, or thinly-cut, dry-cured bacon

3 large free-range eggs, hard-boiled

4 Little Gem lettuces, separated into leaves

FOR THE DRESSING

1 tbsp cider vinegar

1 level tsp smooth German mustard (or a little less Dijon)

$^1/_2$ rounded tsp natural cane sugar

1 large free-range egg yolk

4 tbsp double cream

a little bundle of chives, chopped

a dash of anchovy essence (optional)

Roughly chop the pancetta slices (or bacon). Put the pieces in a cold non-stick frying pan and dry-fry them over a medium heat until crispy. Sieve or finely chop the hard-boiled eggs. Leave to one side.

To make the dressing, whisk the vinegar, mustard, sugar and some salt and pepper in a mixing bowl. Add the egg yolk, and whisk for about 1 minute, until the mixture thickens. Pour in the cream and whisk for a further minute, or until the dressing is thick enough to coat the lettuce. Stir in the chopped chives and, if you like, a dash of anchovy essence. Taste, and adjust the seasoning.

Put the lettuce leaves in a large bowl, pour over the dressing and toss thoroughly until the leaves are well coated. Divide the leaves among the serving plates and scatter on first the chopped eggs, then the crispy bacon. Serve immediately.

Odd though it might seem, the combination of warm, seared smoked salmon with cool, lemony potato salad is a small triumph. The only snag is you'll need to buy a whole side of smoked salmon to get the chunky little escalopes this recipe requires. All I can suggest is that you buy a small side, and use half for this recipe, and the remainder, sliced normally, for other occasions.

The salad will happily sit around in the fridge for a day or so, as long as it's dressed when the potatoes are still hot, and brought to room temperature before serving. The salmon must be cooked to order.

Warm smoked salmon escalopes with potato and sorrel salad

TO SERVE 6

about 600g small, waxy potatoes (eg Jersey Royal, Maris Bard), peeled

a handful of sorrel leaves, finely sliced (or a mixed handful of dill, tarragon, parsley and chives, chopped)

1 small side of Irish or Scottish oak-smoked salmon

a few sprigs of watercress, trimmed

FOR THE MAYONNAISE

1 large free-range egg yolk (or I whole egg if using a liquidiser)

1 level tsp smooth German or Dijon mustard

about 175ml groundnut oil

1 tbsp white wine (or cider) vinegar

about 2 tbsp warm water

YOU WILL NEED

a large griddle pan or large heavy frying pan (preferably not non-stick)

Make sure all the ingredients for the mayonnaise are at room temperature.

You can make the mayonnaise by hand with a mixing bowl and whisk, or in a liquidiser.

Whisk the egg yolk and mustard together, then start adding the oil extremely slowly, whisking constantly. Start with a very fine thread, then gradually increase to a thin stream as the mayonnaise starts to thicken. When the egg has taken up about half the oil, add a little vinegar. Continue pouring in the oil very carefully, making sure it is all incorporated before adding more, then add the rest of the vinegar, and season. The mayonnaise should be a mound of glossy, stiff peaks; to coat the potatoes you will need a thick, pouring consistency, so stir in about 2 tablespoons of warm water. Leave to one side.

Cook the potatoes in simmering, salted water until just tender. Drain, and cut them into large-bite-sized chunks. While they are still hot, toss them gently in the mayonnaise. Just before serving the salad, fold in the sorrel (or the chopped herbs) and adjust the seasoning.

Depending on your appetite and the size of the fish, you will need to allow 2 or 3 escalopes of smoked salmon per person. Cut skin-free slices about 1cm thick on a steep diagonal across the width of the salmon. Put the griddle pan over a high heat and when it is extremely hot, place the escalopes in side by side – you might need to cook them in 2 batches. Cook the salmon for no more than 20-30 seconds, then turn and cook for another 20-30 seconds.

Arrange the escalopes on the serving plates, with a spoonful or two of potato salad and a sprig of watercress. Serve immediately.

Order seafood salad in most Italian restaurants in this country, and you're almost guaranteed to end up gazing mournfully at a heap of tough squid, listless prawns and over-cooked mussels, all slumped in a pool of cheap oil. Make seafood salad at home and it's a different story – but you must buy uncooked mussels and squid, and whole, shell-on prawns, or you might as well go out to the nearest ristorante and order an insalata di mare instead. And end up looking at a pile of tough squid, listless prawns...

The salad is delectable served just as it is, but I think it's even better piled on top of toasted, oil-brushed ciabatta, or pugliese bread.

Although seafood salad is a bit of a fiddle to make, all the work can be done well ahead of time, and the salad will keep well in the fridge for a day or two. Bring it to (cool) room temperature before you serve it, and add the chopped fresh herbs at the last moment.

Seafood and chickpea salad crostini

TO SERVE 8

3 red peppers (or the equivalent good-quality tinned Spanish peppers)

350g shell-on Greenland (North Atlantic) prawns (defrosted, if frozen)

about 350g small-to-medium squid, cleaned and trimmed

2 shallots, peeled and finely chopped

2 cloves of garlic, peeled, crushed and finely chopped

150ml dry white wine

about 1.5kg mussels, cleaned

about 175g cooked cockles, fresh or defrosted if frozen (but not in brine)

1 (424g) tin chickpeas, rinsed and drained

1 mild green chilli, deseeded and finely chopped

a large handful of fresh basil leaves, finely torn

a large handful of flat-leaf parsley leaves, roughly chopped

Preheat the grill to prepare the peppers.

Lay the peppers on the baking sheet and slide it under the grill, fairly close to the elements. Grill the peppers until the skins are completely black, turning them every few minutes with a pair of tongs. Transfer them to a thick plastic bag, seal it, and leave to one side for about 15 minutes: the skins will now peel off like a dream. Finally, deseed the peppers, slice the roasted flesh into strips about 1cm thick, and leave to one side.

Peel the prawns and put the meat in the fridge.

Cut the cleaned squid sacs into 1cm thick rings if the squid is small and fine, or 1cm x 6cm strips if the sacs are a bit larger. Chop any over-long tentacles into bite-sized pieces.

Put the shallots, garlic and wine in a large saucepan over a high heat. Bring to the boil, then immediately toss in the mussels. Cover the pan, and cook the mussels for 4-5 minutes or until they have opened, shaking the pan occasionally. Remove the saucepan from the heat, take off the lid and let the mussels cool. Pick out the meat, discarding any closed mussels, and put it in the fridge. Reserve the saucepan and the mussel juices.

Bring these juices to a gentle simmer, and toss in the squid. Cook, uncovered, for 1 minute or until the flesh has turned opaque. Do not cook any longer or it will toughen. Remove and cool the squid, then put it in the fridge with the mussels and prawns.

FOR THE DRESSING
the grated, or finely
chopped zest of 1 lemon
about 1 tbsp lemon juice
6 tbsp extra-virgin olive oil

YOU WILL NEED
a heavy baking sheet;
a small piece of muslin,
or a very fine sieve

Strain all the cooking juices through a piece of muslin or fine sieve into a small saucepan. Bring to the boil. Boil hard, uncovered, until the shellfish stock is reduced to about 4 tablespoons. Remove the saucepan from the heat and leave the stock to cool before putting it in a small bowl in the fridge.

To make the dressing, whisk the lemon zest and juice with salt and pepper, then whisk in the olive oil to make a thick emulsion. Now whisk in the reduced shellfish stock, and taste. Add a little more oil or lemon juice if necessary.

To assemble the salad, mix the prawns, mussels, squid and cockles (and any extra juices) with the red peppers, chickpeas, chilli and dressing. Season with salt and pepper to taste. Just before serving, add the basil and parsley, and toss the salad again.

Summery main courses

The way I look at it, you can't have too much fish and shellfish, especially in summer, when our native lobsters are at their most succulent, and there's a faint chance that the salmon will be as wild and sinuous as Ricky Martin. Served with stiff, glossy, home-made mayonnaise, there's no better lunch than a fish or shellfish salad. But by the end of the summer, the delights of even properly cooked cold salmon can pall. It's then that you might like to consider one of these slightly more adventurous recipes.

I freely admit that this Indonesian salad has a daunting array of ingredients. But, believe me, the combination of just-crisp vegetables and deeply savoury peanut butter sauce (happily called 'bumbu') is really good. And, on the plus side, there's no skill involved, just patience.

Don't worry about being too exact with the various quantities of vegetables – it's not as if you're constructing the London Eye. Equally, palm sugar is desirable, but not absolutely vital. Nor is shrimp paste, which is Indonesia's answer to anchovy essence, and can be found in most Asian shops.

No salad really likes hanging around, but you can prepare the vegetables a few hours ahead. The peanut sauce will keep for up to a week, refrigerated (and any surplus is terrific served with grilled chicken or barbecued pork). As the sauce firms up considerably when it's cold, you may need to whisk in a little warm water to restore a thick, pouring consistency.

Gado-gado salad with peanut sauce

TO SERVE 4

FOR THE PEANUT SAUCE
2 tbsp groundnut oil

2 cloves of garlic, peeled, crushed and finely chopped

1 shallot, peeled and finely chopped

2 bird's eye (or hot) red chillies, deseeded and finely chopped

1 large-thumb-sized knob of root ginger, peeled and grated

2 as-they-come tbsp palm sugar (or light muscovado)

1 tbsp dark soy sauce

1 tbsp fresh lime juice

1 tsp shrimp paste (optional)

1 (400ml) tin coconut milk

1 (340g) jar organic crunchy peanut butter

To make the sauce, heat the vegetable oil in a medium-sized saucepan or frying pan over a medium heat. Tip in the garlic, shallot and chillies, and fry for 5-6 minutes, stirring occasionally, until lightly coloured. Stir in the ginger, sugar, soy sauce, lime juice, shrimp paste (if using), and a little salt. Bring the contents to the boil, whisking. Remove the pan from the heat and whisk in the coconut milk and peanut butter thoroughly.

Return the pan to the heat, bring the sauce to the boil and simmer for 1 minute, stirring constantly. Remove from the heat and allow to cool, stirring occasionally to incorporate any oil which breaks out.

Fill the saucepan with water, add some salt, and bring to a rolling boil. Blanch the vegetables (which means lightly cooking them in boiling water) and refresh the vegetables (which means cooling them rapidly in ice-cold water), in the following order: carrots – 3 minutes; French beans – 2 minutes; cabbage – 2 minutes; beansprouts – 1 minute. Use a slotted spoon, or Chinese spider, to scoop them in and out of the water. When they are cool, drain the vegetables thoroughly: they should be neither flabby nor raw, just tender.

'The combination of deeply savoury peanut butter sauce (happily, called 'bumbu') and just-tender vegetables is really good'

FOR THE SALAD

2 large carrots, peeled and cut into thin batons

about 170g fine French beans, topped and tailed, and halved

1/4 white cabbage (about 200g), core discarded, the leaves finely shredded

about 150g beansprouts

about 300g cooked, peeled, waxy potatoes (eg Maris Bard, Charlotte), cut into thick slices

3 large tomatoes, quartered and deseeded

3 large free-range eggs, hard-boiled, peeled and quartered

1/4 cucumber, deseeded and cut into batons

2 spring onions, trimmed and finely sliced

a small handful of fresh coriander leaves, chopped

about 8 fresh mint leaves, roughly chopped

1 (100g) packet prawn crackers

YOU WILL NEED

a very large saucepan

To serve the salad, pile the carrot, French beans, cabbage and beansprouts in the middle of a large flat platter, arrange the potatoes, tomatoes and eggs around the edges, then scatter the cucumber, spring onions, coriander and mint over the top.

Adjust the consistency of the peanut sauce. Pour it over the salad or, if you prefer – as I do – give everyone their own little bowl of sauce, to use as liberally or sparingly as they wish. Similarly, you can scatter the prawn crackers over the salad, but I prefer to serve them in a separate bowl, too.

Le grand aïoli is a Provençal recipe which shares its name, confusingly, with the garlicky mayonnaise called aïoli that's a feature of the same dish. Traditionally, le grand aïoli includes salt cod, chickpeas and snails. Now I adore salt cod, but it's difficult to obtain unless you happen to live near a Portuguese deli (although sometimes a good French or Italian deli will sell it, too), and the quality can be very iffy. Salt cod is also a bit of a palaver to prepare, so I've substituted Madagascan prawns (crevettes), but you could use a few thick fillets of poached fresh cod, if you prefer.

Other ingredients you might like to include are cauliflower, celery, tomatoes or mushrooms, which will make the aïoli more grand than petit. And as long as the food police aren't on patrol, there's nothing to stop you using any cooked fish, vegetables or chicken that would taste good dipped into the powerful mayonnaise. Le petit aïoli isn't something you'd want to hike around the countryside for a picnic but it makes a truly splendid and highly convivial al fresco lunch, albeit a very messy one.

The aïoli can be prepared 24 hours ahead, and kept in a cool place. The vegetables can all be prepared ahead, too, but should not be cooked until they are needed, as an aïoli should be a combination of warm and cold ingredients.

Le petit aïoli

TO SERVE 6
FOR THE AÏOLI
(garlic mayonnaise)
5 large cloves of garlic, peeled and crushed
3 large free-range egg yolks (or 2 whole eggs and 1 egg yolk, if using a liquidiser)
about 300ml groundnut oil
about 125ml light, extra-virgin olive oil
the juice of half a lemon
1-2 tbsp lukewarm water

Before you make the aïoli (mayonnaise), make sure all the ingredients are at room temperature. Although it's traditional to make the mayonnaise in a pestle and mortar, you can use a liquidiser. It's also traditional to wield the pestle the whole way through the process, but I find it easier to use a small sturdy whisk once the mayonnaise has started to thicken.

Put the crushed garlic cloves in the mortar, add a large pinch of coarse sea salt and pound with the pestle, until the garlic is almost a purée. Add the egg yolks and bash them around until they are blended with the garlic.

Mix the two oils in a jug, and dribble them very slowly into the mortar, pounding and stirring as you go. As the aïoli thickens, you can increase the dribble to a thin stream, but always make sure the oil has been thoroughly incorporated before adding more. When the aïoli stiffens up very dramatically, add a small squeeze of lemon juice and a touch of lukewarm water to bring it back to a very thick, glossy emulsion, rather than an almost solid, sticky mass. Once all the oil has been incorporated, taste the aïoli, adding a jot more salt, lemon juice or water, as necessary; the flavour should be powerful, but nutty and well-rounded, not brutish.

'As long as the food police aren't on patrol, there's nothing to stop you using any cooked fish, vegetables or chicken that would taste good dipped into a powerful mayonnaise'

FOR THE SALAD

6 globe artichokes

about 1kg small, waxy potatoes (eg Jersey Royal, Maris Bard, Charlotte), peeled or scraped

about 400g organic carrots, top, tailed and peeled

about 200g fine French beans, topped and tailed

24 large cooked Madagascan prawns or crevettes

1 fennel bulb, trimmed, the outer leaves discarded, and cut into sixths

6 large free-range eggs, hard-boiled and peeled

about 100g Kalamata (or other black) olives

YOU WILL NEED

a large mortar and pestle; a very large saucepan

To prepare the artichokes, first slice off the top third of the leaves, then cut off the stems. Cook the artichokes in a large saucepan of boiling salted water, uncovered, for about 30 minutes. To test if they are cooked, scoop an artichoke out of the water with a slotted spoon or spider, and pull at a bottom leaf: if it comes away cleanly, the artichokes are ready. Remove the artichokes from the pan and leave them to drain thoroughly, upside down, then keep them warm.

In the meantime, cook the potatoes, carrots and French beans. I always cook them in the same saucepan as the artichokes, starting with the potatoes, then the carrots and, finally, tossing in the French beans after I've removed the artichokes. Whether you cook the veg in separate saucepans of salted boiling water, or like this, the secret is to time them to be ready at the same time – by 'ready', I mean neither floppy, nor crisp, but tender.

To assemble the petit aïoli, arrange all the ingredients attractively on a large colourful platter – the warm, cooked artichokes, potatoes, carrots and French beans, and the crevettes, fennel, cold hard-boiled eggs and black olives. Serve the mayonnaise straight from the mortar, or in a bright, pottery bowl. The idea is that everyone helps themselves, dipping and dunking into the aïoli. A basket of crusty baguette would not go amiss, nor would a bowl for the debris.

It's sad that we're so bludgeoned by food fashions in this country. Sad, because there's a danger that when the next fad comes along, something good will get ditched because it's deemed old hat. Well, Mexicans have never tired of the spiky, fresh, spirited dressing-cum-sauce they call salsa – and I hope we don't either. As an accompaniment to a piece of densely-fleshed salmon, salsa makes total sense, cutting through the richness with aplomb. It also contrasts very successfully with the creamy champagne sauce (which can be made with dry white wine if you're feeling hard-up).

I much prefer salmon escalopes to salmon steaks. The difference is that a steak, cut straight through the fish, is difficult to cook accurately as it is composed of a very thick section and a very thin section (plus some unfriendly bones). For an escalope, the fish is split lengthways into two sides (like smoked salmon), skinned and boned, then cut across widthways into evenly sized pieces. One side of a whole 3-$3^{1}/_{2}$kg salmon should realise six good-sized escalopes.

Don't let the apparent complexity of this rather smart recipe deter you; much of the work can be done in advance – and I promise the result is really worth the effort. The salsa ingredients can be prepared up to 4 hours ahead, but should only be assembled at the last minute; the champagne sauce can be prepared to the point where the cream is added, then left in the fridge overnight; and the salmon only takes 10 minutes to cook. If you haven't got any fish stock, make up the equivalent amount with a level tablespoon of Marigold Swiss vegetable bouillon powder.

Escalope of salmon with champagne sauce and tomato, ginger and basil salsa

TO SERVE 6

FOR THE SALMON
100ml cold water
100ml dry white wine
6 thick escalopes salmon
30g unsalted butter

FOR THE SALSA
4 good-sized tomatoes, deseeded and chopped into medium dice
1 shallot, peeled and finely chopped
a thumb-sized knob of root ginger, peeled and grated
1 tbsp rice vinegar (or a little less fresh lime juice)
1 tbsp caster sugar
2 tbsp Thai fish sauce
about 12 fresh basil leaves, finely torn or shredded

FOR THE CHAMPAGNE SAUCE
about 550ml fish stock
150ml champagne (or dry white wine)
8 large fresh basil leaves, plus about 12 more, finely torn
425ml whipping cream

YOU WILL NEED
a large roasting tin, lightly buttered

Preheat the oven to 180°C (fan), 200°C (conventional), gas mark 6.

Mix all the ingredients for the salsa in a bowl, except the basil which should be added just before the salsa is served. Leave to one side.

To make the sauce, pour the fish stock and champagne into a medium-sized saucepan and place it over a high heat, uncovered. When the liquid reaches the boil, throw in the whole basil leaves, and boil rapidly for 15-20 minutes until the liquid has reduced to about 5 tablespoons. Remove the pan from the heat, discard the basil leaves, and whisk in the cream. Put the pan back on a high heat, bring the contents back to the boil and continue boiling for 3-4 minutes until the sauce has thickened a little and is the consistency of... well, sauce. Season and stir in the torn basil leaves. Keep the sauce warm while you cook the salmon.

Pour the water and wine into the roasting tin, and put in the escalopes, side by side. Dot them with butter, and season. Cover the tin tightly with foil, and bake the salmon for 8-10 minutes, or until the flesh has turned from a translucent deep pink to an opaque pale pink. (Please don't cook the escalopes any longer or they will be mealy and dry – like the salmon at most weddings.) Remove the escalopes with a fish slice and drain them on a pad of kitchen paper.

To serve, spoon some sauce on to each warmed serving plate, then gently place a salmon escalope on top. Finally, using a slotted spoon, put a tablespoon or so of the tomato salsa on top, deliberately letting some of it fall off into the sauce. Serve immediately.

There is endless debate about the kindest way to kill lobsters (and, whichever way you look at it, that means boiling them alive, or stabbing them with a knife), but from my own experience I am certain that plunging the creatures straight into rapidly boiling, heavily salted water is the quickest method. Fortunately for me, I can't say whether it's also the most painless.

I've tried the alternative method of putting the lobsters into cold or tepid water, and bringing them gently to the boil (a procedure that is supposed to render them unconscious before they quietly pop their clogs), but they really didn't seem to like it. Of course, faint hearts will pretend lobsters emerge prone and pink from the sea. However you choose to square your conscience, it's an inescapable fact that a lobster is the most divinely perfect, fantastically gorgeous, quintessentially marvellous crustacean in the world.

Bathetic though it may sound, a good chip is equally God-given, but choosing the right potatoes is as difficult as finding the right mascara. (That's one for the girls.) The Belgians are perfectionists in this matter – potatoes, not mascara – and swear by Bintje. You could use Desirée or Maris Peer if you prefer waxy-textured chips, but for the traditional, fat, slightly floury British chips, I'd recommend Maris Piper. One thing's for sure, the best chips do not come out of a freezer bag or a microwave, whatever Iceland – that's the supermarket not the country – says.

The blessed unguent which binds lobster and chips in blissful union is, of course, mayonnaise. Dip a pearly-white chunk of sweetly saline, spanking-fresh lobster into a bowl of glistening, home-made mayonnaise, and it's perfection. Do the same with a hot, crisp, tender chip, and it's perfection. Dip the lobster alternately with the chips... and heaven is at your lips, and fingertips.

The mayonnaise can be made 24 hours ahead and kept cool, the chips can be prepared and part-cooked (blanched) up to 12 hours ahead, and the lobsters can be cooked a few hours ahead.

Cold lobster with tarragon mayonnaise and chips

TO SERVE 2

FOR THE MAYONNAISE

2 large free-range egg yolks (or 1 whole egg and 1 egg yolk, if using a liquidiser)

1 rounded tsp smooth German or Dijon mustard

250ml groundnut oil

50ml light extra-virgin olive oil

1-2 tbsp lemon juice

about 1 tbsp warm water

1 tsp Pernod (or Ricard)

about 1 tbsp chopped fresh tarragon

Preheat the oil in the deep-fat fryer to 150°C initially, for the chips, then raise it to 180°C; place the wok or saucepan over a low-to-moderate heat first, then raise the temperature to moderate-to-high.

Before you make the mayonnaise, make sure all the ingredients are at room temperature.

You can either make the mayonnaise by hand with a mixing bowl and a whisk, or in a liquidiser. Mix the oils in a good pouring jug. Whisk the egg yolks and mustard together, then start adding the oil extremely slowly, whisking constantly. Start with a very fine thread at first, then gradually increase to a thin stream as the mayonnaise starts to thicken. When the eggs have taken up about half the oil, add a tablespoon of lemon juice. Continue trickling in the oil very carefully, making sure it is all incorporated before more is added,

'A lobster is the most divinely perfect, fantastically gorgeous, quintessentially marvellous crustacean in the world. And a good chip is equally God-given'

FOR THE LOBSTER AND CHIPS
2 live native lobsters, about 650g each

600g potatoes, peeled and cut into 1cm-thick chips

YOU WILL NEED
a huge saucepan, with lid; a deep-fat fryer, or a wok or large saucepan half-filled with groundnut oil

until the mayonnaise is a glossy, thick, sticky emulsion. Whisk in the warm water, then taste the mayonnaise, adding a little salt, and a jot more lemon juice, as necessary. Finally, stir in the Pernod and tarragon. Leave the mayonnaise in a cool place.

Boil a huge saucepan of water, throw in four big handfuls of sea salt, then plunge in the live lobsters, holding them around their midriffs. They won't like it, but clamp the lid on and within seconds they'll be quiet (dead). Bring the water back to the boil, and cook for 15-20 minutes. Remove the lobsters, run them under cold water for 5 minutes and then leave them in a cool place. Cut the lobsters in half down their backs, using a heavy knife. Remove the grey matter, and the long black thread that runs down the body meat. Tear off the claws and crack them open with a mallet. Keep the lobsters very cool but preferably not in the fridge, unless it's a very hot day and they're not going to be eaten for a while.

Soak the chips in cold water for 15-30 minutes, so that some of the starch leaches out. Drain, and pat them completely dry using clean tea towels. Fry the chips for about 6 minutes, or until they are very lightly coloured and tender to the point of a small knife. Drain them. The chips can now be held for anything up to 12 hours, but carry straight on if you want to eat them immediately.

Turn the heat up to 180°C, put the chips back in the oil and fry for 1 minute, or until they are crisp and golden. Drain the chips thoroughly, sprinkle them lightly with salt, and serve immediately with the lobster and mayonnaise.

Among the shellfish cognoscenti there is a tacit agreement that a spanking fresh crab is every bit as good, maybe even better, than lobster. But, unlike lobster, crab contains two singularly different meats. I've always loved the tender, sweet white flakes of claw meat, but the cloying, intense, slightly bitter-flavoured dark crab meat is a completely different game of crustacea. I like it but it's not to everyone's taste. What bugs me is the apparent conspiracy among catering establishments to pretend there is no such distinction: order a fresh crab sandwich in most seaside cafés and it will look as if it's made from Shippam's paste, such is the paucity of white meat.

For this recipe, you'll almost certainly have to pre-order the crab meat from a (good) fishmonger, and it will be undeniably expensive. But probably not as ruinous as the Saturday when my fish delivery didn't turn up; my husband drove all the way from Suffolk to Harvey Nicks Fifth Floor to buy me white crab because I had a precise (insanely, stupidly precise) menu planned for a dinner party that night.

To prevent ending up hot and greasy, I suggest you fry the crab cakes up to 8 hours in advance – to seal and set the crust – then refrigerate them. Then, all you have to do is finish the crab cakes off in the oven just before serving them.

Crab cakes with coconut and tamarind

TO SERVE 4
500g fresh white crab meat
15g desiccated coconut
the thick top layer of coconut milk from an unshaken (400ml) can
a thumb-sized knob of root ginger, peeled and grated
1 tbsp Thai fish sauce
1 tbsp Sharwood's oyster sauce
the grated zest of half a lemon
3 cloves of garlic, peeled, crushed and finely chopped
2 medium eggs, beaten
50-100g fresh, fine, white breadcrumbs
a few dressed salad leaves

FOR THE SAUCE
about half a (320g) bottle Sharwood's plum sauce
1-2 tbsp tamarind juice

YOU WILL NEED
a deep fat fryer or a large wok or saucepan, half-filled with groundnut oil; a baking tray

Preheat the oil in the deep-fat fryer to 180°C; place the wok or saucepan over a moderate heat. Preheat the oven to 160°C (fan), 180°C (conventional), gas mark 4, to cook the crab cakes.

Mix all the ingredients for the crab cakes into a thick wodge, using 50g of breadcrumbs. Add more breadcrumbs only if necessary, and if the mixture is too dry, add a spot more beaten egg.

With clean, wettish hands (keep rinsing them), form the crab mixture into four round, thick patties, and coat them very lightly with the remaining breadcrumbs.

Deep-fry the crab cakes for about 3 minutes, or until they are golden brown, turning them once. Remove the cakes and drain them on a pad of kitchen paper. Stop here, and first cool, then refrigerate the crab cakes if you are serving them later. To finish the cooking, put the crab cakes on a baking sheet, and cook them in the oven for 8-15 minutes, depending on whether they were straight out of the fryer, or have come from the fridge.

Meanwhile, combine the plum sauce and tamarind, adding enough tamarind to give a pleasantly sour jolt to the sweetish sauce. Serve the crab cakes with salad leaves, and a spoonful or two of the sauce.

Here's a beautiful recipe that's as easy to prepare for one as for eight. The inclusion of salmon rather than tuna is not authentic, but *je ne regrette rien*: I think it tastes better and even the French can't agree on what constitutes a true salade Niçoise, anyway. What I would say is that this is a lot more interesting to eat than it sounds, and it looks stunning. (If you do want to feed more people, multiply the ingredients pro rata and, for four or more, change the teaspoons in the dressing recipe to tablespoons.)

There is not much you can do in advance, but the salad only takes about 30 minutes to make, so I don't think this can be classed as a chore. The most taxing part is timing the potatoes and beans so they're ready at the same time.

Warm salmon salade Niçoise

TO SERVE 2

about 250g small, waxy
potatoes, peeled
(eg Jersey Royal, Maris Bard)

55g fine French beans,
topped and tailed

2 large free-range eggs

about 250g salmon fillet,
boned and skinned

a little plain flour

a little olive oil

3 well-flavoured tomatoes,
deseeded and quartered

a dozen or so fresh basil
leaves, roughly torn

a small handful of
black olives, pitted

FOR THE DRESSING

a dab of smooth French
or German mustard

1 scant tbsp red wine vinegar

4 tbsp extra-virgin olive oil

YOU WILL NEED

a large heavy frying pan
(preferably not non-stick)

To make the dressing, whisk the mustard, vinegar and a little salt and pepper together, then whisk in the oil until it has formed a thick emulsion. Leave to one side.

Cook the potatoes and French beans, separately, in lightly salted boiling water, timing them to be ready simultaneously; the beans should be tender but still retain a little bite. Combine them in a mixing bowl with the dressing, toss well, and keep warm.

In the meantime, boil the eggs until the yolks are set, but still slightly creamy – 5-7 minutes depending on whether they started out at room temperature or not. Run the eggs under cold water for a couple of minutes, then peel and quarter them.

Place the frying pan over a very high heat, and leave it for a few minutes. In the meantime, cut the salmon into finger-sized pieces and very lightly oil them. When the frying pan is searingly hot, put in the salmon. If the fingers of salmon are thin (from the tail end), cook them for no more than 1 minute, turning them halfway through; if they are thicker, you might need to cook them on all four sides, rather than just two – it will take about 2 minutes in all. Remove the frying pan from the heat.

Divide the warm potatoes and beans between two Mediterranean-style bowls. Tuck in the tomatoes, then the eggs, and season with salt and pepper. Perch the fingers of salmon on top of the salad, and strew with the torn basil leaves and olives. Drizzle any remaining dressing over the salad, and serve immediately, with crusty bread.

You'll never eat a better lobster dish than this, although lobster thermidor does give it a run for its money. The recipe for the butter was given to me by a chef who had previously worked with us at Hintlesham Hall, as a fresh-faced lad straight out of college. Guy Bossom is now running the kitchens at the People's Palace at the Royal Festival Hall, so you could say he's made it. I don't know where this butter originates (apart from the obvious, the Café de Paris) but it's equally fantastic plastered over steak.

The list of ingredients looks hopelessly long, but it really doesn't take more than about 15 minutes to whizz the butter together, and it can be made days ahead and kept in the fridge - or even frozen for several weeks (and defrosted for about 15 minutes before being used). The lobsters, too, can be cooked a few hours ahead, split in half and cleaned up, ready for the final grilling.

Grilled lobster with Café de Paris butter

TO SERVE 6

6 live (or freshly cooked) native lobsters, about 650g each

4 handfuls of coarse sea salt

FOR THE BUTTER

2 (250g) packets unsalted butter, plus a scrap

3 shallots, peeled and finely chopped

1 clove of garlic, peeled, crushed and finely chopped

1 scant tbsp mild curry powder or paste

50ml dry white wine

4 large free-range egg yolks

4 anchovy fillets, roughly chopped

1 scant tbsp chopped gherkin

1 scant tbsp capers, chopped

1 small fresh bay leaf finely chopped

the leaves of a small sprig of fresh thyme

the leaves of a small sprig of fresh marjoram

1 tbsp chopped chervil (or dill)

1 tbsp chopped parsley

1 tbsp chopped tarragon

1 tbsp chopped chives

the juice of half a lemon

a few drops of Worcestershire sauce

a pinch of cayenne pepper

Preheat the grill just before serving the lobsters. Soften the butter a little before using it.

To make the Café de Paris butter, melt the scrap of butter in a small frying pan over a low-to-medium heat. Toss in the shallots and garlic, and cook them gently for 3-5 minutes until softened, stirring occasionally. Stir in the curry powder (or paste), and continue to cook for 1 minute. Turn up the heat and pour in the white wine, stirring thoroughly. Bubble energetically for 3-4 minutes, until the contents have reduced to a thick paste. Remove the pan from the heat immediately, and leave the shallot mixture to cool.

Put the 500g of butter in a food processor, then add all the other ingredients, including a good shake of fine sea salt. Whizz for as little time as it takes to mix them, then stop the machine and scrape down the sides of the bowl. Add the contents of the frying pan and whizz again, but using the pulse button: do not over-process the mixture as the butter should retain a little texture.

Scrape the butter on to the middle of a piece of clingfilm in a rough sausage shape, cover with the long sides of the clingfilm, then grasp the two short ends and twist them up tightly to form a neat package. Put the butter in the fridge, or freezer.

Boil a huge saucepan of water, throw in four big handfuls of sea salt, then plunge in the live lobsters, holding them around their midriffs. They won't like it, but clamp the lid on the pan and within seconds they'll be dead. Bring the water back to the boil, and cook for 15-20 minutes. Remove the lobsters, run them under cold water for 5 minutes and then leave them in a cool place. (Not the fridge, unless it's a very hot day and they're not going to be eaten for a while.)

'It's hard to believe that there are walking, talking, sentient people who don't like lobster, but apparently it's true. I shouldn't complain – it means there's all the more for me'

YOU WILL NEED
a meat mallet, or hammer

Using a very heavy large knife, split the lobsters down the back, remove the greyish matter in the head and discard it. Pick out and discard the long grey thread that runs down the length of the lobster. The red coral is perfectly edible, but if you prefer to remove that, do so. (It is very good pounded into a shellfish sauce.) Tear off, and crack open the claws, and fill all the spaces in the lobster shell with this gorgeous white meat. Arrange the lobster halves in a big grill pan, and leave in a cool place.

Unwrap the butter and cut it into half-centimetre slices. Cover the entire surface of the lobsters with the butter, then put them under the hot grill and cook for a few minutes, or until the butter is lightly gilded, puffed up, and hot. Serve immediately.

'The soft, creamy rice provides a wonderful textural contrast to the crisp, sticky prawns, as well as a feisty zip of flavour'

The Silver Palate Cookbook

by Julee Rosso and Sheila Lukins, published by Workman Publishing

This book was my first introduction to the vivid, all-embracing vigour of modern American cookery. Written by partners in a New York deli cum traiteur, it positively vibrates with enthusiasm, especially for good ingredients prepared simply. It was also one of the first cookbooks to break from the traditional bit-of-blurb-and-a-recipe layout; the margins are loaded with pertinent quotes, snippets about favourite ingredients and occasions, and advice on presentation. Because it was so ground-breaking, the Silver Palate Cookbook seems as fresh today as it did when it was published nearly 20 years ago.

Cookery writers can never stop themselves fiddling with other people's recipes. I don't think it's anything to do with arrogance, it's just that the words filter through one's brain, trickle down to the palate, and trigger off other ideas. This is a classic example: the original recipe for these griddled prawns comes from the *Silver Palate Cookbook*, but after years of both marinading and not marinading the prawns, I decided it didn't make a blind bit of difference to the final flavour, so why bother?

Having dispensed with the marinade, I then decided to team the prawns with this elegant citrus-flavoured risotto instead. Not only does it taste divine in its own right, but the soft, creamy rice provides a wonderful textural contrast to the crisp, sticky, ham-wrapped prawns, as well as a feisty zip of flavour.

The prawn skewers can be prepared up to 8 hours ahead, and kept in the fridge. The vegetables for the risotto can be prepared in advance, but the rice itself must be cooked to order.

Griddled prawns wrapped in basil and parma ham, with lemon risotto

TO SERVE 4
24 large raw tiger (or king) prawns, peeled
24 very large fresh basil leaves
8-12 slices parma ham (or thinly-sliced pancetta)

FOR THE RISOTTO
4 tsp Marigold Swiss vegetable bouillon powder
750ml boiling-hot water
about 50g unsalted butter
2 shallots, peeled and finely chopped
1 large clove of garlic, peeled, crushed and finely chopped
250g carnaroli (or arborio) rice
50ml dry white wine
finely grated zest and the juice of 1 large lemon
a small handful of fresh basil leaves, roughly torn

To prepare the skewers, wrap a basil leaf around the middle of each prawn, then just enough parma ham to cover the prawn in a single layer, with a small overlap. Thread three prawns on each skewer, through their length, butting each prawn gently up against the next one. Secure the edges of the ham as you thread them on, although it won't matter if they look a bit untidy. Put them in the fridge.

Whisk the Marigold powder and water together in a saucepan, and keep it gently simmering while you make the risotto.

Melt 30g of the butter in a medium-sized sauté pan, or wide, shallow saucepan, over a low-to-medium flame. Gently fry the shallots and garlic for about 5 minutes until slightly softened, but uncoloured. Tip in the rice and stir for about 1 minute until all the grains are glistening. Turn the heat up, pour in the wine, and let it bubble for about a minute, stirring occasionally.

Start adding the hot stock, a ladle or two at a time. Adjust the heat to keep the risotto at a simmer, adding just enough liquid to bathe the rice, not drown it, and stirring almost constantly. As the stock is absorbed add a little more. Continue with this routine for about 20 minutes, then stir in the lemon zest and half the lemon juice, and season with salt, and a generous amount of black pepper.

'And it's a good example of a recipe which I thought I'd invented, only to find it in other cookbooks later on'

YOU WILL NEED

eight 25cm long (about),
bamboo skewers, soaked for
an hour in cold water;
a large griddle pan
or large heavy frying pan
(preferably not non-stick),
lightly oiled

At this point, start testing the rice by biting into a grain. When they are cooked, the grains should be tender – neither gritty, nor soggy, and the risotto should have a wettish, porridgey look – not dry like a pilaf. (Carnaroli rice normally takes about 25-30 minutes to cook, and arborio about 20-25 minutes.) If you run out of stock before the rice has cooked, add a little hot water.

A few minutes before the risotto is ready, put the griddle pan on to a very high heat. When it is searingly hot, put in the skewers of prawns. Griddle them for 2-3 minutes, then turn, and cook for a further 2-3 minutes. When the skewers are ready, the ham should be caramelised and brown, and any visible prawn meat should be opaque.

When the risotto is cooked, remove the pan from the heat and adjust the flavourings, adding more lemon juice if necessary, and seasoning to taste. Stir in the remaining butter and the chopped basil.

Divide the risotto between four warmed serving plates and perch the skewers of prawns on top, 2 per person. Serve immediately.

Cioppino (pronounced cho-*peen*-o) sounds Italian but actually originates from Fisherman's Wharf in San Francisco; a key ingredient is the famous Dungeness crab. Obviously you won't be able to buy them here, but if you can't find crab of any description at all, substitute mussels or clams. Neither is it mandatory to use monkfish, although the solid, juicy texture is ideal for this dish: any firm white fish will do instead.

This is a meal for those who really like to get stuck in, pulling the crab apart with their hands, vigorously sucking out all the little flakes of meat, and painstakingly licking the juices off their fingers. It's slop-and-slurp food at its very best, and probably more appropriate to serve to good mates, rather than stuffy strangers.

Happily, the bulk of the work (which is making the broth) can be done up to 24 hours ahead. The fish can be cut up and prepared in advance as well, as long as it's very fresh. (I'm appalled that so many supermarkets only give you 24 hours to use their fish: it just goes to show how long it's been out of the water, because really fresh fish will still be good after several days in the fridge.) It will then take about 10 minutes to finish the cioppino.

Cioppino

TO SERVE 6

30ml olive oil

1 large onion, peeled and finely chopped

2 large carrots, peeled and finely chopped

3 cloves of garlic, peeled, crushed and finely chopped

1 red chilli, deseeded and finely chopped

5 large well-flavoured tomatoes

1 (200g) tin chair de tomate (or 2 tbsp tomato purée)

2 bushy sprigs fresh oregano

2 bushy sprigs fresh thyme

250ml light red wine (eg Beaujolais)

550ml boiling-hot water

2 whole, medium-sized, cooked crabs (*not* dressed)

about 600g fresh monkfish tail

12 large raw tiger prawns (shelled or unshelled)

a small handful of fresh basil leaves, chopped

a small handful of fresh flat-leaf parsley, chopped

YOU WILL NEED

a really large saucepan (5-6 litres); a meat mallet or hammer

Heat the oil in the saucepan over a low-to-medium heat. Put in the onions and carrots and fry them gently for 15 minutes, until soft and lightly coloured. Add the garlic and chilli, and fry for 3 minutes.

In the meantime, blanch the tomatoes and, when they're cool enough to handle, peel off and discard the skins. Cut the tomatoes in half, scoop out and discard the seeds, then chop the flesh into small dice.

Add the chopped tomatoes, chair de tomate, oregano, thyme, wine and water to the saucepan. Season, and bring to the boil. Put a lid on the pan, reduce the heat to very low, and simmer the broth gently for 45 minutes. (If preparing the cioppino in advance, this is the point you should stop: cool and refrigerate the broth until needed.)

Prepare the crab: break off the claws, wrench them in half, and crack them partly open. Chop the fine-shelled dome of white body meat inside the shell into quarters. (Don't use the brown meat for this recipe, and discard the feathery feet from the claws and the grey gills which surround the body.) Leave the crabs to one side.

Prepare the monkfish tail(s): cut down either side of the backbone to make two fillets and remove every scrap of the thin membrane which covers the flesh. Cut the fillets into large-bite-sized chunks.

Ten minutes before the broth is ready, spoon out about 500ml into another smaller saucepan. (If you're cooking the broth in advance,

'This is a meal for those who really like to get stuck in, pulling the crab apart with their hands, vigorously sucking out all the little flakes of meat, and painstakingly licking the juices off their fingers'

do this when you reheat it.) Place the saucepan over a low-to-medium heat, and when the broth is simmering gently, add the monkfish. Cover and cook for 3-5 minutes, until the chunks of fish are opaque. Remove the pan from the heat, and leave to one side, with the lid off.

Remove and discard the thyme and oregano stalks from the big saucepan of broth. Put in all the bits and pieces of crab (exactly as you've prepared it), and the raw prawns. Stir well, and simmer the broth for 3-5 minutes, covered, until the prawns have turned pink (if they've still got their shells on), or the flesh has turned opaque (if they're already peeled). Taste the broth with a clean spoon, and adjust the seasoning, adding a little more salt if necessary.

Stir in the chopped basil and parsley, then tip in the monkfish and the broth it was cooked in. Stir gently, being very careful not to break up the fish, and heat through for 1 minute. Serve immediately, dividing the fish, shellfish and broth between six warmed bowls.

Fresh scallops are so beautiful it's a shame to muck them around too much. The sweet, tender flesh only requires the barest cooking (in fact, they are wonderful raw) so any recipe which asks for them to be stewed for eternity should be eschewed. How many scallops you serve will depend on your pocket, but don't be tempted to buy the less expensive but pretty tame queen scallops – you'd be better off buying some spanking fresh, extremely cheap mackerel fillets instead.

You don't have to be Maigret to realise that sauce vierge is French, but super-sleuths reading the recipe will discern that it's actually more a dressing than a sauce. As such, it is extremely easy to make; more importantly, the vibrant, simple flavours go brilliantly with scallops.

I like letting the shallots and garlic mellow in the vinegar for 2-12 hours, but it is not absolutely essential: the tomatoes, basil and olive oil should be mixed in just before the dressing is needed. The pancetta can be cooked up to 12 hours ahead, and kept cool – but not in the fridge or it will toughen up.

Scallops with sauce vierge and crisp pancetta

TO SERVE 4

12-16 large scallops, cleaned and trimmed

a little plain flour

a little olive oil

50g thinly-cut pancetta, grilled or fried until crisp

FOR THE SAUCE VIERGE

1^1/$_2$ tbsp red wine vinegar

1 large shallot, peeled and finely chopped

2 cloves of garlic, peeled and finely chopped

150ml extra-virgin olive oil

4 medium-sized well-flavoured tomatoes, cored, deseeded and chopped into small dice

a handful of fresh basil leaves, roughly torn

YOU WILL NEED

a large heavy frying pan (preferably not non-stick)

To make the sauce vierge, pour the vinegar into a small bowl and stir in the chopped shallot and garlic. Marinate for 2-12 hours. Just before serving, whisk in the olive oil, then stir in the diced tomatoes and basil. Season with salt and pepper.

To cook the scallops, heat the frying pan over a very high heat until it is shimmeringly hot. Meanwhile, season the scallops with salt and pepper, dust them very lightly with flour, and then smear them equally lightly with a little olive oil. Now put the scallops into the frying pan, and sear for 2 minutes – without poking or fiddling with them. Turn the scallops over, and cook for another minute. (If you are using the corals, lightly oil and flour them as you did the white meat, but only cook them for about 1 minute on each side.)

Remove the golden-crusted scallops from the pan, and serve immediately, dribbled with the sauce vierge, and a wafer or two of crisp pancetta on top.

'You don't have to be Maigret to realise that sauce vierge is French, but super-sleuths reading the recipe will discern that it's actually more of a dressing than a sauce. As such, it's a doddle to make, but more importantly, the vibrant, simple flavours go brilliantly with scallops'

'The idea of flavoured butters is pretty old hat but, as I keep telling young chefs who think creativity is the be-all and end-all, old hat – as long as it tastes good – is not to be dismissed'

Lobster mayonnaise and bacon sandwiches are both Palaeolithic hat, but I'd rather eat them any day than pan-fried pink bream with date and parsnip purée.

I wish chefs would stop trying to reinvent the wheel, full stop. There are more than enough ideas and recipes out there already: if only they'd understand that originality in the kitchen is not as important as producing something that's lip-smackingly good to eat. There may well be an art to cooking but the result should be more than a pretentious still-life. The whole point – indeed, the entire reason – is that the food should be worth eating.

The trouble stems from a combination of youth, burgeoning manhood (most chefs are male), and the complete lack of social conditioning and cultural input that exists in most restaurant kitchens. And it's perpetuated by chefs who, although senior in years, are equally callow when it comes to social development. In consequence, there is little or no understanding that cooking is not about creative ego and technical competence, but about producing food that is deeply, viscerally pleasing to the diner.

After the diatribe, here's a jolly good chicken recipe which requires quite a bit of fannying about. But, the butter can be prepared up to a week ahead (or longer, if frozen), and the rest of the preparation can be completed up to 24 hours in advance. If you have a deep-fat fryer, you can fry the chicken to seal and brown the crust, then finish it off later in the oven; this has the advantage that you don't end up looking shiny and faintly hysterical. Otherwise, shallow fry the chicken to order in a large frying pan.

Pinenut-crusted chicken stuffed with basil butter

TO SERVE 4

4 free-range chicken breasts, skinned, but with the wing joint still attached

FOR THE BASIL BUTTER

a small handful of basil leaves, chopped

a few sprigs of flat-leaf parsley, chopped

2 tbsp pinenuts, toasted

2 tbsp finely grated parmesan

3 cloves of garlic, peeled, crushed and finely chopped

1 tbsp extra-virgin olive oil

125g unsalted butter, softened

FOR THE COATING

200g fresh, white, finely grated breadcrumbs

30g parmesan, finely grated

30g pinenuts, finely chopped

2 large free-range eggs, beaten

about 70g plain flour, seasoned

Preheat the deep-fat fryer and/or the oven, according to the cooking method you select – see below. You can cook the chicken in one of three ways: deep-fry at 160°C for 12-15 minutes until thoroughly cooked and golden brown; deep-fry at 190°C for 3-5 minutes to seal the crust, then bake in a preheated 160°C (fan), 180°C (conventional), gas mark 4 oven for 15-20 minutes; or, shallow-fry the chicken in a pre-heated frying pan over a medium heat in about 55g unsalted butter and 4 tablespoons olive oil for 15-20 minutes, turning once or twice.

For the basil butter, put all the ingredients except the butter into a food processor and whizz to a smooth paste. Add the softened butter and seasoning, and whizz for a few seconds to combine. Scrape the butter on to a piece of clingfilm, and twist it into a neat sausage-shaped packet. Refrigerate (or freeze) until firm.

Remove the little fillets from the underside of each chicken breast, and place them between two layers of clingfilm. Beat them out with a meat mallet or rolling pin, keeping the fillets the same length, but increasing the width – these will act as poultry Elastoplast later on. Leave to one side.

Make a pocket in each chicken breast: turn the breast smooth-side down, then cut a slit from top to bottom, but not quite to each end, nor through to the other side. Flatten the knife, and slide it down each side of the cut, as if you were filleting a fish, and again not piercing completely through.

YOU WILL NEED

a meat mallet, or rolling pin;
a deep-fat fryer, or a large wok
or saucepan half-filled with
groundnut oil

Divide the basil butter into four, and stuff each pocket. Place the beaten-out fillets on top of the cut, and bring the edges of the breast up to enclose the butter, and cover the fillet as much as possible. Smooth the flesh into the shape of a bulging cigar, then put the chicken in the fridge to chill thoroughly.

To coat the chicken, first combine the breadcrumbs, parmesan and pinenuts and spread them out in a large dish. Put the eggs in a shallow bowl, and the flour in another dish. Using one hand, lightly flour the chicken, then swoosh it through the egg, through the flour again, back through the egg, and finally roll it in the crumb mixture – that's flour, egg, flour, egg, breadcrumbs. Chill the coated chicken breasts for at least an hour, and up to 24 hours before cooking them.

Serve the chicken immediately, either with some plain noodles or boiled potatoes.

I freely confess that this is a hybrid recipe: salsa verde is a piquant, parsley-based dressing usually served with bollito misto – a gusty Italian dish of hot, poached meats – not these delicate egg and breadcrumbed chicken escalopes. But it works, the verdant, sprightly sauce giving a welcome edge to the richly-crusted meat. By using balsamic vinegar in the salsa verde I've committed another culinary outrage, but I like the slightly sweet, velvet note it gives. The downside is that the balsamic vinegar turns the dressing a rather forbidding colour; if it upsets you, omit it and use 2 tablespoons of the red wine vinegar instead.

The salsa verde can be made up to 24 hours ahead and kept in a cool place, preferably not the fridge. Prepare the escalopes up to 2 hours ahead and refrigerate them – the cooking time is only 4 minutes.

Chicken escalopes with salsa verde

TO SERVE 4

4 free-range chicken breasts, boned, skinned and trimmed

55g plain flour

2 large free-range eggs, well beaten

115g fresh, white, fine breadcrumbs

3 tbsp olive oil

30g unsalted butter

FOR THE SALSA VERDE

a large handful of flat-leaf parsley leaves, roughly chopped

6-10 fresh mint leaves, roughly chopped

1 large clove of garlic, peeled and finely chopped

1 rounded tbsp capers, rinsed and roughly chopped

2 large anchovy fillets, roughly chopped

1 tbsp balsamic vinegar

1 tbsp red wine vinegar

100ml robust extra-virgin olive oil

YOU WILL NEED

a pestle and mortar; a meat mallet or heavy rolling pin; a baking tray lined with clingfilm; a very large frying pan

Put all the ingredients for the salsa verde, except the oil, into a large mortar. Grind everything together with the pestle, then slowly add the oil, grinding all the time. The finished sauce should be a rough-textured emulsion – something like a sloppy pesto. Set to one side, in the mortar. If you haven't got a pestle and mortar, use a food processor; using the pulse button, mix everything roughly together, then slowly pour in the oil.

To prepare the escalopes, first detach the little fillets which lie under the breast. Then place both breast and fillets between two layers of clingfilm and beat the meat out to about 1/2cm thickness.

Season the flour generously with sea salt and black pepper, then put the flour, egg and breadcrumbs into 3 separate dishes or bowls. Flour each escalope, dip it into the beaten egg, and then the breadcrumbs, shaking off the excess each time. (If you want a thicker crust, repeat the last 2 coatings.) Put the finished escalopes on to the lined baking tray, and refrigerate for a minimum of 30 minutes, and up to 2 hours.

You will need to cook the escalopes in two batches: put the frying pan over a fairly high heat, and when it is hot add the oil and butter, swirling it around. When the foam subsides, place as many escalopes in the pan as will comfortably fit. Fry for about 3 minutes, then turn and fry for a further 3 minutes until the crust is golden-brown, and the chicken is cooked. Remove and drain the chicken on a pad of kitchen paper, and keep it warm while you carry on with the frying. (Add more oil and butter, if necessary, remembering to heat it well before putting in the chicken.)

Serve the escalopes as soon as possible, putting the salsa verde on the table so that everyone can help themselves to a spoonful or two. Something like spinach or ruby Swiss chard, and a rich potato gratin would make a good accompaniment.

A dish from my childhood, this is the epitome of old-fashioned, uncomplicated cooking. The pink, moist ham served with a jug of densely freckled parsley sauce, a mound of pistachio-green broad beans, and freshly-dug Jersey Royals is a triumphant testament to the toothsome simplicity of traditional British cooking, and makes a perfect, unpretentious summer lunch.

Prepare and cook the broad beans up to 24 hours in advance. Have all the root veg prepared and ready to cook with the gammon. This is not a recipe to hurry, but there's very little real work involved.

Hot gammon with parsley sauce and broad beans

TO SERVE 8

FOR THE GAMMON
about 1.8kg British prime middle-cut gammon
1 medium onion, peeled and quartered
1 medium carrot, peeled and quartered
1 small leek, roughly chopped
1 stick celery, roughly chopped
2 bay leaves, fresh or dried
12 black peppercorns
2 stalks of parsley (taken from the amount given below)

FOR THE PARSLEY SAUCE AND BROAD BEANS
55g butter
40g plain flour
568ml full cream milk
150ml gammon stock (taken from the cooking liquid)
150ml double cream
2 big handfuls of flat-leaf parsley, finely chopped
a few scrapings of fresh nutmeg
about 700g shelled weight broad beans (fresh, or frozen and defrosted), cooked and individually peeled

YOU WILL NEED
a very large saucepan, with lid; a piece of muslin, or a clean tea towel

Put the gammon in a large saucepan and cover it with cold water. Put the lid on the pan, and bring slowly to the boil, over a medium heat. Reduce the heat immediately, skim off any scum that rises to the top, then throw in all the other ingredients, and simmer very gently for about 80 minutes, with the pan half-covered. (The recommended time for cooking ham is 25 minutes per pound – in old money – but I think 20 minutes is nearer the mark, if you like moist ham.)

Remove the gammon from the stock (reserving 150ml of it for the sauce, and the rest for a lentil soup, if you like). Peel off and discard the skin, and leave the gammon to rest in a warm place for 15-20 minutes with a piece of stock-moistened muslin or a tea towel draped over it to stop the meat drying out.

To make the sauce, melt the butter in a medium-sized saucepan over a low-to-medium heat. Whisk in the flour, and cook this roux for a couple of minutes, then vigorously whisk in the milk and 150ml gammon stock, getting the whisk right into the corners of the saucepan. Bring the sauce to the boil, whisking almost constantly, and as soon as it has thickened, turn down the heat and gently simmer for about 15 minutes, whisking frequently.

Add the cream, chopped parsley, a lot of ground black pepper and a few scrapings of nutmeg. Cook for another 3-4 minutes, then taste and adjust the seasoning. If the sauce is too thick – it should be a rich, pouring consistency – add a little more stock.

If the beans need re-warming, toss them in a little melted butter in a large frying pan or saucepan, over a low-to-medium heat.

To serve, carve the gammon into thick slices, pile a mound of beans on each plate, and pour some parsley sauce over the top. Decant any remaining parsley sauce into a warmed jug to put on the table.

Summery puddings

Of all the chapters, this is the one that could have gone on for ever. I suppose it's partly because I only make puddings when I'm entertaining, and I do far more of that in the summer than in the winter. But it's also because the variety, beauty and exuberance of summer fruits is so inspiring, be it a punnet of sweet, aromatic English strawberries, a bag of fat, juicy, white cherries, or a bowl of those bruise-dark, Scottish raspberries served with a big jug of thick, yellow Jersey cream.

French toast, eggy bread, pain perdu, poor man's omelette, they're all the same thing: namely slices of thickly-cut, crustless white bread, soaked in a mixture of egg and milk, and then fried in sizzling butter until lightly gilded. One of my favourite brunch dishes is French toast piled high with razor-thin, crisp bacon and trickled with dark-amber maple syrup – utter and complete bliss.

French toast can be sweet as well as savoury. I dreamt up this recipe a few years ago, and the combination of aromatic eggy fritters and cool, zippy fruit salsa is stunning. Serve it on informal occasions when you don't mind carrying on a high-decibel conversation from the kitchen, because although the salsa can be made 1-2 hours ahead, the French toast must be fried to order.

Sweet French toast with peach, lime and mint salsa

TO SERVE 4

FOR THE SALSA
3 firm-but-ripe peaches (or nectarines)
1 small fresh lime
a few fresh mint leaves, roughly chopped
1 tbsp caster sugar, or to taste

FOR THE FRENCH TOAST
175ml full cream milk
1 large free-range egg, well beaten
2 tbsp caster sugar
1-2 tbsp amaretto liqueur
4 (1cm thick) slices good-quality white bread, crusts removed, halved
55g unsalted butter
a little caster sugar

YOU WILL NEED
a large non-stick frying pan

For the salsa, first peel the peaches. Put the fruits in a heat-resistant bowl and pour a kettle-full of boiling water over them. Leave for 1 minute, then drain and remove the skin as soon as the peaches are cool enough to handle. Quarter them and cut the flesh into small dice. Leave to one side in a mixing bowl.

Remove the peel and pith from the lime with a small knife. Cut out the segments, discarding the membrane. Chop the flesh into tiny dice, and add them to the peaches, squeezing in the juice from the debris. Stir in the mint and sugar. The salsa should be sparklingly fresh and tangy, but add a little more sugar if it is too tart. Leave the salsa to one side.

Whisk the milk, egg, sugar and amaretto together in a shallow dish. Soak the bread in the mixture for about 5 minutes, turning the slices once – the bread should be saturated but not hopelessly soggy.

Place a large non-stick frying pan over a fairly high heat. Put in the butter, and when the sizzling stops, slip in the soaked bread. Fry the slices for about 3 minutes, then turn and fry them for a further 2 minutes, or until the French toast is lightly patched with gold. (Reduce the heat if it's browning too quickly.)

Drain the French toast on a pad of kitchen paper, sprinkle with caster sugar, then serve immediately, with a small mound of salsa.

Of all the summer fruit tarts, apricot is the best. It's not as got-up and showy as strawberry tart, nor as wimpish as peach tart – simply a perfect marriage of looks, texture and taste.

I am talking about home-made tarts, of course, because whatever the filling they are invariably better than commercial ones. The reason is partly because factory-made pastry has to be like corrugated cardboard to stand up to the travelling, and partly because food manufacturers don't like spending money on things like ground almonds. Served with thick crème fraîche, this sun-drenched ambrosial apricot tart is better than kissing John Malkovich – and I should know. (I wish.)

The pastry case can be baked up to 48 hours ahead if you seal it, tin and all, in a foil packet. Don't assemble and finish the tart until a few hours before you serve it. The tart will keep in a cool place for up to 2 days, but the pastry gets soggier as the hours go by.

Apricot frangipane tart

TO SERVE 6-plus
200g caster sugar
300ml hot water
4 tbsp amaretto liqueur
about 1kg fresh firm-but-ripe apricots, halved and stoned
2-3 tbsp runny apricot jam

FOR THE PASTRY
225g plain flour
1 rounded tsp icing sugar
1 level tbsp caster sugar
a pinch of fine sea salt
140g cold unsalted butter, roughly cubed
1 large free-range egg yolk
3 tbsp ice-cold water

FOR THE FRANGIPANE
85g caster sugar
85g unsalted butter, softened
55g plain flour
140g ground almonds
2 large free-range eggs, beaten
1 tsp orange flower water
a few drops of almond essence/extract

Preheat the oven to 170°C (fan), 190°C (conventional), gas mark 5 for the pastry case; and 160°C (fan), 180°C (conventional), gas mark 4 to cook the tart.

First, make the pastry: whizz the flour, sugars and salt together for a few seconds in a processor, then add the butter and whizz again, until the mixture looks like coarse breadcrumbs. Whisk the egg yolk and water together and pour into the flour mixture. Process again until the pastry has collected in a ball around the spindle. Form the pastry into a thick disc, wrap in clingfilm and leave to rest in the fridge for a minimum of 30 minutes, and up to 2 days.

Take out the pastry and return it to (cool) room temperature, then roll it out thinly. Line the tin – making sure you don't stretch the pastry – then trim the edges. Return the pastry case to the fridge and chill for at least 30 minutes. Now line the pastry with foil and pour in ceramic baking (or dried) beans to weigh it down. Bake for 12-15 minutes in the preheated oven. Remove the foil and the beans, and continue to bake for another 5-6 minutes. The pastry should look dry, but blond rather than brown. Remove the tin and leave the pastry case to cool in it.

For the apricots, combine the sugar and water in a wide, shallow saucepan, and bring it to the boil over a high heat, stirring initially to dissolve the crystals. Pour in 3 tablespoons of amaretto, and reduce the heat so the syrup gently simmers. Tip in the apricots, cover the pan, and poach the fruit very gently for 3-4 minutes – longer if the apricots aren't very ripe – until they are tender but still holding their shape. A few collapsed halves is not a disaster. Remove the apricots from the syrup with a Chinese spider or slotted spoon, and leave them to cool. (Keep the syrup to use at a later date for a sorbet.)

'Served with thick crème fraîche, this sun-drenched ambrosial apricot tart is better than kissing John Malkovich – and I should know'

YOU WILL NEED

a 25cm diameter x 2.5cm deep, loose-bottomed tart tin, buttered; ceramic baking (or dried) beans

In the meantime, make the frangipane filling. Combine all the ingredients in a food processor and whizz until the mixture is thick and smooth.

To assemble the tart, smooth the frangipane over the bottom of the pastry case, then arrange the apricot halves concentrically, starting around the perimeter and working into the middle. Use any collapsed apricots to fill in gaps.

Bake the tart on the middle shelf of the oven for 40-45 minutes, or until the frangipane is golden. Just before the tart is ready, heat the remaining amaretto and the apricot jam in a small saucepan over a medium heat, and whisk it together. As soon as the tart comes out of the oven, brush this glaze over the apricots. Leave the tart to cool for 20-30 minutes before serving.

If I were Michael Howard I would have been quietly flattered by that 'something of the night' accusation. It certainly surprised those of us who'd had him sewn up as something of the gents' outfitters. Compared to other soft fruits you could say that blackcurrants have something of the night about them, too, with their inky juices and sultry aroma, but they do need a good culinary wooing before they give up any hint of their real glory.

In this combination of crisp chocolate pastry and creamy blackcurrant filling, I am not sure whether the knock-down-gorgeous Pucci purple or the taste is the more startling. However, even if you have to don your Raybans first, this tart is a sweet, sharp, voluptuous delight.

The pastry case can be baked up to 48 hours ahead if you seal it, tin and all, in a foil pouch. The blackcurrant purée can be made 2-3 days ahead, and kept refrigerated. Do the final assembly 3-8 hours before the tart is to be served.

Blackcurrant bavarois tart with chocolate pastry

TO SERVE 6-plus

FOR THE PASTRY
200g plain flour
30g cocoa powder
2 tbsp caster sugar
a pinch of fine sea salt
140g cold unsalted butter, roughly cubed
1 large free-range egg yolk
3 tbsp ice-cold water

FOR THE BAVAROIS
about 350g fresh blackcurrants (or frozen and defrosted)
225g caster sugar
3 leaves gelatine
3 tbsp cold water
2 tbsp boiling water
425ml double cream, whipped into soft peaks

OPTIONAL DECORATION
a few strings of fresh blackcurrants
the white of one medium egg, well beaten
a little caster sugar
a sprig of fresh mint

Preheat the oven to 170°C (fan), 190°C (conventional), gas mark 5 for the pastry case.

First, make the pastry: whizz the flour, cocoa powder, sugar and salt together for a few seconds in a food processor, then add the butter and whizz again, until the mixture looks like coarse breadcrumbs. Whisk the egg yolk and water together and pour into the flour mixture. Process again until the pastry has collected in a ball around the spindle. Form the pastry into a thick disc, wrap in clingfilm and leave to rest in the fridge for a minimum of 30 minutes, and up to 2 days.

Take out the pastry and return it to (cool) room temperature, then roll it out thinly. Line the tin – making sure you don't stretch the pastry – then trim the edges. Return the pastry case to the fridge and chill for at least 30 minutes. Now line the pastry with foil and pour in ceramic baking (or dried) beans to weigh it down. Bake for 12-15 minutes in the preheated oven. Remove the foil and the beans, and continue to bake for another 5-6 minutes, until the pastry looks dry. Remove the tin and leave the pastry case to cool in it.

To make the bavarois put a medium-sized saucepan over a low-to-medium heat. Throw in the blackcurrants and 170g of the sugar, and stew very gently for 3-5 minutes, or until the sugar and juice have combined to make a shiny syrup. Do not overcook the blackcurrants, or you'll find yourself staring bleakly at a saucepan of jam. Remove the saucepan from the heat, and leave the blackcurrants to cool.

'While strawberries flaunt themselves in an obvious, pick-me-up sort of way, blackcurrants need a good culinary wooing before they reveal the glory of their inky juices and sultry aroma'

YOU WILL NEED

a 23cm diameter x 4cm deep, loose-bottomed tart tin, buttered; ceramic baking (or dried) beans; a large stout conical or round metal sieve

Rest a stout metal sieve over a bowl, and push all the blackcurrant pulp and syrup through; you should end up with about 300ml of gloriously rich purée. Keep this to one side, and discard the blackcurrant debris left in the sieve. (Or if you're feeling very Mrs Thrifty, soak the debris in a bottle of white wine vinegar; a week, and a few shakes later, you'll have a free bottle of blackcurrant vinegar.)

Scissor the gelatine leaves into strips (watch out, it shatters) over a shallow bowl, then cover with 3 tablespoons of cold water. When the gelatine is gloopy (about 5 minutes), pour 2 tablespoons of boiling water over it. Whisk thoroughly, and when it is a completely lump-free, clear liquid, whisk it into the blackcurrant purée. Chill the bavarois mixture in the fridge for about 45 minutes.

Fold the remaining 55g of sugar into the whipped cream.

When the bavarois mixture looks the consistency of sloppy jelly fold it into the whipped cream carefully but thoroughly. Pile the mixture into the pastry case, and refrigerate the tart for about 2 hours, or until it has set.

For the optional decoration, dip the blackcurrant strings first into the beaten egg white and then into the sugar, making sure the currants are evenly and thinly covered. Leave the strings to dry on a wire rack. Do the same with the mint.

There's nothing more rapturous than the cakes at Harry's Bar in Venice. But what nobody tells you about Harry's Bar is that although it's on the Grand Canal you can barely see a thing out of the windows; that during most of the year it is completely full of Americans, who are nice people but not Venetian; that the tables are so tiny, so low and so close together, it's like eating in an over-crowded doll's house; and, that it is the most expensive restaurant in the entire world – well, I think 35 quid for a plate of carpaccio is pretty steep.

But at Harry's Dolce – across the canal on Guidecca – the cakes are just as fabulous, and as the restaurant is far more agreeable, that's where I suggest you go. It's completely impossible to choose between the lemon meringue cake, the chocolate cake, the coffee cake and the zabaglione cake, so I don't. I just skip lunch, and pig out on all of them for tea. There is actually a Harry's Bar cookbook, with a recipe for this cake, but oddly enough it contains sherry rather than the marsala used in a classic zabaglione. The recipe also suggests decorating the cake with meringues, which is fine if you've got a full-time pâtissière on the payroll. I'm happy with the simplicity of the fresh raspberries.

Because the sponge-cake is fat-free, it must be eaten while it's very fresh. If you do want to make the sponge ahead, it would be best to freeze it. The filling can be made 24 hours in advance and kept in the fridge; it will need a good stir, if not a whizz in a food processor, before use.

Zabaglione and raspberry cake

TO SERVE 8

4 large free-range eggs, separated

140g caster sugar

140g plain flour, sifted

FOR THE ZABAGLIONE PASTRY CREAM

3 large free-range egg yolks

115g caster sugar

3 tbsp plain flour

150ml marsala (or medium sherry)

150ml white wine

425ml double or whipping cream, whipped into peaks

about 250g fresh raspberries

a little icing sugar

YOU WILL NEED

a food processor with cake-making bowl and whisking attachment, or a food mixer; a 23cm diameter springform cake tin, lightly oiled and lined with baking parchment; a wire rack

Preheat the oven to 170°C (fan), 190°C (conventional), gas mark 5.

To make the cake, combine the 4 egg yolks and caster sugar, and beat them for several minutes in a food mixer, until the mixture is pale, thick and voluptuous-looking. Whisk the 4 egg whites into firm peaks that hold their shape. Using a metal spoon, fold a little of the whisked egg whites into the egg mixture, then fold in the remainder, trying to preserve as much air as possible. Just as deftly and lightly, fold the flour into the egg mixture, about a fifth at a time.

Pour the swollen, floppy mixture into the prepared cake tin and bake it on the middle shelf of the preheated oven for 10 minutes. Turn the oven down to 160°C (fan), 180°C (conventional), gas mark 4, and bake the cake for a further 15-20 minutes, until golden and firm to the touch. Take the cake out of the oven, and turn it out on to a wire rack to cool – but don't remove the baking parchment from the base for 30 minutes.

To make the pastry cream, beat the egg yolks and sugar just as you did for the cake. When they are thick and creamy, beat in the flour, marsala and white wine. Scrape the mixture into a medium-sized saucepan, and place it over a medium heat. Bring the contents to the boil, whisking vigorously. When the pastry cream thickens dramatically, and looks like condensed milk, reduce the heat and cook for a further 2 minutes, still whisking constantly. Remove the saucepan and plunge the base into ice-cold water. Keep whisking for a minute or two, then leave the pastry cream to cool thoroughly. When it is cold, fold in the whipped cream.

To assemble the cake, first slice it into three thin layers using a sharp bread knife. Place the first layer on a cake stand or flat plate, spread it evenly with half the zabaglione cream, then scatter on about half the raspberries. Place the second layer of cake on top and cover with the rest of the zabaglione cream and more raspberries. Put the third layer of cake on top, press down gently but firmly, and dust lightly with icing sugar. Decorate the cake with a few remaining raspberries and serve within 6-8 hours.

I freely admit to a slight obsession with meringue. It's partly because I always seem to have egg whites left over when I'm doing a big entertaining number, but mostly it's because meringue puddings look so frivolous, and everyone seems to love eating them. Whether it's huge puffs of swirly, crisp-but-sticky meringue served plainly with raspberries and Jersey cream, or a more complicated creation such as a pavlova or roulade, meringue is first on everyone's lips.

The title of this recipe sounds unbelievably naff, and might do serious damage to my credibility, but, image aside, this is a really gorgeous confection of meringue, whipped cream, rum, pineapple and coconut – so gorgeous that instead of serving it after an elegant dinner you might want to slather it over your naked body and invite Brad Pitt round for a midnight feast instead. (Or, Jennifer, if you prefer.)

The meringue can be made up to 8 hours ahead. Parts of the filling can also be pre-prepared, but should not be combined until the final assembly. The finished roulade will keep in a cool dry place for a few hours. If you store it in the fridge, it will be okay for up to 2 days, but the meringue will soften.

Piña colada roulade

TO SERVE 8-plus

FOR THE FILLING
half a ripe pineapple, peeled and cut into small cubes
3 tbsp dark rum
1 (284ml) carton whipping cream
25g natural caster sugar

FOR THE MERINGUE
30g desiccated coconut
2 tbsp white rum
275g natural caster sugar
1 heaped tsp cornflour
5 large free-range egg whites
1 tsp vinegar (preferably fruit or cider vinegar)

Preheat the oven to 130°C (fan), 150°C (conventional), gas mark 2.

For the filling, put the pineapple and rum in a bowl and leave to macerate for 2-6 hours, stirring occasionally. Whisk the cream and sugar into soft peaks that just hold their shape, and leave in the fridge.

Before you make the meringue, mix the coconut and white rum in a small bowl, and leave it to soak for about 30 minutes. Once the coconut has softened, tip it on to a pad of kitchen paper and pat off the excess liquid. Sieve the sugar and cornflour together and leave both to one side.

In a large, grease-free bowl, whisk the egg whites until they form stiff, satiny peaks: you should be able to turn the bowl upside down without any calamity. Whisk in the vinegar, then a large tablespoon of the sugar mixture. Lightly fold in the rest – about a fifth at a time – using a large metal serving spoon. The object is to retain as much air in the mixture as possible. Gently fold in the coconut.

'Meringue desserts look so frivolous and everyone seems to love eating them, whether it's a puff of crisp-but-sticky meringue filled with whipped cream, or a lavish fruit-laden pavlova'

YOU WILL NEED

a Swiss roll tin or a heavy 35cm x 25cm x 2.5cm baking tray, lightly oiled, and lined with baking parchment

With a palette knife, spread the meringue lightly and evenly over the lined tin, leaving about 1cm clearance round the edge for the meringue to expand. Slide the tin on to the middle shelf of the oven and cook for 20 minutes. Reduce the heat to 100°C (fan), 120°C (conventional), gas mark 1/2, and cook for a further 25-30 minutes, until the meringue is lightly coloured, puffed-up and firm. Remove the meringue from the oven, and leave in the tin to cool.

Cut off a piece of clingfilm several centimetres longer than the tin, and stretch it out on a clean work surface. Slide a knife around the edges of the tin to free any stuck-on bits. Carefully up-turn the meringue on to the centre of the clingfilm. Gently peel off the parchment – don't worry if any of the meringue collapses or breaks off, it's all recoverable.

To assemble the roulade, drain any remaining rum from the pineapple and whisk it into the cream, then gently fold in the pineapple. Spread this filling over the meringue, leaving a 3cm border at the best-looking short edge. Roll up the meringue, starting with the worst-looking short edge – many congratulations if both edges are beautiful. Tuck in the first roll as tightly as you can, using the clingfilm to help the process, and finish with the tail underneath. Pat the roulade to firm up any cracked bits then transfer it to a pretty serving dish.

Eton Mess is the glorious concoction invented at that eponymous college to celebrate King George III's birthday on the Glorious Fourth (of June). But there seems to be some confusion about what constitutes an authentic Mess. According to some authorities, Eton Mess is a confection of plain ice-cream, strawberries, strawberry jam and whipped cream. Nowadays it more usually comprises crushed strawberries and meringues, bound together with whipped cream. Well, here's another scrumptious version – or travesty, depending on your alma mater.

The Mess also provides a golden opportunity to cheat. Buy in a 500g tub of ready-made fresh custard, and a packet of good-quality (M&S) meringues, and the pudding will take minutes. Home-made meringues will keep in an airtight tin for a few days, and the custard can be made 48 hours ahead and refrigerated. The Mess takes no time to assemble, but it will keep in the fridge for a few hours.

Raspberry mess

TO SERVE 6
1 (250g) tub mascarpone
about 600g fresh raspberries
about 350g crème fraîche

FOR THE MERINGUES
3 large free-range egg whites
175g caster sugar

FOR THE CUSTARD
425ml full cream milk
1 vanilla pod, split lengthways
(or a few drops of vanilla
essence/extract)
6 large free-range egg yolks
115g caster sugar
1 level tbsp cornflour

YOU WILL NEED
a large, heavy baking sheet
lined with baking parchment;
6 (350ml) wineglasses, or
similar capacity glass dishes

If you are going to make the cheat's version, all you need do is mix the custard with the mascarpone, then layer the ingredients in each glass in the following order, bearing in mind that the tablespoon measurements do not need to be super accurate:

1 50g raspberries
2 3 tbsp custard and mascarpone mixture
3 crumbled meringue
4 1 tbsp crème fraîche
5 50g more raspberries
6 2 tbsp custard and mascarpone mixture
7 crumbled meringue
8 1 tbsp crème fraîche
9 a few raspberries for decoration

If you are going to make the labour-of-love version, preheat the oven to 100°C (fan), 120°C (conventional), gas mark ½ for the meringues.

First make the custard: heat the milk and vanilla pod in a saucepan until just below simmering point. In the meantime, whizz the egg yolks, sugar and cornflour together in a food processor (or with an electric hand whisk) until the mixture is thick and creamy. Take the milk off the heat and allow it to infuse for 15-20 minutes. Remove the vanilla pod, then pour the milk on to the egg yolk mixture and pulse for just long enough to blend – the custard should not be too aerated and bubbly.

Quickly, but thoroughly, rinse out the milk pan, and pour the custard mixture back in. Return the saucepan to a medium-to-high heat and bring the contents to the boil, whisking almost continuously. Still whisking, reduce the heat and simmer the thickened custard for 1 minute. Remove the pan from the heat and plunge the base into a bowl or sink of ice-cold water. Continue whisking for 2-3 minutes until the custard has cooled a little, then leave it to chill thoroughly, stirring occasionally. (If you're using vanilla essence/extract instead of the vanilla pod, add it now.)

To make the meringues, whisk the egg whites in a clean, grease-free bowl until they form stiff, glossy peaks which don't fall out when you turn the bowl upside down. Whisk in a large tablespoon of sugar, then fold in the rest – about a fifth at a time – using a large metal serving spoon. The object is to retain as much air as possible.

Using a tablespoon, dab small, evenly sized mounds of the meringue on to the baking sheet – it doesn't matter about the shape as you're going to break them up later. Place the tray on the middle shelf of the oven and cook the meringues for 90 minutes, turn off the heat and leave for a further hour. Remove the meringues, and leave to cool.

Whisk the cold custard and mascarpone together until completely smooth. Put 18 raspberries aside for decoration, then fill the glasses in the same way as described at the beginning of the recipe.

Serving strawberries with a sprinkling of ground black pepper is a French trick, and one that brings out the flavour in a very surprising fashion. It was while pondering this tradition that I first thought of the idea of making a green peppercorn-flavoured ice-cream to go with strawberries. My head chef, Brendan Ansbro, then ran with the idea, adding a positive pharmacy of different peppers. Dodgy though this spicing might sound, it actually produces a warmly aromatic ice-cream that's no more peculiar than cinnamon or ginger. If you can't find the Japanese or Szechuan peppercorns, substitute a little cardamom and star anise. The flavour won't be the same, but will still have an agreeable spiciness to it.

Both the ice-cream and the syrup can be made ahead, but remember home-made ice-cream doesn't have the Methuselah-like life span of commercial stuff; because it doesn't contain any stabilisers, the texture will deteriorate after a few days. (But when it's fresh, it's fantastically better than anything you can buy.)

Poached strawberries with five-pepper ice-cream

TO SERVE 4

FOR THE STRAWBERRIES
110g caster sugar, plus 1 tsp more
200ml hot water
50ml orange liqueur (Grand Marnier, Cointreau)
1 tbsp lemon juice
a small scrap of butter
28 large ripe strawberries
12 green peppercorns, rinsed and drained

FOR THE ICE-CREAM
275ml full cream milk
275ml double cream
¼ tsp ground black pepper
10 green peppercorns, drained, rinsed and finely crushed
a pinch of cayenne pepper
a pinch of Japanese pepper (sansho)
½ tsp Szechuan peppercorns, finely crushed
100g caster sugar
7 large free-range egg yolks

YOU WILL NEED
an electric ice-cream-maker or a 1-litre non-reactive container

To make the syrup, put the sugar and half the water in a small saucepan, and place it over a very low heat. Stir the sugar to dissolve the crystals, then raise the heat and boil, uncovered, until the syrup is light golden. Plunge the base of the pan into cold water, then stir in the rest of the water. Add the orange liqueur and lemon juice.

To make the ice-cream, put the milk, cream and peppers into a pan over a low heat, and slowly bring to the boil, uncovered. Leave to infuse for 15 minutes off the heat. Whizz the sugar and egg yolks together in a processor until they are pale and thick. Add the infused milk, whizz for a second to combine, then pour the mixture back into the saucepan. Place the saucepan over a medium heat and bring the custard to just below the boil, whisking constantly. As soon as it thickens, plunge the base of the pan into cold water. Whisk for a few minutes, then leave to cool thoroughly, whisking frequently.

Strain the custard, then churn it as normal in the ice-cream maker. If you haven't got a machine, pour the custard into a non-reactive container, and freeze for about 6 hours, stirring it thoroughly 3 or 4 times to reduce the size of the crystals and ensure a smooth texture.

To finish the dessert, melt a scrap of butter in a pan over a medium heat, and add the teaspoon of sugar. When the butter starts to brown, tip in the strawberries and toss them for about 90 seconds.

Pour the reserved syrup into the pan, add the green peppercorns, and toss for another minute, or until the strawberries have just started to soften. Serve immediately, with the ice-cream.

'The taste of cold, peppery ice-cream and strawberries poached in a spicy syrup is unusual, but not freaky'

'The tart, luscious sloe gin syllabub makes a really magnificent contrast to the sweet, crunchy, marshmallowy meringue'

There is something very Seventies about pavlova, but I adore it – always have and always will. Over the years I've served it with a multitude of different fruits and fillings, but I think this one is a real winner. Admittedly, the pavlova is nicest when I use my own home-made sloe gin, but that might have something to do with it having a higher alcohol content than the shop-bought stuff. I suggest you adjust the amount of brandy according to the provenance of the gin. The pavlova works very well with bottled cherry compôte, but if you prefer use fresh cherries, gently poached. Either way, the tart, luscious sloe gin syllabub provides a really magnificent contrast to the sweet, crunchy, marshmallowy meringue.

Now a small tip: instead of lining a baking sheet with parchment and then drawing a neat circle on it, as most experts advise, I find it far easier to pile the meringue on to an appropriately sized cake-tin base – but it's up to you.

The syllabub can be made up to 24 hours ahead, and kept refrigerated. The pavlova can be made 3-24 hours ahead, and kept covered in a cool place: don't fill it until a few hours before needed. Once made, the pavlova will keep in the fridge for up to 2 days, but will become progressively squidgier.

Pavlova with cherry compôte and sloe gin syllabub

TO SERVE 8-plus
55g caster sugar
2 tbsp fresh lemon juice
1-3 tbsp brandy
150ml sloe gin
1 (284ml) carton double cream
1 (600g) jar cherry compôte or about 500g fresh cherries, stoned and gently poached

FOR THE MERINGUE
280g caster sugar
1 rounded tsp cornflour
5 large free-range egg whites
1 tsp vinegar (preferably fruit or cider vinegar)

YOU WILL NEED
a large, heavy baking sheet lined with non-stick baking parchment, or the base of a 23cm diameter cake tin, similarly lined and the edges very lightly oiled

Preheat the oven to 130°C (fan), 150°C (conventional), gas mark 2.

First make the meringue. Sift the sugar and cornflour together, and set aside. Whisk the egg whites in a clean, grease-free bowl until they form firm, shiny peaks. Whisk in the vinegar, then a large tablespoon of the sugar mixture. Lightly fold in the rest – about a fifth at a time – using a large metal serving spoon. With a palette knife, spread the meringue evenly in a solid circle on the baking parchment, leaving about 1cm clearance round the edge for the meringue to expand, if using the cake-tin base. Using the back of a spoon, make a shallow depression in the centre, and build up the sides as high as you can.

Place the tin on the middle shelf of the oven, and cook the pavlova for about 25 minutes until it is risen, and a light pinky-brown. Reduce the heat to 120°C (fan), 140°C (conventional), gas mark 1, and cook for a further 50 minutes. Without opening the door, turn off the heat and leave the pavlova inside for 2-6 hours. Remove the pavlova from the oven and cool thoroughly before taking off the parchment.

To make the syllabub, combine the sugar, lemon juice, brandy and sloe gin in a large bowl and whisk for about a minute to dissolve the sugar. Pour in the cream and continue to whisk until the mixture forms soft, floppy peaks that just hold their shape.

Pile the syllabub in the middle of the pavlova, spreading it out to the edges, then spoon the cherry compôte on top.

These little fritters are quite dramatically good. The contrast between the warm, soft pastry cream and the crisp, golden coating is sublime, and the juicy cherry buried in the centre only adds to the pleasure. Classy as well as clever – I have my moments.

The pastry cream should be made at least 3, and up to 48 hours ahead, and kept refrigerated. The uncooked fritters also need to spend 3-24 hours in the fridge. However, if you are wondering which batter-fingered, grease-spattered masochist wants to faff around at the last minute with egg, breadcrumbs and a deep-fat fryer, don't worry. You can fry the fritters up to 8 hours ahead, keep them cool (not in the fridge), and then give them a couple of minutes in the fryer to warm through. Your complexion will remain as cool and wan as vanilla ice-cream.

Cherry custard fritters

TO SERVE 4
115g natural caster sugar
4 level tbsp cornflour
425ml full cream milk
5 medium free-range egg yolks,
lightly beaten
2 tbsp cherry brandy
15g unsalted butter, melted
12 large cherries, stoned
(either bottled or fresh)

FOR THE COATING
55g icing sugar, sifted
2 large free-range eggs, beaten
about 115g fresh fine
white breadcrumbs

YOU WILL NEED
a deep-fat fryer, or a large
saucepan or wok half-filled
with groundnut oil; a 12-hole
mini-muffin tin, lightly oiled

Preheat the oil to 180°C in the deep-fat fryer; place the wok or saucepan over a moderate heat.

To make the pastry cream, combine the sugar and cornflour in a medium-sized saucepan, then whisk in the milk. Place the saucepan on a medium heat and bring the contents to the boil, whisking almost constantly. Once the mixture has thickened, cook for a further minute, then remove the pan from the heat and whisk in the egg yolks. Replace the saucepan on the heat and cook for 2 minutes, still whisking. Remove the pan again, plunge the base into ice-cold water and whisk for a minute or two while the pastry cream starts to cool, then stir in the cherry brandy. Put it in the fridge to chill thoroughly.

Line the mini-muffin tin with a sheet of clingfilm, pushing it down into the holes as best you can, then brush the hollows with melted butter. Plop a teaspoon of chilled pastry cream into each hollow, then plant a cherry in the middle. Mound another teaspoon of pastry cream over the top, and seal firmly. Put the tin in the fridge, and leave the uncooked fritters to chill for 3-24 hours.

For the coating, put the icing sugar, eggs and breadcrumbs into three separate dishes. Coat each ball of pastry cream in the following order: icing sugar, egg, breadcrumbs, egg, breadcrumbs, then put them back in the fridge for at least 30 minutes, and up to 8 hours.

Fry the fritters for about 3 minutes, or until they are golden brown. Drain them on a pad of kitchen paper, then dust with icing sugar, and serve immediately. If the fritters have been cooked, re-fry them for a minute or so at 160°C – just long enough to warm them through.

I feel a trifle disingenuous putting this recipe into the summer section because although pineapples and passion fruit are both available all year round, they are really at their best during the winter months. It's the idea of tart-but-sweet fruit combined with frosted, aromatic sorbet that makes the recipe so appropriate for summer. Whatever the season, there's no doubt that pineapple and passion fruit are splendid together, both fruits sharing an intense flavour, and tongue-pricking vivacity.

Of course, the sorbet can be made ahead, though not a whole lifetime. Freshly made sorbet is infinitely nicer than one that's been sulking in the freezer for several months: ideally, make it up to 48 hours in advance. The pineapple can be prepared up to 48 hours ahead, too, and refrigerated.

Fresh pineapple with passion fruit sorbet

TO SERVE 6

half a large ripe pineapple, peeled, cored, and cut into long thin slices

FOR THE SORBET

568ml hot water

450g granulated sugar

8-10 passion fruit, depending on size and ripeness

a little fresh lemon juice, to taste

YOU WILL NEED

an electric ice-cream maker or a 1-litre non reactive container

To make the sorbet, combine the water and granulated sugar in a medium-sized saucepan, and bring it to the boil over a medium heat, uncovered, stirring occasionally. Remove the pan from the heat after 1 minute of fast boiling, and leave the syrup to cool thoroughly.

Cut the passion fruits in half. With a sharp teaspoon, scrape all the pulp and seeds into a food processor and whizz for a minute or so, to separate the flesh and juice from the seeds. Using a plastic scraper, scrape every last bit into a sieve resting over the saucepan containing the sugar syrup.

Using a metal spoon, push and pound the passion fruit pulp into the syrup. When every scrap of juice is through, stir the syrup, and taste. Add enough lemon juice to cut the sweetness of the sorbet and bring out the flavour. Don't go mad: remember that the sorbet will not taste quite as sweet when it is frozen, nor do you want to end up with lemon sorbet rather than passion fruit sorbet.

Pour the syrup into the ice-cream maker, and churn it as normal. If you haven't got a machine, pour the syrup into a plastic (or non-reactive) container, and freeze it for about 6 hours, stirring thoroughly three or four times during the freezing process – stirring reduces the size of the crystals and ensures a lovely smooth texture.

To serve, put a few slices of pineapple on each plate, with a scoop (or two) of passion fruit sorbet on top.

'An extravagant, fantastical whip of alcoholic froth, the whole point of trifle is its utter decadence'

If a pudding can fall from grace then trifle has descended into the inferno. Once an extravagant, fantastical whip of alcoholic froth, this delightful dessert has become nothing more than a red, yellow and white glop over the centuries. (I'm not sure at which point I'm going to confess that I really love Marks & Spencer's individual fruit trifles – my excuse is that I don't think of them as trifles, just a sweet, fattening, out-of-control waste of calories.)

My recipe for apricot and amaretto trifle might be no more historically authentic than your average supermarket's, but I guarantee it's more scrumptious. I've specified dried apricots, which means you can make this trifle all year round, but it would be lovely to use fresh, lightly poached apricots instead.

Go as wild as you like on the decoration – the whole point of a trifle is its decadence. (Which is not an invitation to smother it with hundreds-and-thousands, or lipstick-red glacé cherries.) I like to use those really pretty glacé fruits that come packed in little wooden crates (oh, get her), as well as crystallised violets, angelica, toasted almonds and the like.

You can make the custard, and assemble the base of the trifle at least 48 hours in advance. The whole ensemble will happily survive 24 hours in the fridge, but don't put the final decorations on until the last minute. This is a recipe where it's very difficult to pin the quantities down exactly – a dribble more alcohol here, or a splat of cream there is not going to make too much difference. But using the right-sized glasses or bowls is important.

Apricot and amaretto trifle

TO SERVE 8
24 dried unsulphured apricots
50ml cold water
about 100ml apricot brandy
(or ordinary brandy)
about 100ml amaretto
1 packet trifle sponges
(8 pieces)
about half a jar of good-quality
apricot jam
16 soft amaretti biscuits
568ml whipping cream,
whisked into soft peaks
about 30g flaked almonds,
toasted
24 ratafia biscuits
an assortment of fancy glacéed
fruits, toasted almonds,
crystallised violets and angelica

First make the custard. Heat the milk and vanilla pod in a largish saucepan until just below simmering point. Take the milk off the heat and allow it to infuse for 15-20 minutes. Whizz the egg yolks, sugar and cornflour together in a food processor (or with an electric hand whisk), until the mixture is thick, creamy, and paler than when you started. Remove the vanilla pod from the milk and, with the motor running, slowly pour in the infused milk and pulse for long enough to blend.

Quickly but thoroughly rinse out the milk pan, and pour the custard back in. Return the saucepan to a medium heat and bring it to the boil, whisking almost continuously. As soon as the first bubbles break the surface and the custard thickens to the consistency of whipping cream, reduce the heat and simmer for 1 minute, still whisking. Remove the saucepan from the heat and plunge the base into ice-cold water. Continue whisking for 2-3 minutes until the custard has cooled a little, then leave it to cool completely, stirring occasionally. (If you are using vanilla essence/extract add it now.)

FOR THE CUSTARD

850ml full cream milk

1 vanilla pod, split lengthways (or a few drops of real vanilla essence/extract)

12 large free-range egg yolks

250g caster sugar

2 level tbsp cornflour

YOU WILL NEED

8 (about 300-350ml) small glass bowls or squat tumblers; a large piping bag and fancy nozzle (optional)

Put the apricots, water, brandy and amaretto into a saucepan and place it over a medium heat. Remove the pan as soon as the contents reach the boil, and leave it to one side for about 45 minutes, while the apricots plump up.

Slice the trifle sponges in half horizontally, spread them generously with apricot jam, then sandwich them back together. Put one in each glass or bowl, together with two amaretti biscuits. Divide the apricots evenly between the glasses, then pour over the poaching liquid. The biscuits and sponge should be thoroughly dowsed; tamp the sponge and biscuits down in the liquid, if necessary. Carefully pour on the cold custard, and put the dishes in the fridge (on a tray) for at least 3 hours, and up to 48 hours.

Pile the whipped cream into a piping bag and decorate the trifles as your artistic fancy takes you. (Or if it doesn't take you, spoon the cream on, and swirl it with a fork.) Decorate the trifles with toasted almonds, ratafia biscuits and any other nonsense you like.

The dessert called oeufs à la neige was all the rage in restaurants in the Eighties: I clearly remember Elizabeth David's impatience with chefs who dared to trace inauthentic caramel over the fluffy, poached meringues which float on a pool of marvellously soothing, vanilla-infused custard.

The problem is judging where authenticity begins and ends. Mrs Price, in her 1780 recipe for Floating Island, specifies thinly sliced French rolls, syllabub, sweetmeats, jellies and ratafia cakes – without a hint of meringue, much less custard. This is much the same as the French dessert called îles flottante, but for some reason it's their oeufs à la neige (literally, snow eggs) that we now call Floating Islands. In this recipe I've replaced the normal, plain custard with a nectarine custard. Combined with ethereal meringues, crunchy caramel and sweet fruit, it is completely irresistible – whatever it's called.

Many recipes suggest using the same milk to poach the meringues and make the custard, but I don't like the flavour it gives, and prefer to poach the meringues in water. Another tradition is to form the meringues into egg-shaped quenelles, but I rather like a craggy, St Kilda look – it's entirely up to you.

Although the custard will keep in the fridge for 48 hours, the caramel and meringues should be made no more than an hour or two ahead, and the final assembly should be done at the last minute.

Floating islands
with nectarine custard

TO SERVE 4

FOR THE CUSTARD
500ml full cream milk
1 vanilla pod, split lengthways
4 large free-range egg yolks
100g caster sugar
1 level tsp cornflour
6 ripe nectarines, peeled, stoned and roughly cubed
1 extra nectarine, peeled and finely sliced
2-3 tbsp icing sugar, to taste
2-3 tbsp peach liqueur (or apricot brandy)

To make the custard, put the milk and vanilla pod into a medium-sized saucepan, and place the saucepan over a low-to-medium heat, uncovered. Bring the milk to a bare simmer, then remove the pan from the heat and leave the milk to infuse for 15-20 minutes. Meanwhile, put the egg yolks, sugar and cornflour in a food processor, and whizz for 2 minutes. Remove the vanilla pod from the milk and, with the motor running, slowly pour in the infused milk and pulse for long enough to blend.

Quickly but thoroughly rinse out the saucepan, pour the custard back in and return the pan to a medium heat. Bring the custard nearly to the boil, whisking continuously, and as soon as it has thickened remove the pan from the heat, and plunge the base into ice-cold water. Carry on whisking for a few minutes until the custard has cooled a little and is in no danger of curdling, then leave it to cool thoroughly, whisking occasionally.

Put the roughly cubed nectarines and 2 tablespoons of icing sugar in a blender and whizz to a smooth purée. Taste, and add more sugar, if necessary. As soon as the custard is cold, combine it with the purée, and add the peach liqueur (or apricot brandy – but go easy as it's much stronger) to taste. Put the custard in the fridge.

FOR THE MERINGUES
3 large free-range egg whites
60g caster sugar

FOR THE TOPPING
10g toasted almond flakes
85g granulated sugar
3 tbsp hot water

YOU WILL NEED
a shallow 25cm diameter
glass bowl

To make the meringues, whisk the egg whites until they form firm, shiny, stiff peaks – you should be able to hold the bowl upside down. Using a large metal spoon, fold in the sugar – a third at a time – making sure you use deft strokes to preserve all the air.

Fill a wide, shallow saucepan with about 6cm of water, and bring it to a quiet simmer. Scoop up two or three large tablespoons of meringue and plop them gently on the water, leaving room for expansion. Cook for 2 minutes, then gently turn the meringues and poach them for another minute. Using a fish slice, remove the meringues from the water and place them on a clean tea towel to drain.

Give the custard a quick whisk, pour it into the serving bowl, pile the meringues on top, and sprinkle with the toasted almonds. Tuck the sliced nectarines in between the meringues.

To make the caramel, put the sugar into a small heavy saucepan with the hot water, and stir over a very low heat until the crystals have melted. Turn up the heat, and boil the syrup, without stirring, until it is dark golden. Remove from the heat immediately, and trickle the caramel over the meringues in a lacy web. (There may be too much, but it's difficult to make less.) Wait 10-15 minutes for the caramel to harden before serving.

Until I was six years old, we used to take a house in Broadstairs for the month of July – how terribly English. I can remember little, except being attacked by a huge pack of ravening dogs – it was probably one small dachshund – and the café where, once a week, I was allowed to have a stupendously extravagant Knickerbocker Glory, layered with chopped (real) fruit and scoops of myriad-flavoured Italian ice-cream. The only problem this greedy girl-child had was in deciding whether the banana split might not be the better choice.

I can still picture it – the long, moulded-glass dish with halves of banana propped against the sides, scoops of vanilla ice-cream crammed in the middle and, smothering it all, clouds of whipped cream bristling with toasted almonds. Most importantly, I could choose which sauce to have – important because banana split normally came with strawberry sauce, but I much preferred chocolate. Decades later, I'd prefer not to be seen in a ruched cotton bathing suit with matching sunhat, but I still love banana split.

Of course, you could buy all the components for a banana split, but I've given a recipe for the chocolate sauce, at least, because it's difficult to get a commercial one worth eating – unlike vanilla ice-cream. As for the cream, this is the one and only time I can countenance the idea of buying a can of fluffy aerosol cream. It's quite revolting, but for some arcane reason it's right with banana split. If you can't bring yourself to stoop so low, then whip real cream into soft peaks with some caster sugar.

Banana split

TO SERVE 4

4 large ripe bananas, peeled and cut in half lengthways

8 large scoops good-quality vanilla ice-cream

1 can aerosol cream (or about 300ml whipping cream, whisked with caster sugar, to taste)

about 4 tbsp almond flakes, toasted

thick, fan-shaped wafers (optional)

FOR THE CHOCOLATE SAUCE

175g bitter dark chocolate (min 55 per cent cocoa solids)

150g double or whipping cream

25g unsalted butter

YOU WILL NEED

4 traditional, long boat-shaped, glass dishes

Melt the chocolate with the cream and butter in a medium-sized saucepan over a very low heat. Bring the sauce to just below simmering point, stirring frequently, then remove from the heat. Leave until tepid, stirring occasionally.

To assemble, line each dish with the split bananas, stuff 2 or 3 scoops of ice-cream in between, then pour on the chocolate sauce. Smother the whole lot with whipped cream, sprinkle with toasted almond flakes, and stab with a wafer, if you like. Serve at once.

'To ensure every quivering mouthful of this delicate pudding is as good as it can be, use perfect, wholesome, fresh ingredients'

A light, silky, baked egg custard – properly made – is a joyous creation, and about as traditionally British as you can get. To ensure every quivering mouthful of this delicate pudding is as good as it can be, use perfect, wholesome, fresh ingredients; organic milk and cream, the freshest free-range eggs, natural sugar and real vanilla. Otherwise, you might as well nip down to the nearest baker's and buy one of those leaden, yellow, cornflour-crammed custard tarts.

Serve the custard with fresh berries and a slick of thin cream. It can be made up to 12 hours ahead, and kept cool.

Baked egg custard

TO SERVE 8
425ml full cream milk
300ml double cream
the zest of 1 orange
2 tbsp dark rum
140g natural caster sugar
5 large free-range eggs
4 large egg yolks
a few drops of real vanilla
essence/extract
a few gratings of nutmeg

YOU WILL NEED
a 25cm diameter x 5cm deep
ovenproof dish

Preheat the oven to 100°C (fan), 120°C (conventional), gas mark 1/2.

Put the milk, cream and orange zest into a largish saucepan over a low-to-medium heat, and slowly bring the contents to a simmer. Immediately remove the pan from the heat, pour in the rum, and leave the milk to infuse for about 15 minutes. In the meantime, whisk the sugar, whole eggs and yolks until thoroughly combined. Strain the milk on to the egg mixture (discarding the zest), stir well, and add the vanilla essence.

Pour the custard mixture into the dish, grate on a little nutmeg, and bake on the middle shelf of the oven for 60 minutes, or until the custard has set – gently push the top with a finger to test.

Leave the custard to cool to room temperature before serving.

Summery lunches

Long, lazy, hazy summer days, and lunch as well. Oh what joy. Perhaps it's because most of us work these days, but the idea of sitting down to lunch with a bottle of chilled white wine seems faintly decadent. I always feel I'm on holiday even if I'm just in the back garden. These recipes are not quite as casual, or two-people oriented as the summery suppers, but neither are they formal main courses. Whether it's a creamy risotto, buttery-crisp tart or gutsy salad, they are all redolent of summer – and you can eat most of them with just a fork.

Arabella Boxer is a cookery writer who deserves great acclaim. Admittedly, the innovative design of her 1964 *First Slice Your Cookbook* (in which the spiral-bound pages were colour-coded and sliced into three parts – starters, main courses and puddings), has always been fêted as a triumph of design. But despite the fact she was food editor of *Vogue* for many years (or perhaps because of it), her delectable recipes have never received riotous public recognition.

Arabella Boxer was writing about both Mediterranean and Middle-Eastern food long before it was really fashionable (rather like Robert Carrier), but she also writes with equal intelligence and ability about traditional English and French cooking. What's particularly fascinating (and admirable) is that while she is overt in her preference for vegetables, herbs and light food, none of her recipes are remotely prissy or wishy-washy. In fact, they epitomise the best of modern, healthy cooking.

I can't for the life of me find the recipe that sparked off this fresh, zappy dressing – it shouldn't really be called a sauce – but I've no doubt Arabella Boxer was the inspiration.

If you can't be bothered to blanch and peel the tomatoes it doesn't matter, but it would be nice – you might even feel like a proper cook. The recipe takes about 15 minutes, and should be cooked to order.

Linguine with raw tomato sauce

TO SERVE 4

6 large well-flavoured tomatoes

about 5 tbsp fruity, extra-virgin olive oil

1 large shallot, peeled and finely chopped

about 400g good-quality dried linguine

a pinch of caster sugar

a handful of basil leaves, roughly torn

a small handful of flat-leaf parsley, chopped

Put the tomatoes in a heat-resistant bowl and pour a kettle of boiling water over them. Leave for 1 minute, then drain. When cool enough to handle, peel off the skins, then deseed and roughly chop the tomatoes into small dice.

Heat 3 tablespoons of the olive oil in a medium-sized sauté pan (or shallow saucepan) over a low-to-medium heat. Tip in the shallot and gently fry it for a few minutes, until soft and slightly golden.

Meanwhile, boil the linguine in plenty of salted water, following the instructions on the packet. Drain, and toss in a tablespoon or two of oil.

Add the tomatoes and a pinch of sugar to the sauté pan, turn up the heat, and cook for about 45 seconds, stirring. Add the basil and parsley, and season with a little salt and lots of black pepper. Cook for a further 30 seconds, still stirring, then toss the linguine in the sauce, and serve.

The New First Slice Your Cookbook

by Arabella Boxer, republished by Grub Street Publishing

While it's great to see this book back on the shelves with half-new and half-revised recipes, it isn't quite as glorious as the first edition illustrated by Alan Cracknell. However, as that is long out of print (a first edition now costs about £60), regrets are pointless. Even better than either of these books (as far as the recipes go) is A Visual Feast (1991 Random House), which is also out of print – so why bother telling us, I hear you snarl. Well, only because if you ever find a second-hand copy of this ravishingly beautiful book with photos by Tessa Traeger, buy it instantly. The recipes are just beautiful.

You either like saffron or you don't. Personally, I think it's gorgeous, not just for the fantastic colour, but also for the unique, slightly tannic, toasted-herbage flavour. Where it all goes wrong is if you overdo it – too much saffron is like too much vanilla, overpowering and unpleasant. Risotto and saffron are a classic combination (think of paella), but in this recipe I've tempered it with the smokiness of the red peppers, as well as the sweetness of the garlic.

The usual risotto pre-preparation advice applies; you can roast the peppers, fry off the base vegetables and make up the stock several hours ahead, but don't start cooking the rice until it's actually needed.

Red pepper, garlic and saffron risotto

TO SERVE 4

1 large, firm, whole head of garlic

2 large red peppers (or the equivalent good-quality tinned Spanish peppers)

4 rounded tsp Marigold Swiss vegetable bouillon powder

1 litre boiling water

70g unsalted butter

1 shallot, peeled and finely chopped

1 hefty pinch of saffron threads

300g carnaroli (or arborio) rice

3 heaped tbsp finely grated parmesan

YOU WILL NEED

a fairly large sauté pan or wide, shallow saucepan

Preheat the grill to prepare the peppers.

Cut a slice right the way across the head of garlic – as if you were cutting the top off an egg – so the tips of the cloves inside are revealed. Bring a small saucepan half-filled with water to the boil, throw in the head of garlic and leave it to simmer, uncovered, for 5 minutes. Drain off and discard the water. Break the head apart when it's cool enough to handle, gently skin the cloves, and leave aside.

Place the fresh peppers on a rack close to the grill elements. Leave them until the skin is completely blackened, remembering to turn them every few minutes with a pair of tongs. Put the peppers in a stout plastic bag, seal it, and set aside for about 15 minutes. The skin will now peel off like a dream. Remove and discard the stem and seeds, and slice the flesh into thin strips.

Combine the Marigold powder with 1 litre of boiling water in a medium-sized saucepan. Keep this stock at a very gentle simmer over a low flame while you are making the risotto.

Melt 40g of butter in the sauté pan over a low-to-medium flame. Gently fry the shallot for 3-4 minutes, then stir in the saffron threads, and cook for a further minute. Add the rice and stir thoroughly for another minute or so, until all the grains glisten.

Start adding the hot stock, a ladle or two at a time. Adjust the heat to keep the risotto at a simmer, adding just enough liquid to bathe the rice, not drown it, and stirring almost constantly. As the stock is absorbed add a little more. Continue with this routine for about 20 minutes, then stir in the garlic and red peppers, and season.

Start testing the rice by biting into a grain. (Carnaroli rice normally takes 25-30 minutes to cook, and arborio 20-25 minutes.) When it's ready the grains should be tender – neither gritty, nor soggy, and the risotto should have a wettish, porridgey look – not dry like a pilaf. If you run out of stock before the rice has cooked, add a little hot water.

Finally, remove the pan from the heat and stir in the remaining 25g of butter and the parmesan. If the risotto stiffens up too much, add a spot more hot water. Serve immediately.

Egg and bacon pie is a real family favourite – I genuinely remember my old dad wrapping a wedge of pie in greaseproof paper and shoving it in his pocket to take to work for lunch. He also wore a cloth cap, worked down the mines, got paid a farthing a week and still had enough at the end of the week for a fish and chip supper – or do you think that's stretching it a bit far?

Anyway, back to food: I've got a thing about cooked pastry that's been refrigerated. It ends up tough but soggy, and completely defeats the purpose of pastry which is not only to act as a farinaceous coffin, but to be a crisp, crumbly, buttery delight in itself. And it doesn't matter whether it's a sugary-sharp apple pie or a rich, savoury quiche Lorraine, good pastry adds a vital textural foil, as well as flavour. Which is all a precursor to saying that if you can, keep this tart cool without putting it in the fridge. My ancient mama, for whom the laws of food hygiene are a vestigial spectre, used to plonk the egg and bacon pie on the kitchen table, and leave it there. Mind you, it was scoffed pretty quickly.

The pie and the mustard dressing can be made at least 24 hours ahead, and kept cool, but the salad should not be dressed until required.

Egg and bacon pie with cos salad and mustard dressing

TO SERVE 6

FOR THE PIE
225g plain flour
85g cold unsalted butter, roughly cubed
55g lard
1 large free-range egg yolk
3 tbsp ice-cold water
about 300g dry-cured streaky bacon
12 large free-range eggs
1 small free-range egg whisked with 2 tbsp milk for the egg wash

FOR THE SALAD AND DRESSING
1 level tbsp smooth French or German mustard
1 tbsp white wine vinegar
3 tbsp groundnut oil
1 tsp caster sugar, to taste
4-6 tbsp whipping cream
2 heads cos (or romaine) lettuce, trimmed

Preheat the oven to 170°C (fan), 190°C (conventional), gas mark 5.

Make the pastry: whizz the flour and a pinch of salt together for a few seconds in a food processor, then add the butter and lard and whizz again, until the mixture looks like coarse breadcrumbs. Whisk the egg yolk and water together and pour into the flour mixture. Process again until the pastry has collected in a ball around the spindle, then take it out and divide it into 2 lumps, one twice as big as the other. Press each lump into a thick disc shape, wrap in clingfilm and rest in the fridge for 30 minutes or up to 2 days.

While the pastry is resting, slightly overlap the rashers of bacon in a large, non-stick, cold frying pan, then place it over a low heat. Cook for 6-8 minutes, turning the rashers once (and discarding any fat or liquid that seeps out), without letting it brown. Take the bacon out and drain it on a pad of kitchen paper. (You might need to cook the bacon in two batches.)

Remove the pastry from the fridge, return it to (cool) room temperature, then roll the larger piece out thinly. Line the tin with it, then trim the pastry, leaving enough drooping over the edges to form a seal with the lid.

Arrange half the bacon rashers in the pastry case, cutting the odd rasher to fit, if necessary. Carefully break the 12 large eggs over the

'My ancient mama, for whom the laws of food hygiene are a vestigial spectre, used to plonk the egg and bacon pie on the kitchen table, and leave it there. Mind you, it was scoffed pretty quickly'

YOU WILL NEED
a 23cm diameter x 4cm deep loose-bottomed tart tin, lightly buttered; a heavy baking tray

bacon, trying to keep the yolks whole. Season generously with salt and pepper – the bacon is not as salty as you might imagine, and eggs are very bland – and lay the rest of the rashers on top.

Roll the remaining pastry out into a circle that's a little larger than the tin. Place this on top of the pie, brush both edges with water, and then pinch them together firmly. Now brush the egg wash over the pie. Cut out a few leaf-shapes from the pastry trimmings, brush them with the egg wash too, and appliqué them on top of the pie in a decorative swirl. Finally, cut a few small slashes in the lid, then chill the pie for at least 30 minutes.

Put the baking tray in the oven to heat up, then slide the pie on to it and bake for 45-50 minutes, or until the pastry is golden brown. Remove the pie from the oven and leave it to cool in the tin.

To make the mustard dressing, whisk all the ingredients together, except the cream. Add this last, whisking in enough to make a thick, floppy dressing that will coat the lettuce fairly thickly, but still leave a bit of poke to the mustard flavour.

Leave the small lettuce leaves whole, but tear the bigger ones in half or in thirds. Toss them in the dressing, and serve them with the pie at room temperature.

'Lentil salad, especially with tapenade or anchoïade, is spectacularly good; served with eggs boiled to the point where the yolks have coalesced to a fondant cream, it's sensationally good'

With a few honourable exceptions, I think the south of France has some of the worst restaurants in the entire country. One of the high spots in a plethora of pretentious and unsatisfactory menus is the frequent presence of an oily, earthy lentil salad.

Simon Hopkinson – the chap I'd like to cook my last meal on earth – gave a terrific recipe for lentil salad with anchoïade toasts in Sainsbury's *The Magazine*, some years ago. However, when staying with friends in Provence recently, I had to make do with what was in the store cupboard and, to my surprise, discovered that not only did I prefer lentil salad with tapenade, I preferred tapenade without anchovies in it – strange, since I adore anchoïade. Something else I discovered is that it's much quicker, and even tastier, to cook the lentils in Marigold stock, rather than with the normal bevy of pot vegetables and herbs.

The lentil salad can be made ahead and, in fact, will positively benefit from slouching around in the dressing for a day or two. The tapenade will keep for at least a week in the fridge – both are best served at room temperature. The toasts will survive a few days in a sealed container lined with kitchen paper. Only the eggs will be best if they're not cooked more than a few hours before they are needed.

Lentil salad with soft-boiled eggs and tapenade toasts

TO SERVE 4
6 large free-range eggs
12 slices of (slim) baguette
extra-virgin olive oil
about 250g lenticchie di Umbria or Puy lentils, rinsed
1 tbsp Marigold Swiss vegetable bouillon powder
1 large stick celery
a handful of flat-leaf parsley
a few sprigs of fresh tarragon

FOR THE TAPENADE
250g black olives, stoned
2 tbsp capers, rinsed and drained
2 cloves of garlic, peeled and crushed
2 tbsp extra-virgin olive oil
1 tbsp brandy

FOR THE DRESSING
1 tbsp smooth French mustard
1 tbsp red wine vinegar
1 clove of garlic, peeled, crushed and finely chopped
100ml extra-virgin olive oil
100ml groundnut oil

YOU WILL NEED
a heavy baking sheet;
a pestle and mortar

Preheat the oven to 200°C (fan), 220°C (conventional), gas mark 7 for the toasts.

Bring the eggs to room temperature and boil them for exactly 6 minutes. Run them under cold water for a few minutes, then peel and halve. Leave them to one side.

Lay the slices of baguette on the baking tray and drizzle each piece with a generous quantity of olive oil. Bake for about 10 minutes, or until golden brown and crisp. Remove from the oven, and cool.

Put the lentils in a large saucepan, cover them with water by about 3cm, and stir in the Marigold powder. Bring to the boil, then reduce the heat and simmer, half-covered, for about 30 minutes, or until just tender. Keep testing them – they shouldn't be overcooked and squishy.

To make the tapenade, either smash all the ingredients into a rough paste in the pestle and mortar, or pile them into a food processor, and whizz to a rough paste using the pulse control. Set aside.

To make the dressing, whisk the mustard, vinegar and garlic together, then gradually add the oils, whisking continuously to make a thick emulsion. Season with salt and pepper, and pour the dressing into a bowl large enough to take the lentils.

Drain the lentils, then put them in the bowl with the dressing, and toss thoroughly. Finely chop the celery, parsley and tarragon leaves and stir them in. (If the salad is going to be refrigerated, don't add the parsley and tarragon until an hour or so before serving.)

Spoon the lentil salad on to serving plates, and garnish with the eggs, and the toasts spread generously with tapenade. If there's too much, refrigerate the surplus to eat with drinks at a later date.

The evolution of the omelette is probably not something which exercises your mind unduly – it didn't mine, until I started writing this. But it is a bit odd that the French like their omelettes moist, runny and made in seconds, whereas the Spanish and Italians prefer to nurture their tortilla and frittata to a creamy solidity. Different cooking styles are often dictated by the availability of fuel – long, slow-cooked food in areas abundant with fossil fuels, and quickly-fried dishes in those without – but that hardly applies here. Ah well, another little mystery, along with why cats always want to walk on computer keyboards.

Use really fresh eggs: the large quantity of fresh herbs, and powerful, nutty parmesan will boost the flavour of ordinary eggs, but nothing can replace the creaminess, colour and sheer vitality of an egg laid by a chatty, plump, shiny-feathered, carmine-combed free-range chicken.

The vegetables can all be prepared several hours in advance, but the frittata shouldn't hang around more than a couple of hours; it's best eaten tepid, or at cool room temperature.

Courgette, potato and herb frittata

TO SERVE 6

225g courgettes, finely grated

30g unsalted butter

2 tbsp extra-virgin olive oil

2 cloves of garlic, peeled and finely chopped

1 bunch of spring onions, trimmed and finely sliced

a large handful of flat-leaf parsley, coarsely chopped

3-4 sprigs fresh mint, the leaves finely chopped

4-5 sprigs fresh tarragon, the leaves finely chopped

10 large free-range eggs

about 10 scrapings of nutmeg

55g parmesan, finely grated

about 250g waxy potatoes (eg Maris Bard, Charlotte), peeled, cooked and cut into bite-sized chunks

2 baked ciabatta, or similar rustic bread (optional)

YOU WILL NEED

a food processor with a fine julienne blade, or a grater; a 28cm diameter, non-stick frying pan with heat-resistant handle

Preheat the oven to 130°C (fan), 150°C (conventional), gas mark 2.

Put the courgettes in a colander, salt them vigorously, and leave them for about 30 minutes. Rinse the courgettes under cold running water, and leave to drain for 1-2 minutes. Pile them into the middle of a clean tea towel, and wring them completely dry. The courgettes will now be jammed into a tight ball, which you'll need to tease out.

Melt the butter and 1 tablespoon of olive oil in the frying pan over a low-to-medium heat. Tip in the garlic, spring onions and courgettes and gently fry for about 10 minutes, stirring occasionally, until they have softened and are very slightly coloured. Remove the pan from the heat and add the herbs, then season with salt and pepper. Scrape everything into a bowl and leave aside, reserving the frying pan.

Lightly beat the eggs, season with nutmeg, salt and black pepper, and stir in the parmesan. Place the frying pan over a lowish heat, and put in the remaining oil. Pour about a quarter of the egg mixture into the pan, and leave it for about 2 minutes to set. Remove the pan from the heat and evenly distribute the vegetable mixture, including the cooked potatoes. Replace the pan on the heat, pour on the rest of the eggs and cook the frittata very gently for about 5 minutes.

Transfer the frying pan to the oven and continue cooking the frittata for 10-15 minutes, until the egg has set. Don't be tempted to raise the heat, or the frittata will be unpleasantly bouncy. Remove the pan from the oven (remembering that the handle is very hot) and cool the frittata for about 15 minutes in the pan. Slide it on to a large serving plate, and cut it into wedges. Serve with a dressed salad, or sandwiched in chunks of ciabatta.

This tart looks so magnificent, and tastes so good, it would make a great centrepiece for a summer party. Made from ewes' milk, Greek feta is pickled in a brine solution, which gives it its sparkling, salty flavour and distinctive crumbly texture. The key word is Greek (or Cypriot); feta made elsewhere is a poor pastiche.

Like most tarts, this one is best eaten when it's either warm or at room temperature, rather than piping hot or stone cold. You can make the pastry up to 48 hours ahead, bake the pastry case up to 24 hours ahead (and keep it wrapped in foil, in its tin), and roast the vegetables up to 24 hours ahead. Complete the final cooking between 1 and 4 hours before the tart is going to served.

Feta and Med veg tart

TO SERVE 8-plus
1 large red pepper, deseeded and quartered
1 fennel bulb, trimmed, and cut into large-bite-sized chunks
3 medium courgettes, cut into large-bite-sized chunks
8 medium well-flavoured tomatoes, halved and deseeded
8 tbsp extra-virgin olive oil
8 sprigs of fresh thyme, leaves only
350g Greek feta, patted dry and cut into bite-sized chunks
5 large free-range eggs
300ml double cream
2 cloves of garlic, peeled, crushed and finely chopped

FOR THE PASTRY
350g plain flour
a pinch of fine sea salt
210g cold unsalted butter, roughly chopped
2 small egg yolks, lightly beaten
5 tbsp cold water

YOU WILL NEED
2 large heavy baking trays; a 30-32cm diameter x 4cm deep loose-bottomed tart tin, lightly buttered; ceramic baking (or dried) beans

Preheat the oven to 170°C (fan), 190°C (conventional), gas mark 5 for the pastry case; preheat the oven to 200°C (fan), 220°C (conventional), gas mark 7 for the vegetables.

Whizz the flour, salt and butter in a food processor until the mixture looks like coarse breadcrumbs. Whisk the egg yolks and water together and pour into the flour mixture. Process again until the pastry has collected in a ball around the spindle. Form the pastry into a thick disc, wrap it in clingfilm and leave to rest in the fridge for a minimum of 30 minutes, and up to 2 days.

Take out the pastry and return it to (cool) room temperature, then roll it out thinly. Line the tin – making sure you don't stretch the pastry – then trim the edges. Return the pastry case to the fridge for at least 30 minutes. Now line the pastry with foil and pour in the beans. Bake for 12-15 minutes in the preheated oven. Remove the foil and beans, and bake for another 5-6 minutes. The pastry should look dry, but blond rather than brown. Remove the tin and leave the pastry case to cool in it. (If you're carrying on straightaway with the recipe turn the oven up now to roast the vegetables.)

Toss the vegetables in the oil and arrange on the baking trays. Scatter over the thyme leaves, season and put the trays in the oven. Roast the vegetables for 30-40 minutes until they are soft and gilded around the edges. Drain off (and discard) some of the juices halfway through. Remove the trays and cool the vegetables thoroughly, then cut the red pepper into large-bite-sized pieces.

Distribute the vegetables and feta evenly in the pastry case. Whisk the eggs, cream and garlic together and carefully pour it between the chunks. Don't overfill the pastry case, as the custard will stick to the tin, and the vegetables and feta look prettier peeking out. Place the tart carefully on a middle shelf in the oven and bake it for 25-30 minutes, until the custard has just set and the feta chunks are golden.

I'm a real sucker for seafood salad whether it's as a light, teasing prelude to a serious meal, or the meal itself. And Brown Owl would also like to remind you that squid is not the least bit rubbery when it's cooked properly. That means it must be cooked for no more than 2 minutes, or no less than 40 minutes – anything in between spells Dunlop. I've specified baby squid deliberately, because it's tender and the best size to be cut into rings. If you can only find medium-sized squid, don't cut the tubes into rings, but into fairly thin strips instead.

The finished salad needs to marinate for a few hours, but can be made up to 24 hours ahead, and refrigerated. Bring it back to room temperature before eating, or half the flavour will be lost.

Chargrilled squid, potato and onion salad with lime dressing

TO SERVE 4

16 walnut-sized waxy potatoes (Maris Bard, Charlotte, Anya), washed and halved lengthways

3 tbsp extra-virgin olive oil

2 red onions, peeled

2 red peppers, grilled, peeled, deseeded, and cut into strips (or the equivalent Spanish tinned peppers)

2 mild red chillies, deseeded and finely chopped

a small bunch of fresh coriander, chopped

about 500g squid, cleaned, and cut into (about) 1cm rings

FOR THE DRESSING

the grated (or finely sliced) zest of 2 limes

3 tbsp fresh lime juice

2 tbsp Thai fish sauce

2 cloves of garlic, peeled, crushed and finely chopped

1 tbsp caster sugar

125ml groundnut oil

YOU WILL NEED

a large griddle pan or large, heavy frying pan (preferably not non-stick); a large roasting tin

Preheat the oven to 180°C (fan), 200°C (conventional), gas mark 6 for the potatoes.

For the dressing, whisk the first five ingredients together, then add the oil, whisking continuously, to make a smooth emulsion.

Put the griddle over a very high flame, and leave it to get as hot as possible. Toss the potatoes in 2 tablespoons of olive oil, shake off any excess, and place them on the griddle, cut-side down. Leave the potatoes for 5 minutes, then transfer them to the roasting tin, season with salt and bake in the oven for 15-20 minutes, or until tender.

In the meantime, cut the onions into eighths, slicing downwards so each wedge is held together by a little bit of the root. Dip the wedges into the same oil, shake off any excess, and cook them on the hot griddle for about 5 minutes, turning once or twice, until coloured. Add them to the potatoes, and cook them for at least 10 minutes or until tender. Remove the vegetables from the oven, and leave them to cool. Combine the potatoes, onion, red pepper, chilli and coriander in a large mixing bowl, pour in the dressing, season, and toss well.

Cook the squid in two batches. First, toss it in the remaining tablespoon of oil, and season. Heat the griddle over a very high flame until it is searingly hot. Throw in the squid, including the tentacles (chopped into less scary bits, if necessary), and cook for 90 seconds, turning. Remove the squid, and immediately add it to the salad.

Toss the salad once more, then leave it for 2-8 hours in a cool place to marinate, before serving.

If you have ever needed proof that simple food is often the best, this salad is it. Vibrant, snappy green beans are tossed in a light, cream dressing with a little zip of chopped shallot and a few chunks of mild, meaty tuna; the result is the epitome of good honest food.

The tuna you use can make quite a bit of difference, though. Albacore and bonito are considered the best varieties, but it's more important how the fish is packed. Although tuna in brine is undoubtedly less calorific than tuna packed in oil, I don't go for it much. Of course, the oil must be decent quality; none of that generic, light engineering stuff, but good olive oil, or sunflower oil at least. It goes without saying that the tuna should be 'dolphin friendly' – which makes it sound as though there is a piscatorial entertainments committee at the bottom of the Atlantic.

The dressing can be made up to 72 hours ahead and stored in the fridge, but bring it back to room temperature and give it a good whisk before using it – you might also need to add a splash of warm water to obtain the right pouring consistency. There'll be too much for this recipe (it's impractical to make a smaller amount), but you can use the dressing for other salads. The French beans can be prepared up to 24 hours ahead; again, make sure they are not stone-cold when you serve them.

French bean, tuna and shallot salad

TO SERVE 2
250-300g fine French beans, top and tailed
1 (200g) tin tuna steak in oil, drained
1 small shallot, peeled and very finely chopped

FOR THE DRESSING
1 generous tbsp mayonnaise (home-made or bottled)
1 tsp smooth German or French mustard
1 tbsp red wine vinegar
1 tbsp lemon juice
75ml groundnut oil

To make the dressing, put the mayonnaise into a mixing bowl, then whisk in the mustard, vinegar and lemon juice. Slowly pour on the oil, whisking continuously. The dressing should be the consistency of single cream. Season to taste.

To cook the beans, half-fill a largish saucepan with salted water, and bring it to the boil. Toss in the beans, return the water to the boil, and cook them for 2 minutes, uncovered. Drain, then plunge the beans into ice-cold water to stop the cooking and to preserve the colour. Drain the beans again, and dry them gently but thoroughly in a clean tea towel.

Put the beans in a mixing bowl and pour over half the dressing – the rest can be reserved for a later use. Toss the beans until they are well coated, then divide them among the serving plates, and strew chunks of the drained tuna on top. Finally, scatter the salad with the chopped shallot and serve within 30 minutes.

If we are what we eat then we'd better watch out: a bottle of flavoured mineral water I picked up recently contained more chemical junk than a Sellafield skip. As for commercially raised meat, I'd rather have my antibiotics prescribed by a doctor than a farmer. I never buy anything other than free-range chicken but in a recipe such as this, where the chicken is centre-stage, I'd go further and buy organic chicken. On the surface, it would appear much more expensive to buy, but the flavour is so ballsy that by the time you've had a main-course meal from it, then picked off enough bits to make a club sandwich or two, then brewed a punchy-tasting stock from the carcass (to make a risotto or soup), it's cheap at the price.

In this very simple recipe, a good dollop of herby cream cheese is stuffed in between the flesh and the skin of the bird. The chicken is then roasted in a hot oven until the skin turns wonderfully crispy, sticky and golden, while the breast remains moist and juicy. It is very, very good.

The chicken quarters can be stuffed up to 8 hours ahead as long as they are kept in the fridge – but remember to bring them to room temperature before you start the cooking.

Baked chicken stuffed with Boursin

TO SERVE 4
4 large free-range, organic chicken breast quarters (on the bone)
2 (80g) packets (ail et fines herbes) Boursin cream cheese
2 tsp coriander seeds, thoroughly crushed
a little olive oil
125ml double cream

YOU WILL NEED
a well-oiled roasting tin just large enough to take the chicken quarters

Preheat the oven to 200°C (fan), 220°C (conventional), gas mark 7.

Put a chicken quarter on the work surface, with the cut-side facing towards you, then gently poke your fingers between the skin and flesh, and ease the two apart. Push in half a Boursin, massaging the cheese well down towards the wing and away from the opening; smear any excess cheese over the skin. Rub the skin with a little oil, then season generously. Finally, pat on a quarter of the crushed coriander seeds. Repeat with the other chicken quarters.

Put the chicken skin side-down in the roasting tin, and bake for 25 minutes. Turn the quarters over, and cook for another 20-25 minutes, or until they are golden-brown and the juices run clear if you jab the thickest part with a small, sharp knife. Take the chicken out of the roasting tin, and keep it warm.

Put the tin over a fairly high flame, pour in the cream, and vigorously scrape in all the sticky bits that adhere to the bottom. After about a minute, the cream should have reduced to a small amount of toffee-coloured sauce. Remove the tin from the heat, divide the chicken among four warmed plates, and trickle over the sauce, scraping up every last drop. Serve immediately with some plainly boiled potatoes; a watercress salad would be nice, too.

The undisputed king of food-writing in this country is Nigel Slater – nobody else writes as evocatively. But he does have two small flaws; first, he doesn't like saffron and, second, he hates poached eggs with smoked haddock. He says the latter aversion is down to a miserable childhood, but I think it's more prosaic than that – badly cooked eggs are quite revolting, and too many people cook eggs badly – although not Nigel, of course. In my opinion smoked haddock and eggs go together like an owl and a pussycat, as demonstrated by this sublime tart.

I say tart, because a rich egg custard flavoured with anything from mushrooms to lobster, and then baked to a shivering creaminess in a crisp pastry case is every bit as traditionally English as a quiche is French – our culinary heritage might have had its struggles but it does exist. Here's the delectable proof.

The tart is best eaten when it's either warm or at room temperature, rather than piping hot or stone cold. You can make the pastry up to 48 hours ahead, and bake the pastry case up to 24 hours ahead (and keep it wrapped in foil, in its tin). Complete the final cooking between 1 and 4 hours before the tart is going to be served.

Smoked haddock and watercress tart

TO SERVE 4
about 350g undyed,
smoked haddock fillets

3 large free-range eggs

300ml double cream

30g parmesan, finely grated

a large handful of watercress,
the big stalks discarded,
the rest coarsely chopped

a few scrapings of nutmeg

FOR THE PASTRY
225g plain flour

1 level tsp icing sugar

a pinch of fine sea salt

140g cold unsalted butter,
roughly chopped

1 large free-range egg yolk

3 tbsp ice-cold water

Preheat the oven to 170°C (fan), 190°C (conventional), gas mark 5 for the pastry; and 180°C (fan), 200°C (conventional), gas mark 6 for the haddock.

First, make the pastry: whizz the flour, icing sugar and salt together for a few seconds in a processor, then add the butter and whizz again, until the mixture looks like coarse breadcrumbs. Whisk the egg yolk and water together and pour into the flour mixture. Process again until the pastry has collected in a ball around the spindle. Form the pastry into a thick disc, wrap in clingfilm and leave to rest in the fridge for a minimum of 30 minutes, and up to 2 days.

Take out the pastry and return it to (cool) room temperature, then roll it out thinly. Line the tin – making sure you don't stretch the pastry – then trim the edges. Return the pastry case to the fridge and chill for at least 30 minutes. Now line the pastry with foil and pour in ceramic baking (or dried) beans to weigh it down. Bake for 12-15 minutes in the preheated oven. Remove the foil and the beans, and continue to bake for another 5-6 minutes. The pastry should look dry, but blond rather than brown. Remove the tin and leave the pastry case to cool in it.

If you are cooking the tart in one fell swoop, raise the oven temperature for the haddock by 10 degrees now.

'A rich egg custard baked to a shivering creaminess in a crisp pastry case is every bit as traditionally English as a quiche is French – our culinary heritage might have had its struggles but it does exist'

To cook the haddock, pour about 1cm of water into the roasting tin, put the haddock in skin side-down, grind on some black pepper, then cover the tin with a piece of foil. Bake for 10-12 minutes, until the flesh has turned from translucent to opaque. Remove the fish and leave it to cool, and reduce the oven temperature to 160°C (fan), 180°C (conventional), gas mark 4.

Remove the skin and any bones from the haddock, break the fish into big flakes, and strew them evenly in the bottom of the pastry case.

Beat the eggs, cream and parmesan together in a bowl, stir in the chopped watercress, and season with a little salt, plenty of black pepper and a few grindings of nutmeg. Carefully pour the egg mixture over the haddock, making sure that none of it flows over the edges of the pastry, as it will stick to the tin – you might not need it all. Bake the tart on the middle shelf of the oven for 45-50 minutes until it is puffed up and golden, and only just firm to the touch – shivering, rather than solid.

Remove the tart from the oven and leave it to cool in its tin for about 20 minutes before serving.

'Marinating chicken has the most startling effect on its taste and texture. A meat which all too often has the character of a bobble-hat is suddenly transformed into something succulent, juicy and flavourful'

This Malaysian-style marinade includes the usual garlic and onion, as well as aromatic lemon grass, perky fresh ginger, hot chillies and soothing coconut milk. Served with fat, slippery noodles slouched in a gritty peanut sauce, this is chicken with attitude.

Many of the ingredients are duplicated in both the marinade and the satay sauce; prepare them simultaneously, as it will be much quicker than working through each list separately. Despite the length of the lists, it shouldn't take more than about 15 minutes to sort everything out, and the actual cooking time is negligible. The chicken needs to be marinated for 2-8 hours. The satay sauce will keep for at least a week in the fridge; any left over can be used with other grilled meats, Gado-gado, or noodles.

Grilled coconut chicken with noodles and satay sauce

TO SERVE 4

4 free-range chicken breasts, boned but not skinned

about 250g udon or egg noodles

a handful of fresh coriander leaves, roughly chopped

2-3 spring onions, trimmed and finely chopped

FOR THE MARINADE

1 shallot, peeled and roughly chopped

3 cloves of garlic, peeled and crushed

2 bird's eye (or hot) red chillies, deseeded and roughly chopped

1 thumb-sized knob of root ginger, peeled and grated

2 stalks lemon grass, outer layers discarded, the core finely chopped

1/2 tsp turmeric powder

half a (400ml) tin coconut milk, shaken

YOU WILL NEED

a non-reactive ovenproof dish just large enough to take the chicken in a single layer

Preheat the grill to cook the chicken.

Put all the marinade ingredients, except the coconut milk, in a liquidiser or food processor. Whizz until smooth, then add the coconut milk and whizz again to make a thick, sloppy paste.

Lay the chicken breasts skin side-up, and slash them fairly deeply with 3 or 4 parallel lines, then arrange them in the ovenproof dish. Pour over the marinade, and massage it into the chicken. Clingfilm the dish, and leave it in a cool place (though ideally not the fridge) for 2-8 hours, turning the chicken occasionally.

To make the satay sauce, heat the oil in a medium-sized saucepan or frying pan over a medium heat. Tip in the garlic, shallot and chilli, and fry for 5-6 minutes, stirring occasionally, until soft and a light golden colour. Stir in the ginger, sugar, soy sauce, lime juice and a little salt, and bring the contents to the boil, stirring. Remove the pan from the heat and whisk in the coconut milk and peanut butter. As soon as the mixture is smooth, return the pan to the heat, bring the contents to the boil and simmer for 1 minute, stirring constantly. Remove the pan from the heat, and let the sauce cool, stirring occasionally to re-incorporate any oil which might break out.

'A knobbly, spicy, satay sauce is as popular with kids as it is with adults. Even people who hate peanut butter on bread have been known to dip a morsel of chicken into it'

FOR THE SATAY SAUCE
1 tbsp groundnut oil
1 clove of garlic, peeled, crushed and finely chopped
1 small shallot, peeled and finely chopped
1 bird's eye (or hot) red chilli, deseeded and finely chopped
1 thumb-sized knob of root ginger, peeled and grated
1 as-they-come tbsp palm sugar (or light muscovado)
1 tbsp dark soy sauce
1 tbsp fresh lime juice
half a (400ml) tin coconut milk
half a (340g) jar organic crunchy peanut butter

Pour off and reserve any excess marinade from the chicken then place the dish about 25cm from the grill elements – no closer, or the chicken will burn before it's cooked right through. Grill for 15-20 minutes, spooning the reserved marinade over the breasts halfway through.

In the meantime, cook the noodles in a large saucepan of salted water according to the instructions on the packet, timing them to be ready at the same time as the chicken. Gently heat the satay sauce, whisking in 3-6 tablespoons of water to make a thick, pouring consistency.

To serve, toss the noodles in the satay sauce until they are thoroughly coated. Place a blistered chicken breast on each warmed plate, together with a bundle of noodles scattered with chopped coriander and spring onions. Eat immediately.

Although risotto should never be a repository for cast-off food, this particular recipe is a more than acceptable way of using up a cooked chicken breast, or the pickings from a roast chicken carcass. If you want to do it really properly, make a stock from the chicken carcass, and use this in place of the Marigold.

Although I'm not a great fan of celery *per se*, I would never deny its value as a bedrock flavouring agent. Don't be tempted to leave it out of this recipe because it does add an indefinable but important nuance to what is a very soothing, but satisfying risotto. The courgettes are not irreplaceable, however; peas, tiny broad beans or little chips of asparagus would all be equally good.

You can fry off the base vegetables and make up the stock several hours ahead, but don't start cooking the rice until just before the risotto is ready to be served.

Chicken and courgette risotto

TO SERVE 4

4 rounded tsp Marigold Swiss vegetable bouillon powder

1 litre boiling water

85g unsalted butter

1 shallot, peeled and finely chopped

1 large clove of garlic, peeled, crushed and finely chopped

2 sticks celery, finely diced

300g carnaroli (or arborio) rice

100ml dry white wine

2 small courgettes, cut into small dice

2 cooked free-range chicken breasts, skinned and cut into small dice (or the equivalent of other cooked chicken meat)

3 heaped tbsp finely grated parmesan

YOU WILL NEED

a fairly large sauté pan or wide, shallow saucepan

Combine the boiling water and Marigold powder in a medium-sized saucepan, and whisk. Keep this stock at a gentle simmer over a low flame while you make the risotto.

Melt two-thirds of the butter in the sauté pan over a low-to-medium flame. Tip in the shallot, garlic and celery, and gently fry for 4-5 minutes until the vegetables are soft but not coloured. Add the rice and stir thoroughly for a minute or two, until all the grains glisten.

Turn the heat up, pour in the wine and let it bubble away for a minute, stirring all the time. Now start adding the hot stock, a ladle or two at a time. Adjust the heat to keep the risotto at a simmer, adding just enough liquid to bathe the rice, not drown it, and stirring almost constantly. After 5 minutes, put in the diced courgettes. As the stock is absorbed add a little more, and continue with this routine for about 15 minutes. Now stir in the chicken, and season the risotto with salt, and quite a bit of black pepper.

Carry on cooking for a few minutes, then start testing the rice by biting into a grain. When it's ready the grains should be tender – neither gritty, nor soggy – and the risotto should have a wettish, porridgey look – not dry like a pilaf. (Carnaroli rice normally takes 25-30 minutes, and arborio 20-25 minutes.) If you run out of stock before the rice has cooked, add a little hot water.

When the risotto is ready, remove the pan from the heat and stir in the remaining butter and the parmesan. If the risotto stiffens up too much add a dribble of hot water to return it to a soft, creamy mass. Serve immediately.

'Although this recipe uses some typically Italian ingredients, any pure-blooded Ligurian worth his Vespa would be horrified at the idea of applying rigorous heat to pesto. The pasta or gnocchi provides the heat; the pesto is always spooned on cold'

However dubious its authenticity, this is a colourful and dashing meal, which only takes minutes to assemble, and a few more to cook.

Tomato, mozzarella and pesto galette

TO SERVE 6

1 packet (425g) fresh all-butter puff pastry (or frozen and defrosted puff pastry), thinly rolled out

6 large, ripe, well-flavoured tomatoes, cored, and sliced thinly through the equator

3 heaped tbsp pesto (commercial or home-made)

3 tbsp finely grated parmesan

2 balls (about 100g each) cow's milk mozzarella, drained and thinly sliced

YOU WILL NEED

1 or 2 large, heavy baking sheets, lightly buttered

Preheat the oven to 210°C (fan), 230°C (conventional), gas mark 8.

Cut out six circles of pastry, about 15cm in diameter. Prick the pastry with a fork, leaving about 1cm around the edge. Put the pastry discs on the baking sheets, and chill in the fridge for at least 30 minutes.

Arrange the tomato slices, well-blotted, in concentric, overlapping circles on the pastry, leaving the edge clear. Season with salt and pepper, then smear on the pesto. Sprinkle with grated parmesan (including the edge of the pastry), then place 2 or 3 slices of mozzarella on top of the tomatoes.

Bake the galettes on the middle shelf of the oven for about 15 minutes, or until the pastry is puffed up and golden brown – use a palette knife to lift the galettes and check that they are thoroughly cooked underneath. Remove and serve them with a dressed salad.

Summery suppers

Living on the East Coast can be a bugger. A day that's been bright blue, sunny and warm, can turn decidedly nippy by the time supper comes. Being stalwart Brits, we take every opportunity to eat outside, only conceding defeat when the rain becomes torrential. Quickly-made omelettes and scrambled eggs, as well as goat's cheese, taleggio and mozzarella salads, are all perfect for a supper that's likely to be brought to a swift, inclement close.

Stand on virtually any London street and you can take your pick of restaurants toting anything from Bangladeshi and Chinese, to American and French food. Stroll down a calle in Venice and you'll find numerous restaurants offering northern Italian food and... that's it. I am not complaining. Apart from a distressing lack of bacon sandwiches, I could happily live on risotto, prosciutto, carpaccio, calves' liver Veneziana, grilled scampi and polenta for the rest of my life.

One dish which appears on every Venetian menu is risi e bisi, a kind of free-form, soupy risotto of rice and peas that anyone with even the smallest penchant for nursery food will find vastly appealing. This asparagi version of mine tastes every bit as good as the bisi version – in fact, I think it's even more flavoursome – but doesn't sacrifice anything of the texture or simplicity of the original.

As with any risotto-type dish, you can prepare the vegetables and stock a few hours in advance, but the rice itself must be cooked to order.

Risi e asparagi

TO SERVE 2
3 level tsp Marigold Swiss vegetable bouillon powder
500ml boiling water
450g thin-to-medium grade English asparagus
30g unsalted butter
1 large shallot, peeled and finely chopped
150g carnaroli (or arborio) rice
2 tbsp finely grated parmesan

YOU WILL NEED
a medium-sized sauté pan, or wide shallow saucepan, with lid

Combine the Marigold powder and water in a saucepan over a very low heat, and keep it at a very gentle simmer.

To prepare the asparagus, cut off the tips, and put them to one side, then cut off and discard the woody ends from each spear. (If there's time, you can enhance the flavour of the Marigold stock by simmering these trimmings in it for about 20 minutes, before discarding them, but you'll need to add a splash more water.) Cut the spears into small dice.

Melt the butter in the sauté pan over a low-to-medium heat. Fry the shallot for 4-5 minutes, until softened. Throw in the asparagus and stir for about 2 minutes, until all the pieces are buttery.

Pour in half the stock, season with salt, and stir. Bring the contents to a boil, with a lid on, then reduce the heat and cook at a strong simmer for 5 minutes. Add the rice and the rest of the stock. Half-cover the pan with the lid, and cook for a further 15 minutes, or until the rice is tender – but not mushy – stirring occasionally.

Remove the pan from the heat, stir in the grated parmesan, and season well with black pepper, and some extra salt if needed. The finished dish should be of a consistency that's half-soup, half-risotto – a thick, sludgy, wonderful-tasting mess. Serve immediately.

Omelettes are too often seen as a second-rate stand-in for a real meal. But if you use spanking-fresh eggs, good butter and an attractive filling, omelettes can make a very fine meal. Not too much filling, mind – an omelette shouldn't look like a landfill site. And though I'd be the first to agree that cooked avocado is an abomination, it's barely warmed through in this recipe.

I always use two bowls to beat the eggs, three in each: if I only use one bowl the first omelette always ends up larger than the second, however hard I try to divide the beaten eggs equally.

The breadcrumbs can be made a few hours ahead. Otherwise this recipe takes longer to read than it does to make. But if you have got time – some hope – you could blanch and peel the tomatoes first.

Tomato, avocado and basil omelette with garlic breadcrumbs

TO SERVE 2
2 tbsp olive oil
1 clove of garlic, peeled
30g fresh, white, fairly coarse breadcrumbs
45g unsalted butter
2 large well-flavoured tomatoes, deseeded and cut into small dice
half a firm, ripe avocado, peeled and cut into small dice
a few basil leaves, roughly torn
6 large free-range eggs, lightly beaten

YOU WILL NEED
a 20cm diameter omelette pan

Heat the olive oil in a medium-sized frying pan (not the omelette pan) over a medium heat. Toss in the garlic and stir it around for a couple of minutes until it has coloured and flavoured the oil. Pick out the garlic and discard it, then turn the heat up a little. Throw in the breadcrumbs and fry them until they are crisp and golden, tossing them frequently. Remove the breadcrumbs with a slotted spoon, and drain them on a pad of kitchen paper. Reserve the frying pan.

Heat 15g of butter in it over a medium flame. Put in the tomato and cook for 1 minute, stirring occasionally. Add the avocado and basil, and plenty of seasoning. Cook for a further minute, stirring occasionally, until the basil starts to wilt and the avocado is warm. Remove the pan from the heat, and keep the contents warm.

Now cook the omelettes. Place the omelette pan over a very high flame, then put in half the remaining butter. As soon as it stops frothing, pour in half the eggs. As the curds set, draw them into the middle of the pan with a fork, and let the liquid egg flow in to take their place. Once there is a pile of moist, creamy folds in the centre of the pan, and very little liquid egg left, scoop up half the tomato-and-avocado mix with a slotted spoon (discarding the juices), and strew on the omelette. Now scatter on some of the breadcrumbs.

Using a palette knife, flip the edge of the omelette nearest your hand into the middle. Slide the side farthest away from you on to a warmed plate, then gently tip the first folded side over it to form a nice fat roll.

Keep the first omelette warm while you cook the second – neither should take more than about 1 minute to make. Serve, with a final scattering of garlic breadcrumbs over each omelette.

'Eggs aren't just for breakfast but for brunch, lunch and supper, especially when they're scrambled with attitude – or at least a bit of garlic and chilli'

I've given up ordering scrambled eggs for breakfast when we are away on holiday. Too often, what should be a soft, quivering mass of creamy curds manifests itself as an insolent heap of leathery scraps. Mind you, leathery scraps are a positive joy compared to the solid boulders we were served at school – the marvel was how something could be so rubbery and so wet at the same time.

Perfect, creamy scrambled eggs aren't actually that difficult to make, but you must cook them as tenderly and solicitously as a dog licks its testicles. (I don't think Jack's unique in this matter.) Keep the heat very low and stir gently, preferably with a whisk rather than a wooden spoon. (Constance Spry says to use a silver spoon, but that's probably because she was very genteel, and made them in a chafing dish in front of her house guests.)

This Italian-style scrambled eggs has the particular advantage of not tasting at all breakfasty. You could omit the anchovies but they add panache and – for any doubting Thomases – don't taste at all fishy. It's simply not worth bothering to make these scrambled eggs unless you use spanking fresh, free-range (and, preferably, organic) eggs.

All the vegetables, especially the red pepper, can be prepared a few hours in advance, but cook the scrambled eggs at the last moment.

Scrambled eggs alla parmigiana

TO SERVE 4

1 large red pepper (or the equivalent good-quality tinned Spanish peppers)

45g unsalted butter

2 large cloves of garlic, peeled, crushed and finely chopped

1 red chilli, deseeded and finely chopped

12 large free-range eggs, beaten

1 baked ciabatta, halved lengthways

3 medium-sized, well-flavoured tomatoes, deseeded, and chopped into small dice

1 (50g) tin anchovy fillets, drained and roughly chopped

a small handful of fresh basil leaves, finely shredded

about 30g parmesan, finely grated

Preheat the grill to prepare the red pepper.

Place the fresh pepper on a rack close to the grill elements. Leave it until the skin is completely blackened, remembering to turn it every few minutes with a pair of tongs. Put the pepper in a stout plastic bag, seal it, and set aside for about 15 minutes. The skin will now peel off like a dream. Remove and discard the stem and seeds, and slice the flesh into thin strips.

Melt half the butter in a medium-sized saucepan over a low-to-medium flame. Toss in the garlic and chilli and cook them for 3-4 minutes until slightly softened, stirring frequently.

Season the beaten eggs but don't add too much salt if you're using anchovies. Reduce the heat to low and pour the eggs into the saucepan. Whisking frequently to begin with, and continuously as they start to thicken, gently scramble the eggs. It should take 5-10 minutes before they begin to form thick curds, so turn down the flame (or remove the pan from the heat) if they're solidifying too quickly. (Cooked too fast, the curds will be tough rather than creamy.)

While the eggs are scrambling (watch out, bandits at three o'clock, Monty!), toast the cut sides of the ciabatta, then cut each half in two – discarding the heels – and spread with the remaining butter. Keep the ciabatta warm.

Remove the pan from the heat while the eggs are thick-but-pourable, and stir in the pepper, tomatoes, anchovies and basil. Return the saucepan to the heat and continue stirring (use a spoon now rather than the whisk, as a whisk will trap the bits) until you have a very soft, porridgey-looking mass of curds. Immediately remove the pan from the heat, but continue to stir for another 30 seconds, so the eggs at the bottom of the pan do not dry out and harden.

Quickly spoon the scrambled eggs over the four pieces of toasted ciabatta, and sprinkle the grated parmesan on top. Serve at once.

The Constance Spry Cookery Book

by Constance Spry and Rosemary Hume

Good recipes never die, they just grow dusty on the bookshelf, waiting for some ingénue to rediscover them. The Constance Spry Cookery Book was the Mrs Beeton's of the mid-twentieth century, and a recipe book to which my mother referred more than any other. And so it was that my first fumblings in the kitchen were inspired by a woman who was actually a flower arranger, not a cook: it was her partner, Rosemary Hume, founder of 'Au Petit Cordon Bleu', who was responsible for the recipes. Weird or what? Forty years on, I still look in Constance Spry (as this fat tome is affectionately referred to by its aficionados) when I want to know how to cook a classic French or British dish properly. I'm shocked it appears to be out of print, especially since secondhand copies rarely turn up.

'Young goat's cheese has a dense but creamy texture, and a clean, fresh, slightly lemony flavour. It's only very mature goat's cheese that has a viciously astringent kick'

Although warm goat's cheese salad has become a restaurant cliché, it's only because it tastes so good. I'm convinced that those who say they don't like goat's cheese have never tried it, and think it tastes the way an old billy goat smells. Well, it doesn't. Young goat's cheese has a dense but creamy texture, and a clean, fresh, slightly lemon flavour. It's only very mature goat's cheese that has a viciously astringent kick – and I don't like it, either.

While cheese and onion are classic mouth-mates, this dressing is slightly more unusual. The intense flavour of the balsamic vinegar blends beautifully with the mild nuttiness of the oil; the sultanas (which have been marinated in the dressing) add fruity little explosions. Of course, the salad will still taste very good if the dressing is made with red wine vinegar and a mixture of olive oil and walnut oil, or even plain extra-virgin olive oil. When you look at the price tag of balsamic vinegar, you could be forgiven for thinking that it is a big con, but this amazing elixir, made from Trebbiano grapes and fermented in oak or chestnut casks for anything from four to 40 years has such verve and sweet mystery it really is worth its weight in gold.

Although it pains me to say so, it's generally easier to buy logs of French goat's cheese (chèvre) than English goat's cheese. Sliced thickly, chèvre melts very well, but if you stumble over the little fluffy-white drums of English cheese, called Capricorn or Somerset, give them a whirl. Slice each drum around its equator, then grill the halves, cut-side up, until the paste melts as enticingly as a warm Mars bar.

The dressing should be made 24 hours ahead. The croûtons can be made a few days ahead, and kept in an airtight container lined with kitchen paper. The final assembly must take place at the last minute.

Grilled goat's cheese salad with balsamic and sultana dressing

TO SERVE 4
groundnut oil
2 large, thickly-cut slices
of white crustless bread, cut
into medium dice
4 large handfuls of mixed salad
leaves, washed and dried
a few sprigs of fresh tarragon,
the leaves chopped
4 Somerset or Capricorn goat's
cheeses, halved, or 6 (2-3cm
thick) slices of French chèvre

FOR THE DRESSING
1 tbsp balsamic vinegar
1 tbsp red wine vinegar
6 as-they-come tbsp sultanas,
well-rinsed and dried
6 tbsp extra-virgin olive oil

YOU WILL NEED
a heavy baking sheet

Preheat the grill 10 minutes before serving the salad.

For the dressing, combine both vinegars in a small bowl and stir in the sultanas; leave them at room temperature for 6-12 hours. It isn't a disaster if you haven't got time to do this, but the sultanas won't plump up quite as much. Add the oil and season, then whisk vigorously. Leave at room temperature for another 2-8 hours.

To make the croûtons, pour in enough oil to cover the base of a large non-stick frying pan and place it over a medium-to-high heat. When the oil is hot, fry the cubes of bread for a couple of minutes, tossing almost constantly, until a light golden brown. Remove the croûtons with a slotted spoon, and drain them on a pad of kitchen paper.

Before you start grilling the cheese, scoop out the sultanas from the dressing and toss them with the salad leaves and tarragon in a large bowl – but don't dress the salad yet.

To grill the cheese, put the slices or upturned halves on a baking sheet, season, then place under the grill for 3-4 minutes. Depending on the type, the cheese will gently melt, or bubble with a few golden blisters. Remove and keep warm.

Quickly pour some of the dressing over the salad, and toss the leaves thoroughly. Don't use too much dressing – just enough to coat the leaves, not drench them. Divide the salad among the serving plates, and strew on some croûtons. Finally, top each pile of leaves with the grilled goat's cheese. Serve immediately.

I am a real sucker for a rich, savoury tart, be it a modish affair like this one, or a classic quiche Lorraine. The only stipulations are that the custard filling must be deep, rich and creamy, and the pastry as crisp, buttery and short as Jeffrey Archer's memory. This recipe fills the brief on all counts and although the combination of pastry and potato sounds undesirably heavy, by some miracle that's not how it tastes. Coupled with the lemony goat's cheese, sweet peas (no, not a bunch of flowers), and a touch of fresh, zippy mint, this really is an ace summer tart.

You can make the pastry up to 48 hours ahead, and bake the pastry case up to 24 hours ahead (and keep it wrapped in foil in its tin). Complete the final cooking between 1 and 4 hours before the tart is going to served. All custard-based tarts are best served warm or at room temperature, rather than piping hot or frigid.

Potato, goat's cheese, pea and mint tart

TO SERVE 8

FOR THE PASTRY
225g plain flour
1 level tsp icing sugar
a pinch of fine sea salt
140g cold unsalted butter, roughly chopped
1 large free-range egg yolk
3 tbsp ice-cold water

FOR THE FILLING
about 650g small, waxy potatoes, cooked (eg Maris Bard, Charlotte, Jersey Royal)
about 175g fresh white goat's cheese, without rind
about 140g shelled fresh or frozen peas, defrosted
8-12 mint leaves, finely chopped
5 large free-range eggs
150ml whole milk
200ml double cream
a little olive oil

Preheat the oven to 170°C (fan), 190°C (conventional), gas mark 5.

First, make the pastry: whizz the flour, icing sugar and salt together for a few seconds in a food processor, then add the butter and whizz again, until the mixture looks like coarse breadcrumbs. Whisk the egg yolk and water together and pour into the flour mixture. Process again until the pastry has collected in a ball around the spindle. Form the pastry into a thick disc, wrap it in clingfilm and leave to rest in the fridge for a minimum of 30 minutes, and up to 2 days.

Take out the pastry and return it to (cool) room temperature, then roll it out thinly. Line the tin – making sure you don't stretch the pastry – then trim the edges. Return the pastry case to the fridge and chill for at least 30 minutes. Now line the pastry with foil and pour in ceramic baking (or dried) beans to weigh it down. Bake for 12-15 minutes in the preheated oven. Remove the foil and the beans, and continue to bake for another 5-6 minutes. The pastry should look dry, but blond rather than brown. Remove the tin and leave the pastry case to cool in it.

Arrange the cooked potatoes (whole, or cut into large-bite-sized chunks) in the bottom of the pastry case, interspersed with the cheese broken into 8-10 chunks, and a scattering of peas. Strew on the fresh mint, and season liberally with sea salt and black pepper.

'Whether you call it a quiche or a flan, for a great tart the custard filling must be deep, rich and creamy, and the pastry as crisp, buttery and short as Jeffrey Archer's memory'

YOU WILL NEED
a 28cm diameter x 4cm deep loose-bottomed tart tin, buttered; ceramic baking (or dried) beans

Whisk the eggs, milk and cream together and season well. Pour the mixture into the pastry case, making sure some of the pieces of potato and goat's cheese poke through the custard. (You might have some custard mixture left over, but don't overfill the case.) Brush the tops of the potatoes with a little olive oil, then place the tart on the baking sheet in the oven, and cook for 30-40 minutes, or until the custard has set but is slightly trembling, and the tart is golden brown.

Remove the tart from the oven and cool in the tin for about 20 minutes before serving.

'We ate, and life took on new meaning. Nothing could have been simpler than that plate of mozzarella and pear, but it was heaven on earth'

It was Naples, it was horrible, we were hungry, and we couldn't find anywhere to stay – in fact, we didn't particularly want to stay, the town was so ugly. Eventually we ended up in a ghastly hotel with a hideous view, the sea in the distance and the booming beat of an industrial jackhammer close by.

Then we ate, and life took on new meaning. Nothing could have been simpler than that plate of mozzarella and pear but it was heaven on earth; the milkiest, coolest, most drippingly-fresh, tender, vestigially sour, buffalo mozzarella – a whole, huge, smooth, ivory, doeskinned ball of it – and the sweetest, juiciest, most aromatic, meltingly luscious passacrassana pear. It's 20 years since I first ate this magical combination, and I must have eaten it hundreds of times since, but the exuberant fresh simplicity of it never palls. Whoever first thought of it should have been sanctified.

I haven't seen passacrassana pears in the shops for years; apparently they don't travel well. It doesn't matter, though, because the big stumpy Doyenné du Comice (commonly known as Comice) are readily available and, as long as you ripen them gently at home, are every bit as good – if not better. Whatever you do, don't be tempted to substitute Conference as they have as much taste as a policeman in a string vest. Equally, this is not a salad in which to use cow's milk mozzarella, a bland cheese which is perfectly okay when it's gussied up a bit, but hasn't the bravura for a stand-alone performance.

There's absolutely no need to make this salad in advance as it only takes minutes to prepare. The ingredients can be increased pro rata, according to the number of people you want to feed.

Buffalo mozzarella with pears

TO SERVE 2
2 balls (about 100g each) of absolutely fresh, buffalo mozzarella, drained
2 ripe Doyenné du Comice pears, peeled and cored
light extra-virgin olive oil

Either slice the mozzarella or, better still, tear it into raffish, large-bite-sized shards. Slice or quarter the pears, and arrange the mozzarella and pear on serving plates. Season with a generous amount of black pepper and a little salt, then trickle on a good libation of olive oil. Eat, with plenty of crusty bread to wipe the plates clean.

Here's a desperately simple and extremely quick supper with a lovely jumble of colour and flavour. As ever, the dish lives or dies by the quality of the ingredients you use and in this case it will taste infinitely better if you buy whole North Atlantic (or Greenland) prawns rather than the ready-peeled ones. Not only are whole prawns colossally better in terms of taste and texture, but you end up with a pile of (free) shells – heads included – from which you can make a seriously good shellfish stock.

There's nothing mysterious or exotic about crostini. Imagine the Italian equivalent of 'something on toast', and that's about it. Normally, the bread is toasted or grilled, and rubbed with garlic, but here I've lightly fried it.

The prawns can be peeled up to 24 hours ahead, and kept refrigerated, and the vegetables can be prepared a few hours ahead, too. It will then only take about 10 minutes to finish the recipe.

Prawn, mushroom and parsley crostini

TO SERVE 2

about 400g shell-on North Atlantic (or Greenland) prawns

about 8 tbsp extra-virgin olive oil, plus a little extra

4 thick slices ciabatta, cut diagonally

2 sticks of celery, finely diced

3 cloves of garlic, peeled, crushed and finely chopped

225g button mushrooms, wiped and cut in half

a large handful of flat-leaf parsley, coarsely chopped

First peel the prawns, reserving all the debris to make stock at a later date. Put the prawn meat in the fridge.

Pour the olive oil into a large, non-stick frying pan and heat it over a medium flame. When the oil is hot, fry the slices of ciabatta on both sides until lightly coloured but still soft inside, then drain them on a pad of kitchen paper. Keep the ciabatta warm, and reserve the pan.

You will need 3-4 tablespoons of olive oil in the frying pan, so either add or discard some, as necessary. Replace the pan over a medium heat and tip in the chopped celery and garlic. Fry the vegetables for 2-3 minutes until the garlic is a light, nutty brown – no darker – stirring frequently.

Add the mushrooms and some salt, and stir until all the chunks are covered in oil. Fry for about 3 minutes, stirring frequently, until the mushrooms have started to wilt. Finally, stir in the prawns and chopped parsley. Grind on some black pepper, and toss the prawns around for no more than a minute to heat through – they don't need any cooking as such. Put the slices of ciabatta on warmed plates, pile the prawn mixture on top – including all the oily juices – and serve immediately.

In the Far East, fresh ginger is almost mandatory with fish and seafood. Browse through any oriental cookbook and you will be hard-pressed to find a recipe that doesn't include this wonderful zingy flavour. And quite right too, because the combination of sweet, succulent shellfish and zesty ginger is just fabulous. (I ought to mention here that despite North Atlantic prawns being one of my favourite foods, tiger prawns do have some virtues, not least their size, and the fact you can buy them raw.)

The list of ingredients in a stir-fry is always a bit off-putting. But it really doesn't take that long to chop up a few vegetables, and the beauty is that all the preparation can be done a couple of hours ahead, with the actual cooking taking a mere 10 minutes or so. Incredibly tasty, and not too fattening, stir-frys are a regular feature in the Watson household. I chop everything up in the early evening, clingfilm it, and then have a speedy session at the stove in the 20 minutes between my husband coming home, and *EastEnders* or *Coronation Street* starting. Isn't married life bliss?

Tiger prawn, leek and red pepper stir-fry

TO SERVE 4
2 tbsp dark soy
about 4 tbsp black bean sauce
2 tbsp mirin (or 1 tbsp red wine vinegar and a tsp of caster sugar)
2 tbsp dry sherry
3 tbsp groundnut oil
1 mild green chilli, deseeded and finely chopped
2 cloves of garlic, peeled, crushed and finely chopped
2 small red peppers, deseeded and chopped into large dice
3 leeks, trimmed and cut into fine 7cm long strips
a large-thumb-sized knob of root ginger, peeled and grated
500g raw, peeled tiger prawns
1 tbsp fresh lime juice

YOU WILL NEED
a large wok, or very large frying pan

Whisk the soy, black bean sauce, mirin and sherry together in a small bowl. Leave to one side.

Heat the wok over a high flame, then pour in the groundnut oil. When the oil is very, very hot, throw in the chilli, garlic and red peppers, and fry them for 2 minutes, tossing all the time. Add the leeks and cook for a further 2 minutes. The vegetables should be crisp but definitely not raw.

Tip in the ginger (including any juices) and prawns, and cook for about 3 minutes, still tossing, until the prawns have turned from blue-black to brick-pink.

Pour in the soy mixture, and bubble for about 1 minute until the sauce has reduced and thickened a little. Remove the wok from the heat and stir in the lime juice.

Serve immediately, with some fragrant Thai rice, sticky Japanese rice or, if you prefer, egg, udon or buckwheat noodles.

Not all salads could be said to be irresistible, in fact, most of the salads that are served in restaurant chains and motorway cafés bear no resemblance to salad at all – or is it just me that thinks a claggy cheap-mayo mess of tinned sweetcorn, coleslaw, soggy pasta and even soggier potatoes hardly constitutes a salad. Oh, and let's not forget that towering stack of iceberg lettuce leaves; I wonder when they'll be 'grown for flavour'.

After that trenchant blow – what was it Pope said about breaking a butterfly upon a wheel? – let me say this combination of warm earthy potatoes, mushrooms and broad beans, with a jolt of crisp fennel and salty bacon and a squidgy, oozing layer of melted taleggio cheese *is* irresistible.

Taleggio comes from Lombardy and has a pinkish-brown washed rind and a supple, buttery, rich paste – that's the bit you eat. With its fruity, nutty, farmyard flavour, a farm-made taleggio is as good to have on the cheeseboard as it is to melt on top of polenta, risotto or bruschetta. Factory-made taleggio is a lot milder, as you'd expect.

The dressing can be made 24 hours ahead, and all the vegetables can be prepared a few hours ahead. Leave the cooking of the potatoes, and the final assembly, to just before everyone is ready to eat.

Warm taleggio, mushroom and fennel salad

TO SERVE 4

500g small waxy potatoes, peeled (eg Maris Bard, Charlotte, Jersey Royal)

about 175g podded broad beans, cooked and peeled

8 medium-sized chestnut mushrooms, wiped and thinly sliced

half a fennel bulb, outer leaves and core discarded, chopped into medium dice

about 250g taleggio, sliced thinly (without rind)

about 100g thinly-sliced pancetta, roughly chopped

1 heaped tbsp chopped fresh dill (or parsley)

FOR THE DRESSING

1 tbsp cider vinegar

1 tsp smooth French or German mustard

2 tbsp extra-virgin olive oil

2 tbsp groundnut oil

YOU WILL NEED

4 gratin dishes

Preheat the grill to finish the salad.

To make the dressing, whisk the vinegar and mustard together and season, then add the oils. Whisk vigorously until the dressing is thick and emulsified, then leave to one side.

Cook the potatoes in boiling, salted water until tender, then drain them, and put them in a large bowl. Pour the dressing over the potatoes while they are still hot, and toss well. Tip in all the other vegetables, and toss again. Season to taste.

Divide the salad among the four gratin dishes, then place a few slices of taleggio on top. Scatter on the pieces of pancetta, and put the bowls on a baking tray. Slide the tray under the grill, not too near the elements, and cook for 3-4 minutes until the cheese has melted and the pancetta is crisp and brown. Remove the bowls, and sprinkle the dill on top. Serve the salads immediately, with a cold plate under each dish – and a reminder that they are very hot.

At least half the reason I love Venice so much is because I can eat risotto every day – and superlative risotto at that. Go to Da Fiori for the best in the world: the patron's wife cooks, and she doesn't cheat like so many chefs by making the risotto in advance – she just stirs and stirs while you wait. (Even the wait isn't too bad when you can fill the time by noshing on the house's complimentary, and divine, friture of little fishes and shrimps.)

I created this risotto for a cheese supplement I wrote some years ago. I used a fairly strong gorgonzola for the original recipe, but you could substitute any blue cheese, bearing in mind that if you use a mild cheese you might want to add a little more.

As with every risotto, by all means fry off the base vegetables, and prepare the stock ahead of time, but the rice should be cooked to order.

Gorgonzola, broad bean and dill risotto

TO SERVE 4
4 rounded tsp Marigold Swiss vegetable bouillon powder
1 litre boiling water
55g unsalted butter
2 shallots, peeled and finely chopped
300g carnaroli (or arborio) rice
50ml dry white wine
about 175g cooked, shelled and peeled broad beans (fresh or frozen)
about 175g gorgonzola, roughly chopped into large dice
2 heaped tbsp chopped fresh dill

YOU WILL NEED
a fairly large sauté pan or wide, shallow saucepan

Combine the Marigold powder and boiling water in a saucepan, and keep it simmering very gently while you are making the risotto.

Melt half the butter in the sauté pan over a low-to-medium heat. Add the finely chopped shallots and fry gently for 5-6 minutes, stirring occasionally, until they have softened and are very light golden.

Add the rice, and stir for about 90 seconds until all the grains are glistening and buttery, then raise the heat and pour in the wine. Bubble for 1 minute, stirring frequently, before reducing the heat.

Start adding the hot stock, a ladle or two at a time. Adjust the heat to keep the risotto at a simmer, adding just enough liquid to bathe the rice, not drown it, and stirring almost constantly. As the stock is absorbed add a little more. Continue with this routine for about 20 minutes.

Now start testing the rice by biting into a grain. When it's ready the grains should be tender – neither gritty, nor soggy - and the risotto should look wettish and porridgey – not dry like a pilaf. (Carnaroli rice normally takes 25-30 minutes to cook, and arborio rice 20-25 minutes.) If you run out of stock before the rice has cooked, add a little hot water.

When the risotto is almost ready, add the broad beans, gorgonzola and dill, and stir until the cheese has nearly melted. Remove the pan from the heat, then stir in the remaining butter. Serve immediately.

Directory

Food Suppliers

Please note that all wholesalers are happy to supply the name of a local retail stockist

Brindisa Ltd
9b Weir Road
London SW12 0LT

telephone: 020 8772 1600
email: sales@brindisa.com
web site: www.brindisa.com

Wholesale specialist suppliers of Spanish food, including tinned wood-roasted red peppers, almonds, anchovies, dried beans and tuna

Harvey Nichols Food Market
Knightsbridge
London SW1 7JR

telephone: 020 7235 5000
fax: 020 7235 5020
web site: in development

Upmarket supermarket with excellent cheese, meat and fish counters, and specialised grocery section, which stocks Hime tempura mix, Thai fish sauce, mirin, tamarind and buffalo mozzarella

Neal's Yard Dairy
17 Shorts Gardens
London WC2H 9AT

telephone: 020 7407 1800
fax: 020 7378 0400
email: nydmailorder@nydairy.co.uk
web site: in development

Suppliers of the best British and Irish cheeses by mail order, or at their London retail shops

Parma Britishlat
telephone: 020 8334 8012

Importers of Italian food, including besciamella

Athenian Grocery
16a Moscow Road
London W2 4BT

telephone: 020 7229 6280

Small retail shop offering fine Greek and Cypriot produce, including wild figs (in season), fresh herbs, halloumi, feta, pomegranate molasses and harissa

Fiddes Payne Ltd
Pepper Alley
Unit 3b
Thorpe Way
Banbury
Oxfordshire OX16 8XL

telephone: 01295 253888

Wholesaler specialising in a huge range of top-quality spices, vanilla pods and tisane

Fine Italian Foods
Upper Tulse Hill Trading Estate
3 Somers Place
London SW2 2AL

telephone: 020 8671 6622

Wholesaler of a wide-range of Italian produce, including Medusa vongole al naturale

The Oil Merchant Ltd
47 Ashchurch Grove
London W12 9BU

telephone: 020 8740 1335
fax: 020 840 1319
email: the_oil_merchant@compuserve.com

The first, and still probably the best, wholesaler and importer of single estate, and extra-virgin olive oil, including Collona

Knipoch Smokehouse
By Oban
Argyll PA34 4QT

telephone: 01852 316251
fax: 01852 316249
email: smokehouse@knipochhotel.co.uk
web site: www.knipochsmokehouse.co.uk

Family-run smokehouse and mail order company,
supplying superb oak-smoked Scottish salmon

Merchant Gourmet
227-255 Ilderton Road
London SE15 1NS

telephone: 0800 731 3549
web site: www.merchant-gourmet.com

Enterprising and successful wholesaler
specialising in bespoke European food products,
including mi-cuit plums and pumpkin seed oil

Butley-Orford Oysterage
Market Hill
Orford
Suffolk IP12 2LH

telephone: 01394 450277

Family-owned shop, restaurant and mail-order
company specialising in oysters and smoked fish

Emmetts
The Street
Peasenhall
Suffolk IP17 2HJ
telephone: 01728 660250
Village shop and mail-order business
specialising in Suffolk sweet-cure hams,
bacon, and other traditionally-cured hams

The Fresh Olive Company
Unit 1
Hanover West Ind Est
Acton Lane
London NW10 7NB

telephone: 020 8838 1912
fax: 020 8838 1913
email: sales@fresholive.com

A wholesale company offering an enormous
range of excellent olives, as well as antipasti,
vinegars and mustards

MacSween of Edinburgh Ltd
Dryden Road
Bilston Glen
Loanhead
Edinburgh EH20 9LZ

telephone: 0131 440 2555
email: haggis@macsween.co.uk
web site: www.macsween.co.uk

Producers of finest Scotch haggis,
available by mail order

The Wiltshire Tracklement Company Ltd
The Dairy Farm
Pinkney Park
Sherston
Malmesbury
Wiltshire SN16 0NX

telephone: 01666 840851
fax: 01666 840022
email: sales@tracklements.co.uk
web site: www.tracklements.co.uk

A specialist retail and mail-order company, making
superb mustards, sauces and condiments

Equipment Suppliers

Cucina Direct
PO Box 6611
London SW15 2WG

telephone: 020 8246 4300
email: sales@cucinadirect.co.uk
web site: www.cucinadirect.co.uk

Mail-order suppliers of well-designed cookware
and tableware, mostly with a provincial French
bias, including chefs' tongs and cake lifters

The Professional Cookware Company
Cotswold House
449 High Street
Cheltenham
Gloucestershire GL50 3HX

telephone: 08700 707172

Mail order suppliers of kitchen equipment,
tableware and cutlery

Ocean
Ocean Home Shopping Ltd
9 Hardwicks Way
London SW18 4AW

telephone: 0870 2426283
fax: 0870 2426284
web site: www.oceancatalogue.com

Mail-order company offering a small range of ultra-
modern cookware and tableware as part of a larger
range of home products

Lakeland Ltd
Alexandra Buildings
Windermere
Cumbria LA23 1BQ

telephone: 015394 88100
fax: 015394 88300
email: net.shop@lakelandlimited.co.uk
web site: www.lakelandlimited.com

A very efficient mail-order company specialising in a
huge range of everyday kitchen equipment and
tableware, including ceramic baking beans, cake lifters,
whisks, metal spoons and a rather refined Chinese
spider described, hideously, as Lift 'n' Drain

Scotts of Stow
The Square
Stow-on-the-Wold
Gloucestershire GL54 1SS

telephone: 0870 600 4444
fax: 0870 544 9800
email: sales@scottsofstow.demon.co.uk
web site: in development

Mail-order company and retail shop offering a mixed
range of home products including some kitchen
and tableware

David Mellor
4 Sloane Square
London SW1W 8EE

telephone: 020 7730 4259
fax: 020 7730 7240

Retail shop and mail-order company offering
exceptionally well-designed (mostly) British cookware,
ceramics, cutlery and glass

Summerill & Bishop
100 Portland Road
London W11 4LN

telephone: 020 7221 4566
fax: 020 7727 1322
email: in development
web site: in development

A retail shop and mail-order company specialising
in beautiful and eclectic, modern and antique
kitchen equipment, tableware and glassware,
including La Forme baking tins

The Conran Shop
The Michelin Building
81 Fulham Road
London SW3 6RD

telephone: 020 7589 7401
fax: 020 7823 7015
email: conranshop@dial.pipex.com

Retail shop specialising in superbly designed
modern products for the home and kitchen,
including oroshigane – root ginger graters

ICTC Ltd
3 Caley Close
Sweetbriar Road
Norwich NR3 2BU

telephone: 01603 488019
email: ictc@dial.pipex.com
website: www.ictc.co.uk

Manufacturer of exceptional quality saucepans and
kitchen equipment, including Cuisinox

New Cook's Emporium
21 High Street
Ledbury
Herefordshire HR8 1DS

telephone: 01531 623976
fax: 01531 631011
web site: www.cecipaolo.com

A fantastically well-stocked cook's shop with
everything from Italian coffee machines and stoves
to Thai ingredients and a coffee shop cum
demonstration area. Jumping.

Books for Cooks
4 Blenheim Crescent
London W11 1NN

telephone: 020 7221 1992
fax: 020 7221 1517
web site: www.booksforcooks.com

A cook book shop without rival, not just
in London, but anywhere. There's a tiny café
at the back where they cook up recipes gleaned
from the countless books in stock.

Some Favourite Restaurants

The Trinity
Crown and Castle Hotel
Orford
Suffolk IP12 2LJ

telephone: 01394 450205
fax: 01394 450176
web site: www.crownandcastlehotel.co.uk

For being my own lively bistro in our modest,
comfortable hotel, set in a fabulous coastal location,
and serving really good, honest food

The Ivy
1 West Street
London WC2H 9NE

telephone: 020 7836 4751

For unstarchy, courteous service, a great buzz, and
unpretentious eclectic food

Bibendum
Michelin House
81 Fulham Road
London SW3 6RD

telephone: 020 7581 5817

For having the most civilised dining room in London,
and offering perfect service, good food and wonderful
wines (at a price)

The Blueprint Café
1st Floor, The Design Museum
Shad Thames
London SE1 2YD

telephone: 020 7378 7031

For having a wonderful view of the Thames, and a
hugely talented, bright chef, Jeremy Lee, who cooks
gutsy, honest, full-flavoured food

Merchant House
Lower Corve Street
Ludlow
Shropshire SY8 1DU

telephone: 01584 875438

For having one of the best chef/proprietors in the country, Shaun Hill, who cooks intelligent, simple, fuss-free food

Suntory Restaurant
72 St James's Street
London SW1A 1PH

telephone: 020 7409 0201

For being a traditional Japanese restaurant offering attentive service and superlative food, especially the sashimi

Alastair Little
49 Frith Street
London W1V 1TP

telephone: 020 7734 5183

For being owned by a chef-hero, the eponymous Alastair Little, who cooks brilliant food with unmatched vigour, generosity and style

Regatta
171 High Street
Aldeburgh
Suffolk IP15 5AN

telephone: 01728 452011

For being a lively, friendly, ultra-casual seaside restaurant majoring on fresh fish, and owned by my niece and her husband (nepotism rules OK)

The Japanese Canteen
19-21 Exmouth Market
London EC1R 4QD

telephone: 020 7833 3521

For being simple and unpretentious, and serving very cheap Anglo-Japanese food at lunchtime, and excellent, modestly-priced traditional Japanese food in the evening

The Fifth Floor Restaurant
Harvey Nichols
Knightsbridge
London SW1 7JR

telephone: 020 7235 5250

For being lively but comfortable, and having a lovely chef, Henry Harris, who cooks imaginative, modern, bold-tasting food

Altnaharrie Inn
Ullapool
Highland IV26 2SS

telephone: 01854 633230

For being in a fabulously romantic setting, having the shyest chef/proprietor, Gunn Eriksen, and serving the best, and most extraordinary, food in the country

da Fiore
Calle del Scaleter
San Polo
Venice 2202/a

telephone: 00 39 041 721308
fax: 00 39 041 721343

For serving the best risotto in Italy (never mind Venice), and having a comfortable, civilised dining room

Index

A

Afghan rice pudding, 113
aïoli, le petit, 180-1
almonds: apricot
    frangipane tart, 208-9
    marzipan baklava,
    114-15
anchovies, 20
apple tart, French, 92-3
apricots, 22, 24-5
    apricot and amaretto
    trifle, 226-7
    apricot frangipane tart,
    208-9
    hazelnut and apricot
    meringue cake, 103
asparagus: asparagus and
    girolles crostini, 167
    griddled asparagus with
    sesame sauce, 166
    risi e asparagi, 260
aubergines, soy-glazed
    grilled, 43
avocados, 25
    burritos with spicy
    beans and avocado
    salsa, 118
    spinach salad with
    avocado and pancetta,
    168
    tomato, avocado and
    basil omelette, 261

B

bacon: egg and bacon pie,
    238-9
    ham and haddie, 155
baklava, marzipan,
    114-15
bananas: banana split,
    230
    butter-fried bananas
    with orange and
    coconut syrup, 90
beans, 20-1
    borlotti bean and goat's
    cheese pasteles, 147
    burritos with spicy
    beans and avocado
    salsa, 118
    casarecce with porcini
    and pinto beans, 146

Harry's dolce fagioli in
    saor, 46
    Italian beans on toast,
    148
béchamel sauce, 22
beef: steak and kidney
    pie, 77-8
blackcurrant bavarois tart,
    210-11
blinis, 19
bread: croûtons, 28
bread and butter pudding
    with honey, 112
broad beans, 32
    Gorgonzola, broad bean
    and dill risotto, 277
    hot gammon with
    parsley sauce and, 203
buckwheat noodles with
    squash, soy and sesame
    seeds, 143
burritos with spicy beans
    and avocado salsa, 118
butter, 23, 28, 29
    Café de Paris butter,
    188-9
butternut squash:
    buckwheat noodles with
    squash, soy and sesame
    seeds, 143
    butternut and chickpea
    soup, 40
    pappardelle with squash
    and sage pesto, 144
    roast butternut squash,
    garlic and oregano
    risotto, 123

C

Café de Paris butter,
    188-9
cake, zabaglione and
    raspberry, 213
casarecce with porcini
    and pinto beans, 146
celeriac, greens and
    potato soup, 42
cheese, 20
    baked chicken with
    Boursin, 249
    borlotti bean and goat's
    cheese pasteles, 147

buffalo mozzarella with
    pears, 272
    feta and Med veg tart,
    245
    feta and watermelon
    salad, 165
    flat mushroom, red
    onion and mascarpone
    pizza, 128-9
    fried mozzarella with
    pesto and chilli, 170
    Gorgonzola, broad bean
    and dill risotto, 277
    grilled goat's cheese
    salad, 269
    ham and fontina
    pancakes, 132-3
    livarot, rocket and
    potato tart, 127
    macaroni con brio, 119
    omelette Molière with
    parmesan and gruyère,
    126
    penne with kale,
    mascarpone and
    pancetta, 150
    potato, goat's cheese,
    pea and mint tart,
    270-1
    scrambled eggs alla
    parmigiana, 262
    stuffed mushroom
    crostini with smoked
    mozzarella, 134
    tomato, mozzarella and
    pesto galette, 257
    twice-baked spinach
    and Parmesan soufflé,
    62-3
    warm taleggio,
    mushroom and fennel
    salad, 276
cheesecake, pumpkin,
    100-1
cherries: cherry custard
    fritters, 222
    pavlova with cherry
    compôte, 221
chicken: baked chicken
    with Boursin, 249
    chicken and courgette
    risotto, 256

chicken escalopes with
    salsa verde, 202
    fried chicken with
    hazelnut sauce, 80
    grilled coconut chicken
    with noodles and satay
    sauce, 254-5
    pinenut-crusted
    chicken stuffed with
    basil butter, 200-1
chickpeas: griddled squid
    with coriander hummus,
    56
    seafood and chickpea
    salad crostini, 174-5
chillies, 31
chocolate, 27
    banana split, 230
    blackcurrant bavarois
    tart with chocolate
    pastry, 210-11
    chocolate and stem
    ginger pavé, 109
    chocolate zuppa
    inglese, 110-1
cioppino, 194-5
clams, 23
    linguine with parsley,
    garlic and, 136
cobbler, damson and
    almond, 98
cockle, chicory and bacon
    salad, 55
coconut pancakes, 104
cod: seized cod with white
    bean and parsley purée,
    65
    with saffron mash and
    gremolata, 69
coffee, rum and
    cardamom trifle, 106
courgettes: chicken and
    courgette risotto,
    256
    courgette, potato and
    herb frittata, 243
crab, 31
    cioppino, 194-5
    crab cakes with
    coconut and tarragon,
    186
crème pâtissière, 92-3

crevettes with flat mushrooms and garlic, 72

crostini: asparagus and girolles, 167

prawn, mushroom and parsley, 273

seafood and chickpea salad, 174-5

stuffed mushroom with smoked mozzarella, 134

croûtons, 28

cucumber: chilled cucumber and coconut milk soup, 162

curry sauce, mussels with, 59

custard, 32

apricot and amaretto trifle, 226-7

baked egg custard, 231

floating islands with nectarine custard, 228-9

raspberry mess, 216-17

D

dairy products, 25

damson and almond cobbler, 98

duck: confit of duck, 82-3

duck fat, 20

E

eggs, 18, 31-2

baked egg custard, 231

courgette, potato and herb frittata, 243

egg and bacon pie, 238-9

Little Gem salad with egg and bacon dressing, 172

old-fashioned egg mayonnaise, 169

scrambled eggs alla parmigiana, 262

smoked haddock Bénédict, 135

see also omelettes equipment, 35-7

F

fat, 20

fennel and mussel broth, 70

feta and Med veg tart, 245

feta and watermelon salad, 165

fish: fritto misto, 76

see also cod; tuna etc

floating islands with nectarine custard, 228-9

French apple tart, 92-3

French bean, tuna and shallot salad, 248

French toast with peach, lime and mint salsa, 206

frittata, courgette, potato and herb, 243

fritters, cherry custard, 222

fritto misto, 76

fruit compotes, 21-2

fruit salad brûlée, 108

G

gado-gado salad with peanut sauce, 178-9

gammon with parsley sauce and broad beans, 203

garlic, 28

le petit aïoli, 180-1

gravadlax, Thai-style, 54

greens, celeriac and potato soup, 42

H

haggis, potato, bacon and apple fry-up, 149

ham and fontina pancakes, 132-3

ham and haddie, 155

Harry's dolce fagioli in saor, 46

hazelnut and apricot meringue cake, 103

herbs, 32

horseradish, 19

hotpot, not Betty's, 84

I

ice-cream: banana split, 230

deep-fried mincemeat and ice-cream parcels, 105

poached strawberries with five-pepper ice-cream, 218

Italian beans on toast, 148

J

jams, 21

K

kale, penne with mascarpone, pancetta and, 150

L

lamb: not Betty's hotpot, 84

spiced lamb patties with roast vegetables, 156

leeks: chilled sweet potato vichyssoise, 160

leek salad with tarragon, caper and parsley dressing, 163

tiger prawn, leek and red pepper stir-fry, 275

lemon: lemon meringue pie, 94-5

lemon risotto, 192-3

lentils, 21

lentil salad with soft-boiled eggs and tapenade toasts, 242

lettuce: cos salad, 238-9

Little Gem salad with egg and bacon dressing, 172

lime, 25

linguine: with caramelised onions and fried breadcrumbs, 145

with clams, parsley and garlic, 136

with raw tomato sauce, 234

Little Gem salad with egg and bacon dressing, 172

livarot, rocket and potato tart, 127

lobster, 24

cold lobster with tarragon mayonnaise and chips, 184-5

grilled lobster with Café de Paris butter, 188-9

M

macaroni con brio, 119

marzipan baklava, 114-15

mayonnaise: cold lobster with tarragon mayonnaise, 184-5

old-fashioned egg mayonnaise, 169

le petit aïoli, 180-1

meringue: floating islands, 228-9

hazelnut and apricot meringue cake, 103

lemon meringue pie, 94-5

pavlova with cherry compôte, 221

piña colada roulade, 214-15

raspberry mess, 216-17

mincemeat and ice-cream parcels, deep-fried, 105

minestrone soup, Mum's, 140

monkfish: cioppino, 194-5

mozzarella, 20

Mum's minestrone soup, 140

mushrooms: asparagus and girolles crostini, 167
flat mushroom, red onion and mascarpone pizza, 130-1
stuffed mushroom crostini with smoked mozzarella, 134
warm taleggio, mushroom and fennel salad, 276
mussels, 29-30
deep-fried mussel and vegetable tangles, 152
fritto misto, 76
gratin Basque-style, 58
mussel and fennel broth, 70
with red curry sauce,59
mustard, 24

N

nectarines, 24-5
floating islands with nectarine custard, 228-9
noodles: buckwheat noodles with squash, soy and sesame seeds, 143
grilled coconut chicken with, 254-5
nuts, toasting, 27

O

oils, 17, 33
olives, 24
tapenade toasts, 242
omelettes: omelette Molière with parmesan and gruyère, 126
Savoy omelette with peas, pepperoni and potatoes, 124-5
tomato, avocado and basil omelette, 261
onions: deep-fried onion bhajis, 44
linguine with caramelised onions, 145

orange: griddled scallops with Seville orange chutney, 67
Seville pond pudding, 88-9

P

palm sugar, 24
pancakes: borlotti bean and goat's cheese pasteles, 145
coconut pancakes with maple, pecan and rum butter, 104
ham and fontina pancakes, 132-3
saffron pancakes, 74-5
pancetta, 24
Little Gem salad with egg and bacon dressing, 172
pappardelle with squash and sage pesto, 144
passion fruit sorbet, 223
pasta, 23, 28
pastry, 33
pavlova with cherry compôte, 221
peaches, 24-5
sweet French toast with peach, lime and mint salsa, 206
peanut butter: gado-gado salad with peanut sauce, 178-9
grilled coconut chicken with noodles and satay sauce, 254-5
pearl barley stew, confit of duck with, 82-3
pears: buffalo mozzarella with, 272
pear and pinenut salad, 47
peas: spinach, two-pea and leek soup, 41
penne with kale, mascarpone and pancetta, 150
peppercorns, 18
poached strawberries with five-pepper ice-

cream, 218
peppers, 20
red pepper, garlic and saffron risotto, 237
tiger prawn, leek and red pepper stir-fry, 275
pesto, squash and sage, 144
le petit aïoli, 180-1
pies: egg and bacon pie, 238-9
steak and kidney pie, 77-8
piña colada roulade, 214-15
pinenut-crusted chicken, 200-1
pineapple, 29
fresh pineapple with passion fruit sorbet, 223
piña colada roulade, 214-15
pizza, flat mushroom, red onion and mascarpone, 130-1
plums: baked plums on panettone, 96
plum sauce, 24
porcini, casarecce with pinto beans and, 146
potatoes: cod with saffron mash and gremolata, 69
cold lobster with tarragon mayonnaise and chips, 184-5
courgette, potato and herb frittata, 243
haggis, potato, bacon and apple fry-up, 149
livarot, rocket and potato tart, 127
not Betty's hotpot, 84
potato and sorrel salad, 173
potato, goat's cheese, pea and mint tart, 270-1
Savoy omelette with peas, pepperoni and, 122-3

prawns, 20
cioppino, 194-5
crevettes with flat mushrooms and garlic, 72
griddled prawns wrapped in basil and parma ham, 192-3
le petit aïoli, 180-1
prawn, mushroom and parsley crostini, 273
tiger prawn, leek and red pepper stir-fry, 275
tiger prawn tempura, 51
pulses, 20-1
pumpkin cheesecake, 100-1

R

raspberries: raspberry mess, 216-17
zabaglione and raspberry cake, 213
rice, 22-3
Afghan rice pudding, 113
risi e asparagi, 260
see also risotto
risotto: chicken and courgette, 256
Gorgonzola, broad bean and dill, 277
lemon, 192-3
red pepper, garlic and saffron, 237
roast butternut squash, garlic and oregano, 123

S

saffron pancakes, 74-5
salads: chargrilled squid, potato and onion, 246
cockle, chicory and bacon, 55
cos, 238-9
feta and watermelon, 165
French bean, tuna and shallot, 248
gado-gado, 178-9

grilled goat's cheese,
269
leek with tarragon,
caper and parsley
dressing, 163
lentil with soft-boiled
eggs, 242
Little Gem, 172
pear and pine nut, 47
le petit aïoli, 180-1
potato and sorrel, 173
seafood and chickpea
crostini, 174-5
spinach with avocado
and pancetta, 168
warm salmon salade
Niçoise, 187
warm taleggio,
mushroom and fennel,
276
salmon: escalope with
champagne sauce,
182-3
nearly sashimi, 49
Thai-style gravadlax,
54
warm salmon salade
Niçoise, 187
salsas: salsa verde, 202
tomato, ginger and
basil, 183
salt, 17-18
sashimi, nearly, 49
Savoy omelette with peas,
pepperoni and
potatoes, 124-5
scallops, 30
griddled scallops with
Seville orange chutney,
67
nearly sashimi, 49
with sauce vierge and
crisp pancetta, 196
with whipped garlic
butter, 68
seafood and chickpea
salad crostini, 174-5
Seville pond pudding,
88-9
sloe gin syllabub, 221
smoked haddock: ham
and haddie, 153

smoked haddock and
watercress tart, 250-1
smoked haddock
Bénédict, 135
smoked haddock
chowder, 154
smoked salmon, 19
warm smoked salmon
escalopes with potato
and sorrel salad, 173
with pancetta,
horseradish crème
fraîche and blini, 52
sole: Dover sole
meunière, 74-5
sorbet, passion fruit, 223
soufflé, twice-baked
spinach and Parmesan,
62-3
soups: butternut and
chickpea, 40
celeriac, greens and
potato, 42
chilled cucumber and
coconut milk soup, 162
chilled sweet potato
vichyssoise, 160
Mum's minestrone
soup, 140
smoked haddock
chowder, 154
spinach, two-pea and
leek, 41
spinach: spinach salad
with avocado and
pancetta, 168
spinach, two-pea and
leek soup, 41
twice-baked spinach
and Parmesan soufflé,
62-3
squash see butternut
squash
squid, 30
chargrilled squid,
potato and onion salad,
246
fritto misto, 76
griddled squid with
coriander hummus, 56
steak and kidney pie,
77-8

stock powder, 19
strawberries with five-
pepper ice-cream, 218
sugar, 21, 29
sweet potato vichyssoise,
chilled, 160
syllabub, sloe gin, 221

T

tapenade toasts, 242
tarts: apricot frangipane,
208-9
blackcurrant bavarois,
210-11
feta and Med veg, 245
French apple, 92-3
livarot, rocket and
potato, 127
potato, goat's cheese,
pea and mint, 270-1
smoked haddock and
watercress, 250-1
tempura, 19
tiger prawn tempura,
51
Thai fish sauce, 19
Thai-style gravadlax, 54
tomatoes, 18, 31
linguine with raw
tomato sauce, 234
tomato, avocado and
basil omelette, 261
tomato, ginger and
basil salsa, 183
tomato, mozzarella and
pesto galette, 257
tortillas: burritos with
spicy beans, 116
trifle: apricot and
amaretto, 226-7
coffee, rum and
cardamom, 106
tuna, French bean and
shallot salad, 248

V

vanilla pods, 22
vegetables: deep-fried
mussel and vegetable
tangles, 152
feta and Med veg tart,
245

Mum's minestrone
soup, 140
spiced lamb patties
with roast vegetables,
156

W

watercress and smoked
haddock tart, 250-1
watermelon and feta
salad, 165
white sauce, 22

Y

yoghurt, 25

Z

zabaglione and raspberry
cake, 213
zest, 27
zuppa inglese, chocolate,
110-1

**The Publishers would like
to thank the following for
lending props for
photography:**

The Conran Shop
tel: 020 7589 7401

Kara Kara
tel: 020 7591 0891

Nicole Farhi Homestore
tel: 020 7494 9051